Clarinet

Ollie Weston

Exploring Jazz Clarinet

An Introduction to Jazz Harmony, Technique and Improvisation

SCHOTT

www.schott-music.com

Mainz · London · Madrid · Paris · New York · Tokyo · Beijing

About the Author

Ollie Weston is professor of jazz saxophone at the Guildhall School of Music where he currently runs the jazz workshop and jazz MA courses for their junior school. Ollie has enjoyed working in numerous ensembles across the contemporary music spectrum.

Jazz credits include: The London Jazz Orchestra, National Youth Jazz Orchestra, Back to Basie Band, Combustible Alarms, Clarinet Appeal, Enigma Orchestra and the Nelson Riddle Orchestra. As well as performing with numerous smaller groups, he also writes and arranges for his own quartet and co-leads the Zephyr sax quartet.

Ollie has worked in the commercial sector, with session credits for 19 Management, Island Records, Edwyn Collins, Jamie Cullum and Amy Winehouse. He has a great deal of experience as a pit player and has worked in many of London's West End productions including *Chicago, The Rat Pack* and *Blood Brothers.*

He has been keenly involved in jazz education over the last eight years, to his credit many of his pupils have gone on to study music at university or conservatoire level and are hoping to make their careers in music.

Picture Credits

Photographs courtesy of David Sinclair
(www.jazzphotographs.com)
p. 6 Ken Peplowski
p. 10 Johnny Dankworth
p. 26 Tony Coe
p. 86 Gilad Atzmon
p. 120 Acker Bilk
p. 127 Rudi Mahall
p. 158 Alan Barnes
p. 190 Artie Shaw

The audio files are an integral part of this book, which originally came with two CDs. The files can be downloaded on **www.schott-music.com/online-material** using the voucher code **ya2BrfS5**.
Throughout the book we refer to the original CD.

ED 13350D
British Library Cataloguing-in-Publication Data.
A catalogue record for this book is available from the British Library.
ISMN 979-0-2201-3866-9
ISBN 978-1-84761-517-6

Project management, layout and copy-editing by Scott Barnard for MusicPreparation (www.musicpreparation.co.uk)
Cover design by www.adamhaystudio.com
Main cover image: iStock Photo Library

Printed in Germany S&Co.8694

Contents

Introduction

1: The Blues

2: The Major Seventh Chord

3: The Minor Seventh Chord

4: The Seventh Chord

5: Putting it Together

6: Modes of the Major Scale

7: The II-V-I Progression

8: The Minor II-V-I

9: Song and Standards

10: Bebop

11: Style Workout

Conclusion

History and Listening

Introduction

Starting Out

If you've got as far as picking up this book you are probably already interested in jazz on some level – maybe you've been inspired by a particular musician or a jazz tune? Maybe you naturally associate the clarinet with jazz and want to find out what the hype is about? Whatever your motivation, this book will help you on your journey to becoming the jazz musician that you wanted to be when you first picked up the clarinet.

This book will provide you with the knowledge you need to play jazz successfully. Each chapter contains tunes and exercises that will improve your playing in all areas – your technique, reading, creativity, improvisation and theory will all benefit and you will also gain an understanding of the history of jazz and some of its innovators. In short this book will give you a thorough insight into this fascinating art form and free up your inner jazz musician.

What is Jazz?

There are many images and clichés associated with jazz and its musicians – the image of the cool performer nonchalantly receiving inspiration from thin air is a popular one and one that we all aspire to as clarinettists. However, to be that laid back on a gig requires years of dedicated work behind the scenes. Rather than thinking 'it doesn't matter what notes I play – this is jazz!' the journey towards being a fluent jazz musician demands that you acquire a thorough knowledge both of your instrument and of the inner workings of music. You will discover an art form that can be honed and developed as your musicianship grows. Whether playing at home, the concert hall or a basement club you will discover that jazz has become a serious music form played by serious musicians.

It takes time to become a fluent jazz improviser but when you do, the rewards are huge – the excitement of creating new music in front of an audience can't be beaten and once you get 'bitten' by the jazz bug you will find no more satisfying feeling in the musical world.

Improvisation

The biggest concept of all for the aspiring jazz musician is improvisation. The word conjures dread, excitement and misunderstanding in equal measure – the idea that great jazz improvisation comes like a spontaneous bolt of lightning to the special few is misleading.

A great jazz soloist in full flight is indeed incredibly impulsive and creative; however there are many years of methodical work behind the spontaneity. This book will de-mystify improvisation and within a few chapters you too will be improvising with style.

The Clarinet in Jazz

The clarinet was one of the first woodwind instruments to be used by jazz musicians. The rich sound, huge variation of tone and dynamics possible on the instrument have made it a firm favourite with players since the birth of jazz in New Orleans, in the early twentieth century. There are profiles of great clarinettists throughout this book, each with a recommended listening list. Try to get hold of these recordings and listen to them in detail, that way you will hear the subtleties of tone and phrasing that are so important in jazz. The best way to develop as a musician is to listen to as much as possible – the listening lists in this book will provide you with a good starting point for the wealth of great jazz recordings out there.

Notation

This book assumes that you have reached at least a basic level of ability on the clarinet. It is not intended for an absolute beginner. Once you've got the basics of the instrument and are comfortable reading notes and simple rhythms you are ready to go. The exercises in this book will then develop your skills from this point in the same way as a regular tutor book, but with the emphasis on jazz.

Chapter Content

The first four chapters of this book will introduce you to some of the language of jazz – the blues scale and the three main types of chord will be covered in some detail. This makes chapters one to four fairly exercise heavy – these are the hardest chapters in the book, so be ready to play lots of scales and patterns. That said, don't feel you have to master every exercise in every key straight away. Chapters one to four could be seen as a complete section of the book in themselves, covering much of the groundwork for the rest of the book.

Chapters five to eleven focus more on musical concepts and introduce the theoretical side of jazz. The emphasis here is on style and improvisation – there are lots more tunes to play along with, to help you find your feet and start to develop your own style and sound.

Sample Solos

Many of the tunes in this book have a sample solo with them. These are 'improvised' solos in the style of the tune. You can use these to learn the chord progression to a tune and as a stylistic and technical workout but eventually you will want to be playing your own solos. Please feel free to borrow any 'licks' from the sample solos and add them to your own expanding vocabulary of licks!

Backing Tracks

The CD accompaniment to this book contains rhythm section backings to some of the exercises and tunes. These will give you experience of playing with a professional pianist, bassist and drummer which in turn will help you play with a great jazz feel.

Many of the tunes in this book include the clarinet part followed by a sample solo. Play along with these and use them as an audio guide to help you master the style and any awkward rhythms. Ultimately you should be playing the tracks without the recorded clarinet and replacing the sample solos with your own.

The main tunes for each chapter are available as play-along CD backing tracks. Versions with the clarinet are also available as mp3s on the disc – as are many of the workouts and technical exercises.

1 denotes CD track 1

2 denotes mp3 track 2

Where piano parts are fully realized, they have been written so as to appear in the same key as the clarinet. This has been done so that the clarinet player can 'read' the fully realized chords in the home key of the clarinet.

Practice

The old adage is that the more you put in the more you will get out! The great saxophonist **John Coltrane** would practise so much that he often fell asleep with the sax still in his mouth – this might strike you as excessive, but the results are there to be heard in his playing.

Practice is more effective little and often rather than all in one go the night before a lesson or gig. If you can find fifteen to twenty minutes a day you are doing well – otherwise aim for every other day or even three times a week. Having decided to learn, you owe it to yourself to make the most of it – try to find regular practice slots and stick to them. The quality of your practice is as important as the quantity though, so if you have limited time, focus on one exercise and one tune and really try to nail them – this will benefit you much more than rushing a whole chapter.

Above all you should enjoy your playing – there may be times when you find an exercise or tune difficult. You are not alone, everyone who's ever played an instrument has struggled at one time or another – persevere and, who knows, you might be the next big name in the jazz world!

1: The Blues

Any study of jazz would be incomplete without a little prior knowledge of the blues, so this chapter will look at the musical and cultural environment that gave birth to jazz.

As you will see, blues and early jazz are linked in history, and understanding the blues will give you a vital insight into many of the musical styles from the last century to the present day.

The Blues – The Musical Source of Jazz and Popular Music

Legend has it that in the early 20th century, an unknown musician named **Robert Johnson** met with the devil and sold his soul in return for guitar prowess. He returned from this meeting with a sound and style that would change the course of music forever – the blues.

The chances are that you've already heard blues-influenced music: in fact it's hard to find any 20th century popular music that hasn't been touched in some way by the blues. The bent notes, wailing delivery, as well as the spirit and feeling of the blues, have influenced rock, soul, funk, hip hop and R&B. Artists as diverse as **B. B. King**, **Eric Clapton**, **Herbie Hancock**, **Miles Davis**, **Duke Ellington**, **Aretha Franklin**, **James Brown**, **The Rolling Stones**, **Prince**, **Beyonce**, **Kanye West** and **Alicia Keys** love the blues and acknowledge its impact on their music.

The blues developed in the south of the USA in the early 1900s and was the result of a number of different musical cultures meeting and fusing together. African work songs and chants mixed with American folk and gospel music to create a new sound. The songs tell of the tough living at the time: African-American slaves sang of hope and freedom to keep their spirits up whilst working the land. Other musicians played the blues to entertain at home or in bars and theatres. These songs covered familiar human themes of love and loss. The image of an old bluesman – guitar in one hand, whisky bottle in the other – lamenting his woman leaving town has often been used to summarise the blues era, but paints a good picture of the time and its characters.

Further Listening

Bessie Smith / Louis Armstrong – 'St. Louis Blues'

Bessie Smith – 'St. Louis Blues' (You Tube broadcast)

Robert Johnson – 'Crossroad Blues' (tells the story of his meeting with the devil)

Robert Johnson – 'Sweet Home Chicago'

Louis Armstrong – 'Blues In The Night' from *Louis Armstrong Meets Oscar Peterson*

Eric Clapton – 'Before You Accuse Me' from *Unplugged*

B. B. King – 'Every Day I Have The Blues'

'Leavin' Town'

To find out how the blues is constructed in more detail let's analyse the example below – a simple tune in the style of **Bessie Smith** or **Robert Johnson**. Notice how the song is split into three separate 4-bar sections; the first line is repeated with the third line as a conclusion or answering phrase. Listen to mp3 track 1 to hear what this sounds like. After you've got an idea of the melody, play the tune for yourself (attempt to do this throughout this book).

Fig 1.1 'Leavin' Town' 1

This version sounds a little too happy to be a sad blues tune. The melancholic nature of the song (and the style in general) needs to be expressed in the music. Look at the second version of the tune and notice how I've changed the mood by altering certain notes:

Fig 1.2 'Leavin' Town' ('bluesed-up' version)

2

Ollie Weston

The new version sounds far more bluesy. Some simple note changes have created that unique blues sound – over time these specific notes have become synonymous with the blues sound and are called 'blue' notes. Before we discover the relationship between blues and various scales, let's first explain some terminology.

Intervals

Musicians call the distance between any two notes an 'interval'. To find out the interval between two notes, we need to count the letter names between them (including the ones you start and finish on). So, to find the interval between the notes D and A, we would count the letter names from D to A (D, E, F, G, A). There are five letter names between the two notes, therefore we refer to this interval as a 'fifth'. We could apply the same principle but start on a different degree of the scale – let's start on the second note of the D scale which is E and say we want to find the interval between that E and the C above it. We would once again count the notes from E to C (E, F, G, A, B, C), there are six letter names this time, therefore we have an interval of a sixth.

Tones and Semitones

Notice the pattern of tones and semitones marked under the stave. The interval of a second, say from D to E, can also be described as a 'tone'. If we played from D to E♭ – a smaller interval – the distance between the two notes is reduced to a 'semitone' (i.e. half a tone). Semitones are the smallest intervals available to us.

Here is a major scale with the tones and semitones marked:

Fig 1.3a Tones and Semitones within the Major Scale

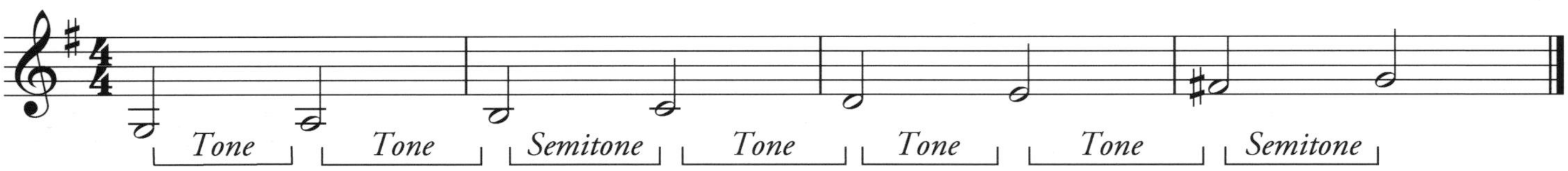

It is this pattern of tone, tone, semitone, tone, tone, tone, semitone that defines the major scale. Pick any starting note and try to follow this tone 'map'. Note that to follow the pattern, you will have to add sharps and flats to keep the intervals consistent – for example here it is in B♭ major:

Fig 1.3b Tones and Semitones within the B♭ Major Scale

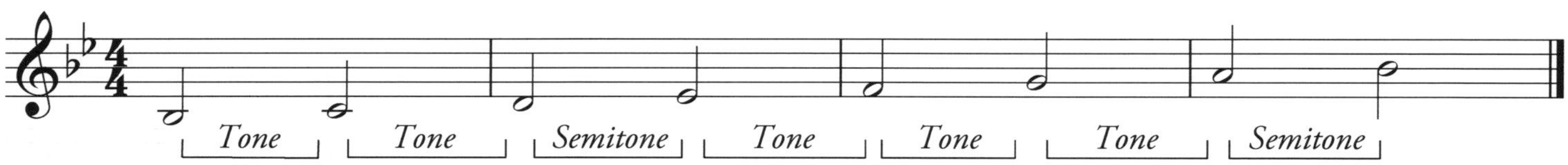

Notice the tone/semitone pattern is exactly the same for B♭ major as it is for G major, only the notes change. The F♯ from G major becomes a natural and B♭ and E♭ are added.

Let's number the notes of the scale from one to eight (as in the example below):

Fig 1.4 Degrees of the Scale

The first note of the scale (the note the scale is built from, using the pattern of tones and semitones above) is called the root note, and the numbered scale tones are often referred to as the 'degrees' of the scale. Looking at the example above we can also see that the degrees of the scale correspond to the interval between that note and the root note – so the third note of the scale is a third above the root, the fifth note of the scale is a fifth above the root, and so on. We will shortly see that it is vital to be aware of root notes as without this the other notes have no reference point.

The Blues Scale

The most important thing to come from the blues is the 'blues scale'. Any melody can be injected with the blues sound by altering certain notes. Blues musicians flatten (lower) the third, fifth and seventh notes of the major scale by a semitone to create a more soulful sound and therefore better express the sadness of the music. The intervals within the scale have consequently changed, but are still described by their relationship to the root; these intervals are now called 'flat' or 'minor' thirds, fifths and sevenths. Here are the new, smaller intervals:

Fig 1.5a **Major Scale with Blues Notes added**

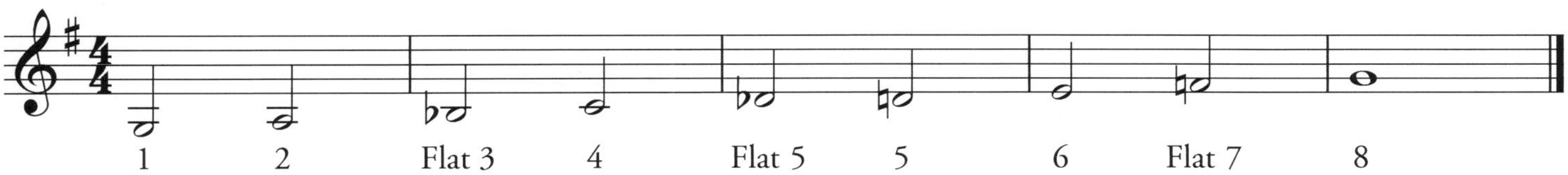

The flattened third, fifth and seventh are the so-called 'blue notes' that typify the sound we're looking for. We then leave out the second and the sixth note as they have no particular bluesy characteristic and we are left with the 'blues scale'.

Fig 1.5b **The G Blues Scale**

Checkpoint

You should now be familiar with the notes of the major scale and the construction of a major scale with tones and semitones. Flattening the third, fifth and seventh creates an alternative set of notes and has a bluesy effect.

Now play 'Leavin' Town' (Fig 1.2) again and identify the blue notes, listen to how they clash with the accompaniment (notes that clash with each other are said to be 'dissonant'). In the blues, dissonance is used to express the mournful quality of the music.

Listen to how the B♭ starts the tune and instantly sets a more gritty tone for the rest of the song. Similarly, the F naturals and D flats are the other blue notes and play a big part in the overall effect. Really dig into the blue notes and play them like you mean it!

Swing Quavers

The other big difference between the two versions of 'Leavin' Town' is the way the quavers are played. In the first (mp3 track 1) they are played evenly or 'straight', in the second (mp3 track 2) they are 'swung'. Swung quavers are a feature of blues music as well as jazz.

Swung quavers are created by making the first quaver of each pair longer than the second. The exact length is down to each individual – different players 'swing' in different ways.

Have a look at the next example:

Fig 1.6a Straight to Swing Quavers

Straight

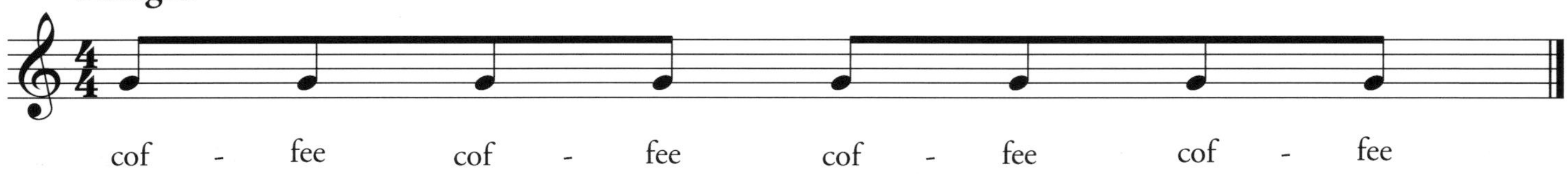

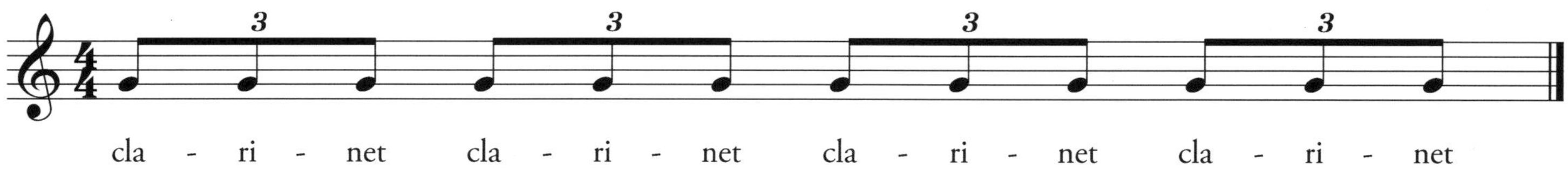

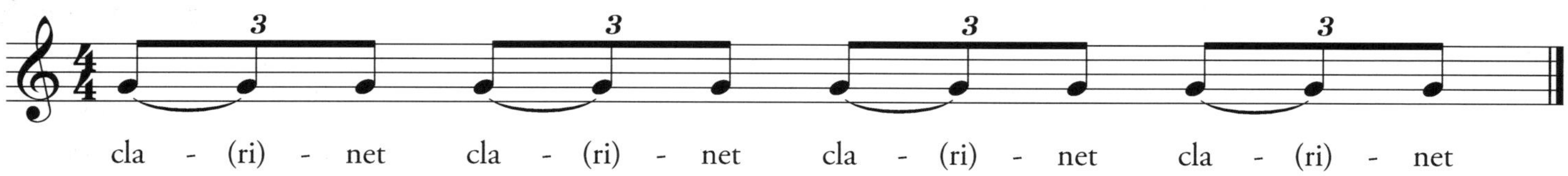

Swing

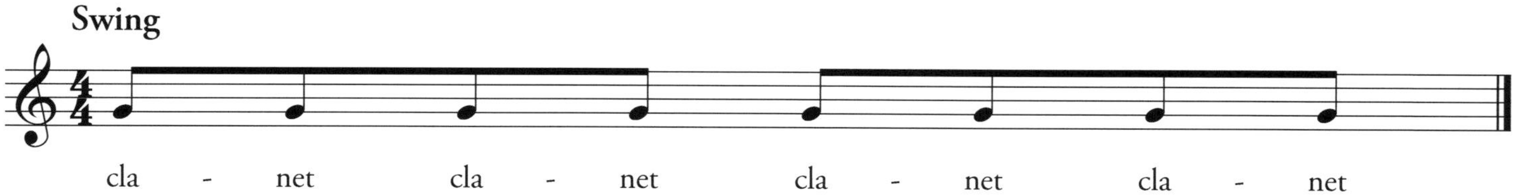

Here is a rough guide using two- and three-syllable words (I've chosen 'coffee' and 'clarinet' but any will do!).

To turn straight quavers into swing quavers, simply think of the word 'clarinet' and leave out the 'ri' syllable. (The third system should sound the same as the fourth.)

It's very rare for swung quavers to be written out for you in a triplet fashion (as above). An instruction is usually given at the top of the page, usually simply the word 'swing' is written. Sometimes the symbols in Fig 1.6b are also given:

Fig 1.6b **Swung Quaver Notation**

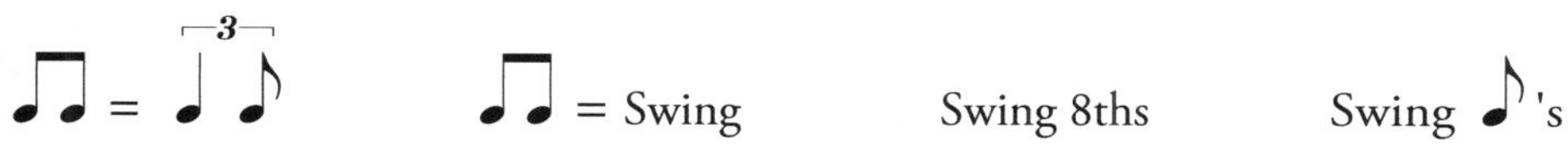

Think of these instructions as a key signature, but for feel. Just like a key signature, they continue until you are told otherwise. Always look out for this – playing straight quavers over a swing groove doesn't sound too good (unless you really know what you're doing). The best way to learn is to listen to great musicians and try to copy their feel. As **Duke Ellington** said "It don't mean a thing if it ain't got that swing!"

Song Form

Few songs or tunes are written straight through from beginning to end with nothing repeated. If you think of popular songs, most have several verses, each leading to a chorus. This verse–chorus pattern is usually repeated several times, making up the body of the song, and can be clearly seen in the majority of today's pop tunes. It is therefore possible to think of songs being built up of different sections. This makes music appealing to the listener and also more memorable and effective in its emotional message. Jazz and blues music is no different – few tunes are 'through composed' (one long, constantly evolving piece) but are instead made up of different sections that are put together and repeated. All the music we will look at in this book is built up of different sections that, when put together, make the 'form'.

Assignment

Here is a simple melody that could be used as a blues tune. Like the first version of 'Leavin' Town' it's too bright and could use an injection of blues. Try to play this tune with a more bluesy approach. You'll need to identify the thirds, fifths and sevenths and make changes to them. Make the new version as bluesy and soulful as possible.

Fig 1.7 Bluesify 'Leavin' Town'

The 12-Bar Blues

One of the most common forms is the '12-Bar blues'. Look again at 'Leavin' Town' (Fig 1.1) and, in particular, notice the three different lines. Each is four bars long and together they make the 12-Bar form. This is then repeated as many times as required for the duration of the tune. Jazz musicians will often refer to the entire form as a 'chorus'; you might be invited to 'take four choruses' of solo on a blues – this would mean playing four times round the 12-Bar progression making a total length of forty-eight bars.

Head and Solos

A jazz performance usually features a rendition of the melody – often referred to as the '**head**' (meaning the start or top of the tune) – and then improvised solos over the same form. Improvised solos started out as individual renditions of the head with the soloists' own embellishments. Over time, these variations became more elaborate and have grown to become an art form in their own right. After the solos, there is a final rendition of the 'head'.

A gig version of 'Leavin' Town' could run like this: head (two choruses), clarinet solo (four choruses), piano solo (four choruses), head (two choruses).

In total the 12-Bar blues progression has been repeated twelve times in this tune. The number of choruses per solo is rarely pre-arranged, it's up to you as the soloist to decide, in the moment, how long to play. The aim is to keep the solo interesting and stop when you think you've said enough!

The 12-Bar Blues Chord Progression

So far we've dealt only with melody and the options available for embellishment and improvisation. We will, over the course of this book, look into what happens underneath the tune as well. You will seldom be called upon to improvise freely on your own with no accompaniment. Usually you will be accompanied by a '**rhythm section**'. Although the name suggests a rank of drummers, the standard jazz rhythm section consists of only one drummer, a bass player (double bass or electric bass) and a chord-playing instrument – usually piano or guitar, or sometimes a percussion instrument such as a vibraphone. The rhythm section provides the platform and musical background for your solos whilst also creating the rhythmic drive, incorporating the pulse, the swing and – equally importantly – the chords. To be a really successful improviser you must be able to navigate a set of chords and play interesting melodic lines over them. The next three chapters will introduce three different types of chord and demonstrate how to play over them.

For now, we're going to focus on the notes that the bass plays. In the example below are the root notes of the chords for the standard 12-Bar blues progression. (In the same way that a scale is based on a root note, chords are also constructed from root notes.)

Fig 1.8a **Root Notes of a 12-Bar Blues**

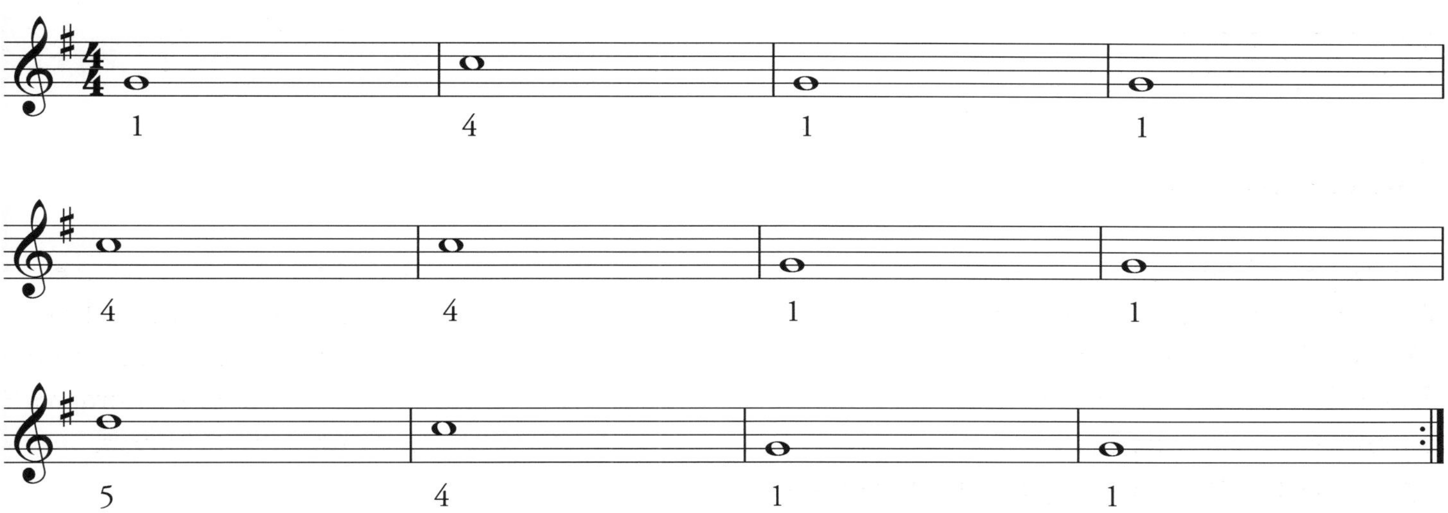

Notice that I've numbered the notes by their relationship to the root in the same way that we numbered notes and intervals previously. We will find out more about the chords later in the book, but for now get used to playing the root notes with mp3 track 2 and listen to how the piano chords change with the bass.

The next example uses the same notes but with a more appropriate rhythm:

Fig 1.8b **Root Note exercise**

Checkpoint

You will now be a bit more clued-up on how a jazz tune is put together. We've looked at how to create swing quavers to give your playing the correct rhythmic drive and covered elements of form and the concept of a repeated section over which both the melody and the improvisation take place. You will also have started to appreciate what the rhythm section do and, by playing along to the root notes of the 12-Bar blues, you will have made steps towards understanding a chord progression.

Assignments and Improvisation Tips

Use Fig 1.9 (below) to compose a simple blues tune or 'head' using the G blues scale (from Fig 1.5b). Aim to compose a three-line theme like 'Leavin' Town'. If this seems overwhelming, remember that you only need three sections to make a 12-Bar blues. A good first line is important, as it is usually repeated to make the second line. The third line is usually different from the first two and acts as an answering phrase. Use the blues scale as your palette of notes – this will make almost anything sound authentic. For rhythmic inspiration you could look at some of the earlier examples in this chapter or start from scratch. Remember the importance of swing quavers – the delivery of the notes is as important as the notes themselves!

Keep it simple! Often the best themes are composed of few notes – one of the most enduring blues heads of all time is **Duke Ellington**'s 'C Jam Blues' which consists of a two-note motif repeated three times – that's it! Trying to be too clever is an easy mistake to make – concentrate on a simple, memorable tune, which will sound great and set you on your way. You may want to start with writing some lyrics first to construct the rhythmic aspect only – sometimes this helps with the phrasing – it's up to you. Try it out over mp3 track 3.

Fig 1.9a **Write your own 12-Bar Blues**

3

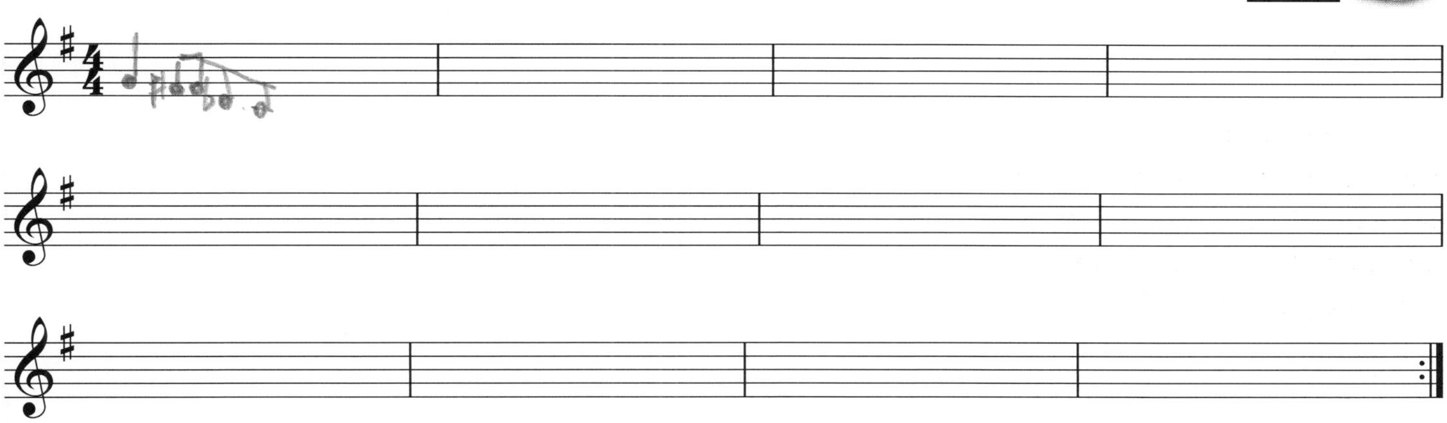

Here's another set of empty staves for you to try a different version.

Fig 1.9b **Write your own 12-Bar Blues**

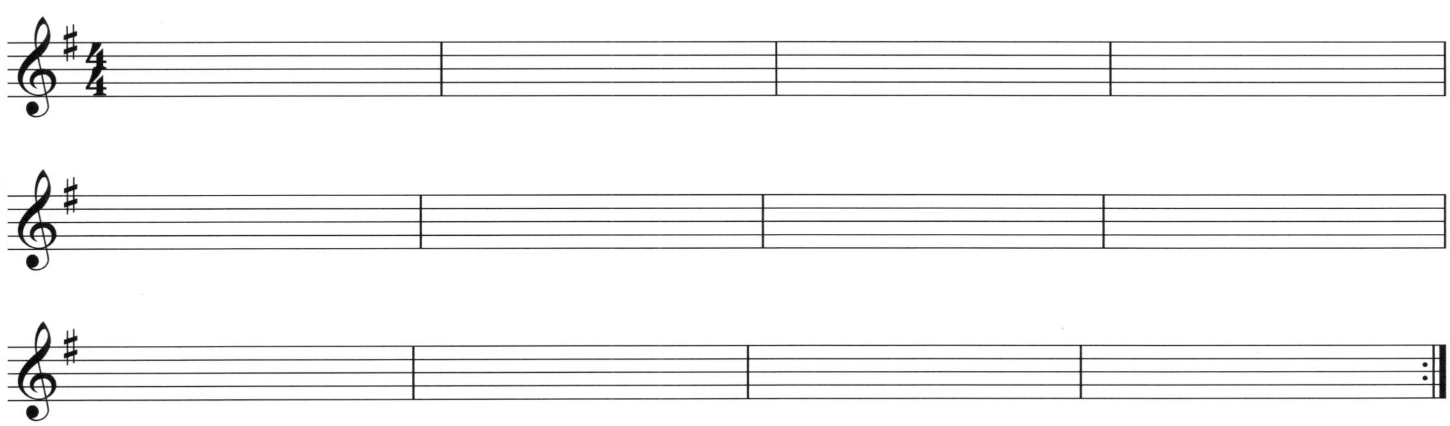

Improvising

After the head, we get to the main business of jazz and blues music – improvisation. We've looked at the running order of a jazz tune and established that after the head we move on to the solos. This is your chance to put everything together that you've learned so far. It may seem daunting at first, but remember that you now know how the blues works and some of the important elements of the sound. Remember also that originally, improvisations developed from extended decorations of the head, so this could be a great place to start. Use either 'Leavin' Town' or the blues you've written in Fig 1.9 and try to vary it for a few choruses. Think about varying the rhythm for example – playing the same notes in a slightly different place works well (i.e. play the same phrase again but start one beat earlier or later).

Sample Solo

Here is a sample blues solo based on 'Leavin' Town'. I've tried to replicate what a soloist might play on a gig, also mixing up what we've looked at throughout this chapter. We start by playing the head twice, then there are four choruses for you to improvise over and the head twice again to finish.

Fig 1.10 Sample Blues Solo – 'Leavin' Town'

4

Ollie Weston

2nd chorus

3rd chorus

4th chorus

Head

Checkpoint

In Fig 1.10 notice how the first chorus develops from the head – the sequences of notes are similar in both their rhythmic phrasing and the note choices made (for example, the first notes of the solo are simply the first two notes of the head repeated).

I then continue to paraphrase 'Leavin' Town' into the next bar: the notes are the same (flattened seventh returning to the root) – but the rhythm is different. I also use the same notes for the third line in both the head and the solo with different rhythms – again serving to paraphrase the original melody.

Notice how the solo uses only the blues scale, yet sustains interest from just these few notes. If you are having trouble getting started, use this solo as a model for now, then try to build on it in the ways we've discussed. Listen to the recorded version (mp3 track 4) to hear it played for you, and then try playing along with the track, paying attention to the swing feel of the quavers.

The last line of the fourth chorus of the solo is the same as the last phrase of the head. Jazz musicians often do this at the end of solos to make a clear ending to their improvisations. (This gives a coherent feel to the solo and lets the following improviser know they're up next.)

Assignments and Improvisation Tips

Now play a version of your blues tune as if you are on a gig – use the backing track (mp3 track 3) as your rhythm section accompaniment. The arrangement will be: the head twice (two choruses), four choruses of solo and twice more round the head to finish – eight choruses in total. Use all the knowledge you have gleaned in this chapter. You have unlocked some of the mysteries of the blues and the authentic touches should now be accessible to you. Whilst trying to be original and creative, you will now have some ideas for what works over this progression. Trial and error is the key – you will find things that you particularly like to play and that resonate with you. As a budding musician these will become the hallmarks of your personal sound and style. Already you will be sounding more and more like a jazz musician.

2: The Major Seventh Chord

As one of the cornerstones of western music, the major key has a familiar, comfortable ring to it. Whilst it may not sound terribly jazzy at first, it seems sensible to start our study of chords and their uses with the major seventh chord, as it is an important building block for effective improvisation. We're going to learn how to build the chord from the root and then look at ways to improvise effectively within the confines of that chord.

First let's number a C major scale so we can investigate building a major seventh chord from it.

Fig 2.1 Numbering a C Major Scale

Fig 2.2 shows the root, third and fifth of the scale. We can build a simple triad (three-note chord) using these notes – much like an arpeggio (which literally means 'broken chord') – where the notes are played individually.

Fig 2.2 Building a Triad

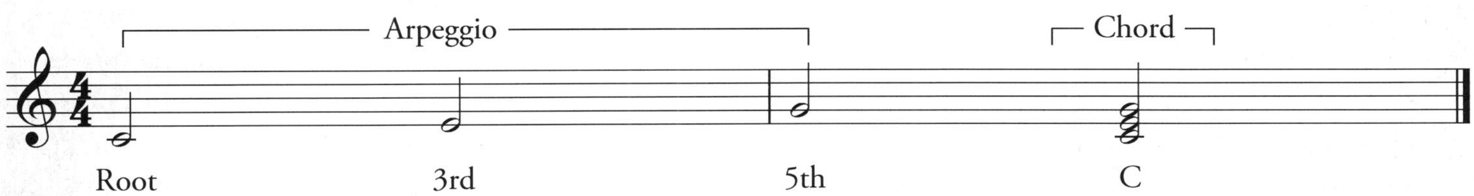

Jazz musicians often add a seventh to chords to make a more distinctive, colourful sound. In this case the seventh note would be B – adding this to our C triad produces a major seventh and creates a lush-sounding chord – C^{maj7}.

The major seventh instantly makes the chord sound sweeter and more jazzy (see the example below).

Fig 2.3 Adding the Seventh to create a C Major Seventh Chord

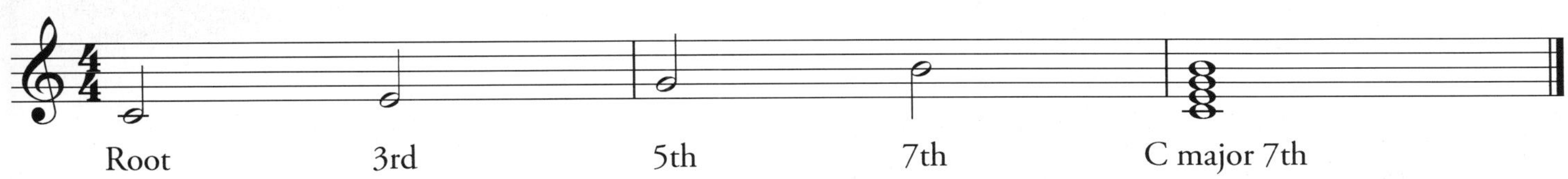

Chord Tones and Passing Tones

If you were to play all the notes of the major scale at once the result would be a dissonant mess, as the ear finds it difficult to separate out too many close notes played at once. The root, third, fifth and seventh of the scale are the notes most often used to make chords as they spell out the key effectively, yet are far enough apart not to clash. These are therefore called the 'chord tones'; whereas the notes in between (the second, fourth and sixth) are called 'passing tones'. This is illustrated in the example below. Chord tones are sometimes also referred to as 'chord notes'. Similarly passing tones are referred to as 'passing notes' – the two terms are interchangeable – so don't worry if you see or hear tones described as notes.

Fig 2.4 **Chord Tones / Passing Tones**

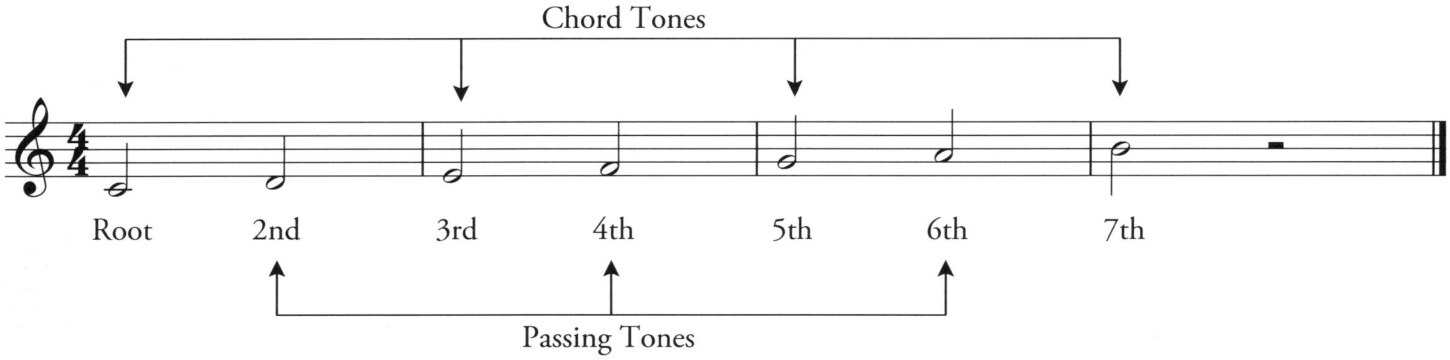

Checkpoint

You will now be familiar with the workings of the major scale and the principles of building a major seventh chord from the root, third, fifth and seventh of the scale. The intervals we looked at in chapter one are relevant to this and the brightness of the major third and the major seventh are the characteristics of the major seventh chord.

Assignments and Improvisation Tips

Using the Backing Tracks

Mp3 tracks 5, 6 and 7 are useful for applying the major chord exercises as we learn them. The tracks consist of 16 bars of each chord. I've arranged the major seventh chords ascending in minor thirds – there is no particular reason for this – but each change of chord does create a nice lift. I've also arranged only four chords per track – this makes it easier to keep your place and restart the tracks if necessary. You will get a real feel for playing with a rhythm section and they will help to keep you in time; like a metronome but with a bit more swing!

Major Scale Workout

Here are all twelve major scales written out, plus the corresponding chord tones written as an arpeggio. Try to identify the important notes of each scale as you are playing it – make sure you can recognize the sound of the root, third, fifth and major seventh and their relevance to the chord. Also make sure you can move between them by using the second and the sixth degrees of the scale – although not as crucial to the sound of the chord, seconds and sixths still have a part to play.

Play each scale and the guide tones over the rhythm section. Remember that the feel is still important so take care to swing hard!

Fig 2.5a **Major Seventh Workout (C, E♭, F♯, A)**

5

6

Fig 2.5b Major Seventh Workout (D♭, E, G, B♭)

7

Fig 2.5c Major Seventh Workout (D, F, A♭, B)

The 12-Key Dilemma

It would be great for us, as jazz musicians, if all music was in a friendly, relatively accidental-free key (no sharps or flats) – C major would be great! However a lifetime of listening and playing in one key would be monotonous and lacking in colour. Different keys have different personalities and the relationships and contrasts between them are one of the fascinating things about music. Unfortunately this means that you will at times be confronted by chords and keys that are littered with sharps and flats, which may feel totally unfamiliar to your fingers. Having to think creatively and navigate a horrendous key can be a tough challenge, but it needn't be insurmountable!

The less familiar keys shouldn't pose a problem to your musical creativity, but are merely a technical problem to overcome on your instrument – if you can hear it in C major, you can also hear it in C flat major. The problem lies in transferring the ideas to a new key. The major scale workout will introduce you to each key and let you familiarize yourself with the scale itself and its chord tones.

Your eventual goal should be to play fluently in all keys – however initially focus on acclimatizing to a few, then transfer your ideas into the less familiar, more fiddly keys. As mentioned, for each exercise there are four keys per track so you can repeat them more easily. The pace you go at is up to you, maybe concentrate on one set of four keys in each practice session. Rather than having all twelve keys on one track, they have been laid out in groups of four making the task more manageable. It's far better to master one set of four keys, than bluff your way through twelve!

It might be frustrating at first, but soon you will be comfortable in more keys and will have done invaluable groundwork for your future playing.

Embellishing Simple Phrases

As we are looking more and more at the theoretical side of chords and their uses in jazz, it's important to remember that the way we play the notes is just as important. Jazz musicians often talk about phrasing and the way other musicians phrase things. Like spoken language, communication is the essential thing. You can hit all the right notes, but played without any expression or sentiment they can sound wooden and forced. Imagine someone talking on and on in a monotone voice, although you understand every word they are saying you would soon find listening to them dull. Suppose your favourite actor is now saying the same words. The changes of tempo and the phrasing they use would certainly keep you riveted. Jazz improvisation is the same in that you must try to instil your playing with the inflections and subtle changes of tone associated with the human voice and effective story telling.

Here is a simple major phrase that would 'work' in a theoretical and technical sense over a major chord.

Fig 2.6a

The phrase fits the chord well, using chord tones. However it can be embellished to give it greater authenticity. Here is the same phrase, but the first note is prepared with a grace note – the flattened fifth, which we already know is synonymous with jazz and blues – this instantly makes this phrase more authentic.

Fig 2.6b

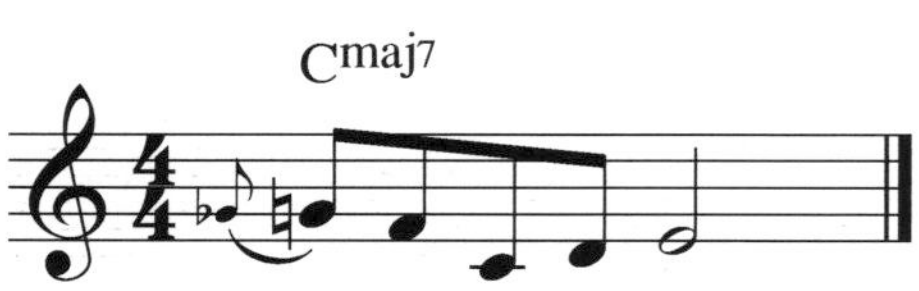

This next variation decorates the second note of the phrase. Adding a triplet instead of a quaver creates a falling effect to the tonic (the C). The first two notes of the triplet aren't as important as the third – the F is the note you are aiming for. Play the G and A more quietly and try to make them 'roll' into the F.

Fig 2.7

Here are the original and embellished versions of the same phrase for all the major chords. Play them over the mp3 backing tracks 5, 6 and 7 and really try to let the embellishments bring the phrases to life.

Fig 2.8 Exercise

Expanding your Major Seventh Chord Repertoire

The major pentatonic scale: as the name suggests, the pentatonic scale is a five-note scale (think of the words pentagon and pentathlon – all are derived from the Greek word 'pente' meaning five). It clearly spells out the major chord, but has a personality of its own.

To build a pentatonic scale, use the root, second, third, fifth and sixth degree of the major scale, as shown below.

Fig 2.9 Major Pentatonic Scale

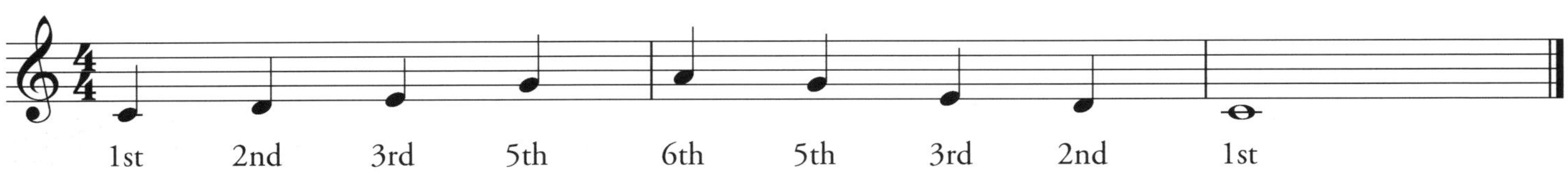

The pentatonic scale is often used over major seventh chords as an alternative to the major scale. It has a funkier edge to it than the major scale, particularly if you play with a strong groove and articulation! Here are some simple patterns to get you started:

Fig 2.10a Major Pentatonic four-note groups

Initially try to accent the first note of each four-note group (beats one and three of the bar). The pentatonic sound relies on its rhythmic punch, as well as its melodic qualities, so make it really swinging!

Here is an octave of the pattern in all 12 keys. Once you're comfortable with this exercise try to extend it over the range of the clarinet. Try to think of these as 'cells' of four notes. You can then start to develop some rhythmic variety too.

Fig 2.10b Pentatonics in all keys

This next exercise moves the pentatonic scale between on- and off-beats for an interesting rhythmic variation. This is similar to the major pentatonic workout, but each group of four notes is separated by a quaver (eighth note) rest. This makes the pattern asymmetrical as the groups of quavers start alternately on both the 'on' and 'off-beats', it can feel odd to play at first, but keep accenting the first note of each four note group and you'll start to develop an interesting rhythmic language.

Fig 2.11a Major Pentatonic four-note groups – Rhythmic Exercise

Here is the rhythmic template for that pattern – the rhythm is written for you, but the notes are left blank: this is signified by a note stem with a cross for a notehead. Take this rhythm and apply it to each of the pentatonic scales in example 2.10b. This will really get your brain and fingers working – you'll soon have your pentatonics nailed!

Fig 2.11b **Pentatonic Rhythmic Template**

Pentatonics in Pop

To hear the major pentatonic used really well, have a listen to the horn section soli (an ensemble solo) in **Stevie Wonder**'s 'Sir Duke'. This is a 16-bar section that serves as a link between the chorus and the next verse (you can hear it at 1:04). By looking at major pentatonics in this chapter, the sound of this **soli** should now sound familiar to you. Check out the way the soli has a strong percussive groove, another feature of good pentatonic playing.

Now revisit the major scale workout (mp3 tracks 5, 6 and 7) and play pentatonic scales and patterns over these – eventually in all keys!

Using the Blues

In chapter one, we learned how to make a blues scale from a major scale. Knowing how to spice up a major chord with an injection of the blues is a useful trick for an improviser and can really add interest and authenticity to your solos. The flattened third, fifth and seventh of the blues scale can be played against chords using the third, fifth and seventh that normally occur in the major scale. The resulting clash gives the music the rough, bluesy edge that we are looking for.

Here's a short major phrase to which we will give the blues treatment. Initially we will play both the flattened 'blue' notes and the regular major ones, then an all-out blues version of the same idea.

Fig 2.12 Blue Note Resolution

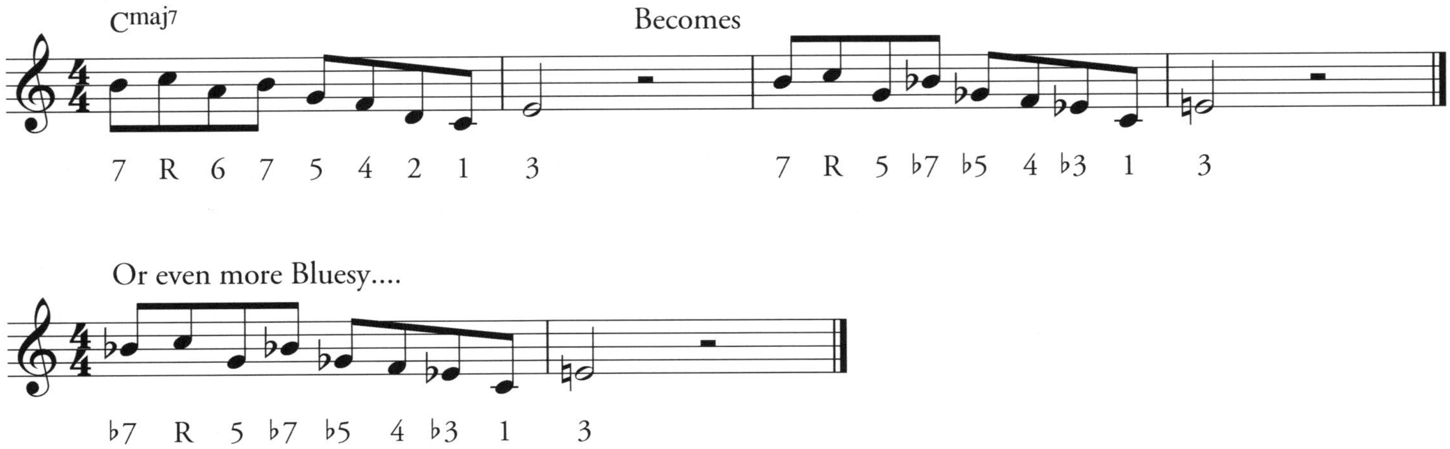

Notice how this short phrase or 'lick' (to use some jazz terminology) ends on the major third. The blues notes have created a clash against the major key that we then 'correct' or resolve in the last bar.

Whilst it feels more natural to resolve the third, you could also leave the blue note unresolved for a moodier sounding phrase – see the next example.

Fig 2.13 Unresolved Blue Note

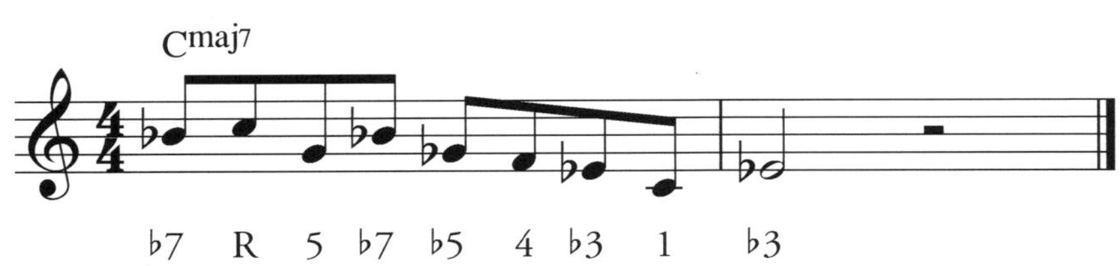

Experiment with the blue notes over the major scale workout (again eventually in all twelve keys). A good starting point is to aim to inject the blues notes into the major scale, not the other way round. You will soon get a feel for when it works and when it doesn't – go with your instinct, there's no wrong way. It's your solo so express yourself as you wish!

Checkpoint

Now you will be familiar with the sound of the major seventh chord. The soft, lush sound of major seventh chords is the basis of many tunes so you will often need to apply ideas founded on them. Use the pentatonic and blues patterns we have covered in this chapter to create your own melodic and rhythmic ideas. The CD tracks can be used to play the exercises as demonstrated or – equally importantly – to solo over and mix everything up.

Here is a tune based on major seventh chords, a good vehicle to try out your new ideas. This is a longer form than the 12-Bar blues in chapter one, and comprises four sections. To make it easier to follow the sections while improvising, each section is denoted by a letter. If you take a look at 'Major 7th Heaven' you'll notice that the first eight bars are repeated, so section 'A' happens twice. At bar 10, the music changes, so these next eight bars are the 'B' section. The last eight bars of the head reprise the 'A' section and so are labelled another 'A' section. The form of 'Major 7th Heaven' is AABA.

8 1

Fig 2.14 **'Major 7th Heaven'**

Ollie Weston

22
Fine
Cmaj7
B♭maj7
A
Solo
26
Cmaj7
B♭maj7
30
Cmaj7
B♭maj7
A2
34
Cmaj7
B♭maj7
38
Cmaj7
B♭maj7
B
42
Fmaj7
B♭maj7
46
Fmaj7
B♭maj7
A
50
Cmaj7
B♭maj7
54
Cmaj7
B♭maj7
D.S. al Fine

Lead Sheets

The style in which the music is displayed for 'Major 7th Heaven' is called a 'lead sheet'. These are often used in jazz to summarize the content of a tune. Because there is going to be improvisation in the tune, a thorough score is seldom used. The aim of a 'lead sheet' is to communicate all of the information that the musicians need in terms of melody, form and harmony.

The top line is probably the most familiar to you, as it is written in standard notation. This is the melody of the tune and the only thing that you will be required to play exactly as written. The lower stave summarizes the rhythm section's activity. The chord symbols tell us which chords are being played, and the rhythm is indicated by the headless notes – the notes of the chords can be 'voiced' (the way a chord is constructed) by the individuals. In the 'A' sections of 'Major 7th Heaven', the rhythm section stick to the groove written. In the 'B' section, the dashes indicate merely the passing of time. The rhythm section will play a swing feel as instructed at the top of the page: the drummer will play a swing drumbeat, while the bass player will 'walk' (crotchets and quaver notes on the bass spelling out the chord tones). The pianist or guitarist is free to fill the spaces as they wish – this is called 'comping' a word derived from 'accompanying'.

Notice how the melody (the head) sticks very closely to the chord tones – the only exception is bar seven where the last note anticipates the chord change by a quaver. This creates rhythmic interest and a bluesy sound. Accent the offbeat quavers in this bar and in bars 16 and 17 for a punchy rhythmic effect. There is also an embellishment in bar five of the 'A' section: the grace note is the minor third resolving up to the major third.

The sample solo (from bar 26 onwards) mixes up the various improvisation ideas we've looked at in this chapter. In bar 27 there is a triplet embellishment (see Fig 2.7) – aim to recreate the falling effect we're looking for. The crucial note is the fourth beat of the bar. Don't spend too long on the triplet and lose the beat!

Try to analyse the solo as you play. It's based around the scales and chord tones of the chords. (N.B. a change of chord requires a change of chord tones) but look for pentatonic scale usage as well as blue notes. 'A2' begins with a major pentatonic pattern, while the last 'A' section has a shot of blues in it to change the mood.

Your Solo

Hopefully you are now eager to get soloing over this 32-bar AABA form. All the chords are major sevenths and there aren't too many accidentals to deal with. Incorporate the topics covered into your solo: major seventh chord tones, pentatonic scales and the blues as well as some of the rhythmic and melodic motifs can all be used to create interesting improvisations.

3: The Minor Seventh Chord

This chapter introduces the minor seventh chord and the minor key in general. As common, if not more so than the major seventh chords we looked at in the previous chapter, the minor seventh chords have a funky edge to them that makes effective improvising quickly possible. We will look at the differences between major and minor keys, as well as some practical ways to unlock the melodic possibilities of the minor seventh chord.

Major and Minor Keys

Most of the music we play can be said to be in a 'key'. This is the specific tonal centre of the music, and the base from which the music is developed. Remember back to chapter two where we numbered the major scale – the 'root' or 1st degree of the scale was our keynote. So a piece based on a C major scale can be said to be in the 'key' of C major. Minor keys work in exactly the same way, but the key difference is the third note. In minor keys, the third degree is lowered by one semitone compared to a major scale. This makes a dramatic difference to the sound of the key and melodies within it. Fig 3.1a is a simple melody played in both the major and minor keys. You will notice that the minor version completely changes to a sadder, darker mood by the simple flattening of one note.

Fig 3.1a Major and Minor Melody

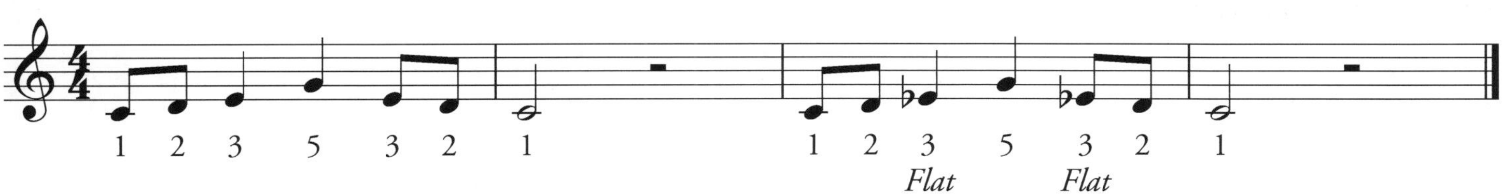

N.B. The terms 'flattened' and 'lowered' or 'sharpened' and 'raised' – are different ways of describing intervals. A flat third is exactly the same as a minor third. In the same way, a major seventh is the same as a raised seventh. All these terms deal with the raising or lowering of notes by a semitone and the resulting change in their purpose as either major or minor. It's good to be conversant with all of them as different people use different terms.

The Minor Seventh Chord

From looking at minor melodies, we know that the third is lowered (compared to a major melody). To build a minor seventh chord we start with the root, third, fifth and seventh of our major scale but flatten the third. This makes a minor chord, but the major seventh creates a dissonance that doesn't sound quite right – to make a clear sounding minor seventh chord we need to flatten the seventh as well.

Let's take a C major seventh chord and turn it into a C minor seventh chord. This is the chordal equivalent of making a major melody minor, as we did in Fig 3.1a.

Fig 3.1b **Major Seventh to Minor Seventh**

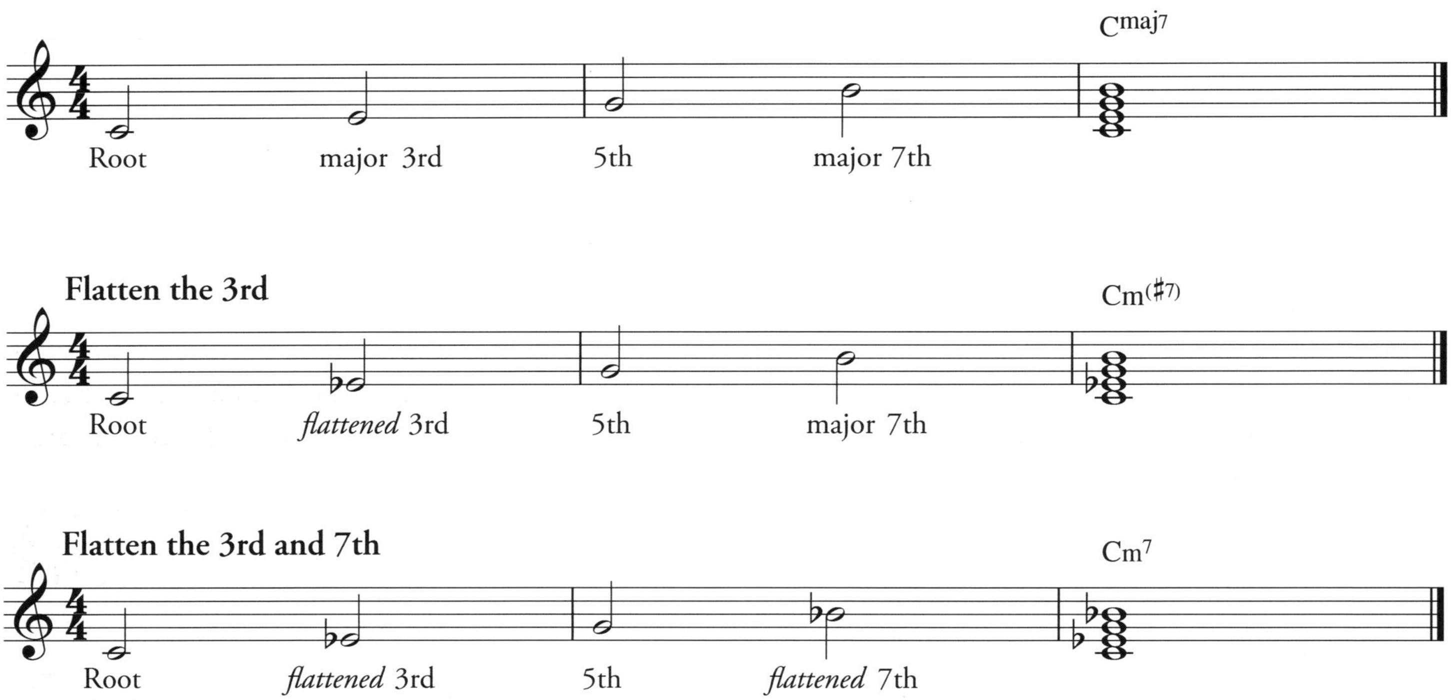

Minor Seventh Chord Passing Tones

In exactly the same way as the major scale, we build minor seventh chords from the root, third, fifth and seventh of our scale. We've seen how to flatten the third and seventh to make a minor seventh chord, if we leave the passing tones (the second, fourth and sixth) untouched, we are left with a minor arpeggio that perfectly spells out the minor seventh chord.

Fig 3.2 **Minor Seventh Chord / Passing Tones**

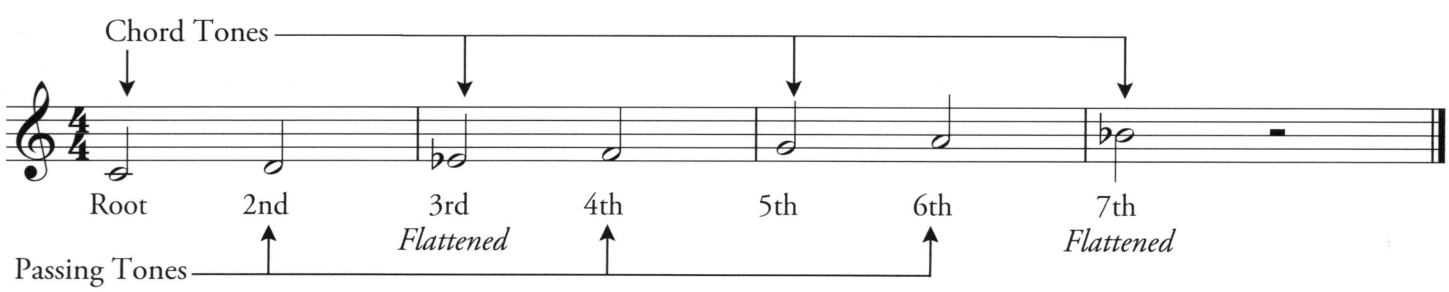

Minor Scale Variations – 'Modes'

While traditional Classical music generally focuses on the major or minor scales and harmony, jazz musicians also use another set of scales called 'modes'. The basic premise of the modes is that the passing tones (second, fourth and sixth) can be altered without changing the fundamental tonality of the chord but can still create a personality of their own. We will explore the modes later in the book but let's focus for now on one of the 'minor' modes, the 'Dorian mode'. I've chosen to start with this one as it clearly demonstrates the sound of the flattened third and seventh. This will help you understand the main chord types and the differences between them.

Fig 3.3 **C Dorian Scale**

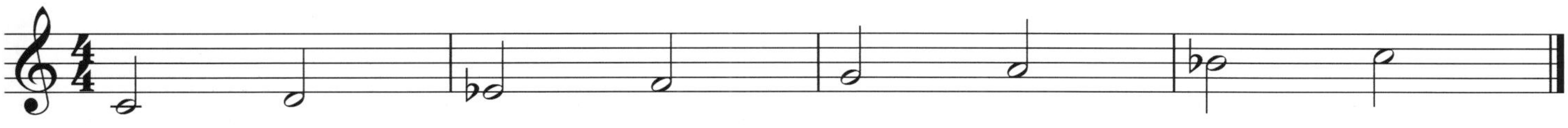

Dorian Mode/Minor Seventh Chord Workout

Play along with mp3 tracks 9, 10 and 11, and get to know your minor sevenths. As in the major scale workout in chapter 2, you have both the scale and the chord tones (root, third, fifth, and seventh) laid out for you. They are organized as before with four keys per track. Try to familiarize yourself with the sound of the scales and the chord tones.

Fig 3.4a

9

10

Fig 3.4b

11

Fig 3.4c

Checkpoint

You should now be clear on the differences between major and minor keys and the major seventh and minor seventh chords used to state these keys.

The minor seventh is a very important part of the jazz chord repertoire and you will be doing valuable groundwork by becoming really comfortable with the scales and chord tones.

Assignments and Improvisation Tips

Listen

You can develop as a musician all the time – not just in your practice slots. Music of all types surrounds us – listen enquiringly to everything you hear and ask yourself if it is in a major or minor key. What purpose is it serving? Is it there to create a specific mood? Music is cleverly used in film, television and advertising. Listen also to your favourite albums and artists and ask similar questions.

Ear Training

Try to take melodies that you know and transform them from major to minor or vice versa. This can sometimes have amusing results as the mood of the song often contradicts the words or the original purpose of the song! For example, a soft lullaby can sound totally out of context in a minor key.

As you are listening to the original, try to hear the melody notes by their relationship to the root. Ask yourself: does this tune start on the root, or the third? Does it ascend or descend?

Successful improvisation depends on being able to play what you hear in your head, in doing so you are both the composer and the performer – transferring your ideas to your fingers is an important skill.

Learn Notes by their Number

We have often referred to notes by their interval from the root, calling them thirds, fifths etc. The faster you can apply these to every key the better. Whilst you are playing your scales, work out which degree of the scale each note is as you are going up and down. You will then be able to recognize and hit the chord/passing tones of any key far more quickly.

Licks

A short phrase that a musician knows well and uses in a variety of situations is called a 'lick'. The idea that all jazz improvisation is totally spontaneous is slightly misleading; all musicians use licks to a certain extent. The ideal is to find phrases of your own that are comfortable for you to play – yet sound awesome! Here is a 'lick' to get you started.

Fig 3.5a Minor Seventh Chord Lick (Cm, E♭m, F♯m, Am)

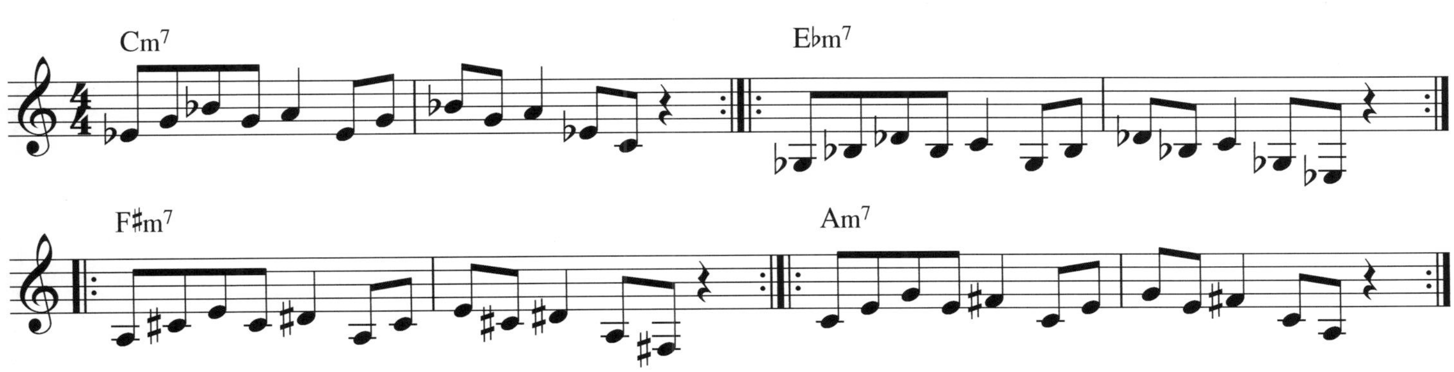

Fig 3.5b **Minor Seventh Chord Lick (C♯m, Em, Gm, B♭m)**

This is a simple but swinging line that spells out the minor seventh chord. Notice how the sixth is used in this lick and how it adds a bright, funky touch to the phrase. Analyse it in each new key and ask yourself how each note relates to the root – are they thirds, sixths, sevenths? Now revisit the minor seventh workout (mp3 tracks 9, 10 and 11) and replicate this lick in all twelve keys. It should become increasingly comfortable for you to play physically, leaving you to concentrate on the swing.

Less is More

By giving you the scale and chord tones for each key, you have all the options laid out in front of you. Don't feel that you have to use all the notes all the time.

The Minor Pentatonic Scale

Just as we had a five-note scale to spell out the major key, the minor key also has its own pentatonic scale. Understanding this will unlock minor seventh chords for you and provide a wealth of ideas to help you build on your Dorian scale improvisations. To transform the major pentatonics quickly to their minor equivalent, we must first look at the relationship between the major and minor keys.

Relative Major/Minor

Every major key has a minor equivalent (and vice versa) that shares its key signature and chord tones. By changing the context in which the notes are used, we can change the mood and therefore the tonality from major to minor. Here is a familiar major pentatonic scale.

Fig 3.6a **Major Pentatonic**

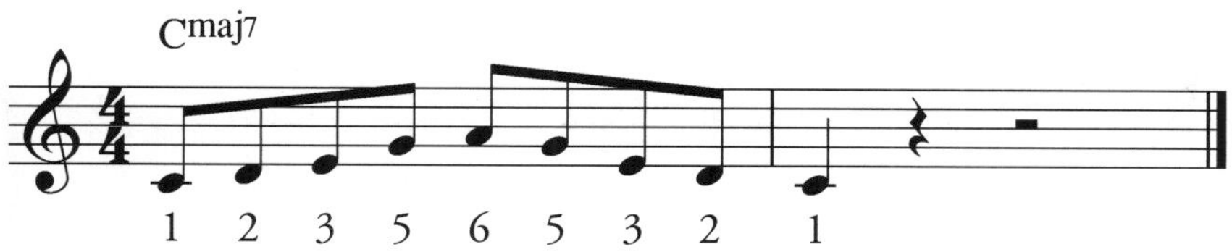

Now I'm going to change the chord symbol from C^maj7^ to Am^7^.

Fig 3.6b **Change of Chord from Major to Relative Minor**

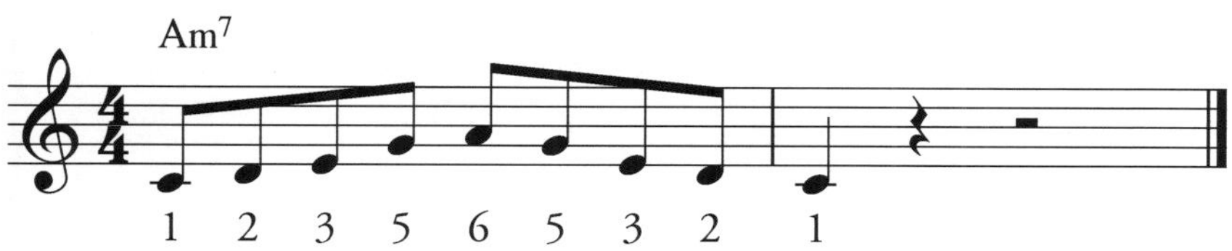

Notice how the numbering is now wrong – the root of the major pentatonic isn't now the root of our new minor chord (the root here should be A). Here it is with the numbers now relevant to the new root:

Fig 3.6c **Notes Numbered correctly according to Root of Relative Minor**

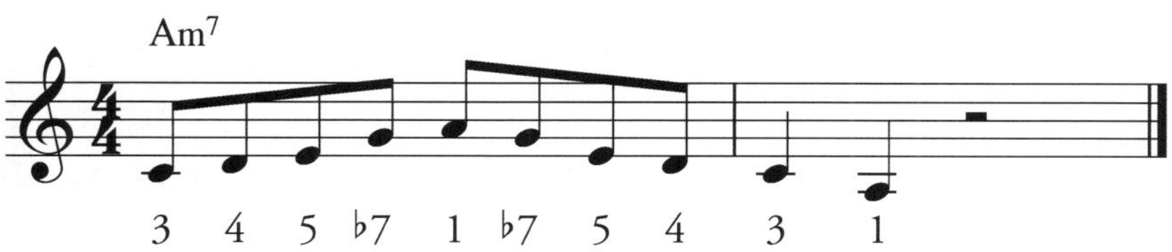

By changing the context (but not the notes), we've created a new pentatonic (A minor) from the C major pattern. These two keys are, respectively, the relative major and relative minor of each other. Note that the root note has changed, but nothing else. The minor pentatonic starts on the sixth degree of the major scale and the major pentatonic starts on the third degree of the minor scale. Here they are written out together.

Fig 3.7 **Relative Major / Minor Pentatonics**

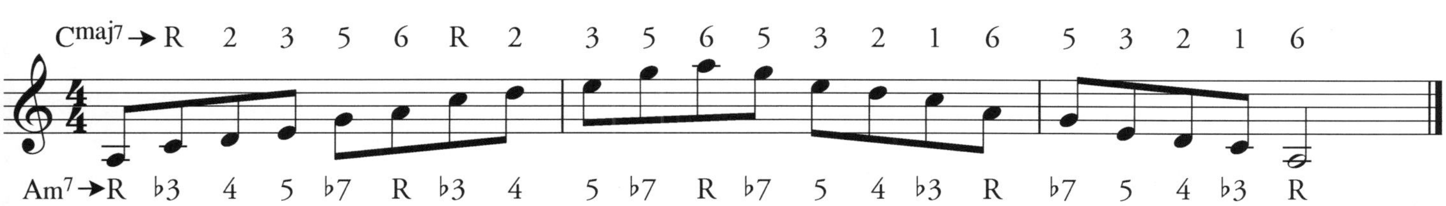

Try to play each with a sense of major and minor tonality as you go through.

This is not to be confused with major and minor pentatonics that start on the same root note – C major pentatonic isn't the same as C minor pentatonic. Here are major and minor pentatonics starting on the same root note. Notice how the scales are built slightly differently: the major pentatonic has the root, second, third, fifth and sixth whilst the minor pentatonic has the root, flattened third, fourth, fifth and flattened seventh.

Fig 3.8 Major / Minor Pentatonics from the Same Root Note

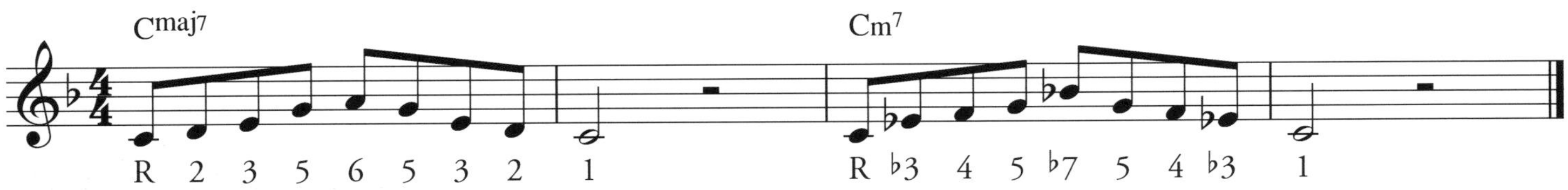

Minor Pentatonic Patterns

Using mp3 tracks 9, 10 and 11 (the same tracks as you used for the minor scale workout) let's try the four-note pentatonic patterns we learned in chapter two. Crucially though they are now in a minor context.

Written in brackets are the relative major keys of each one. As with the major pentatonics, for these to sound really effective they need rhythmic punch as well as melodic accuracy – really swing hard with the rhythm section!

Fig 3.9a Minor Pentatonic Shapes (Cm, E♭m, F♯m, Am)

Fig 3.9b Minor Pentatonic Shapes (C♯m, Em, Gm, B♭m)

Fig 3.9c Minor Pentatonic Shapes (Dm, Fm, G♯m, Bm)

Using the Blues over Minor Sevenths

As we found in the chapter on major chords, injecting lines with a dose of the blues adds a gritty authenticity to solos. The same is true of minor seventh chords. If you compare the minor pentatonic and then the blues scale, you will see that they are in fact very similar:

The only difference between the two is the blues scale's flattened fifth – one of the 'blue' notes. Therefore to impose the blues sound over a minor pentatonic, all you need to do is add a flat fifth to your pentatonic ideas.

Fig 3.10 Minor Pentatonics / Blues Scale Comparison

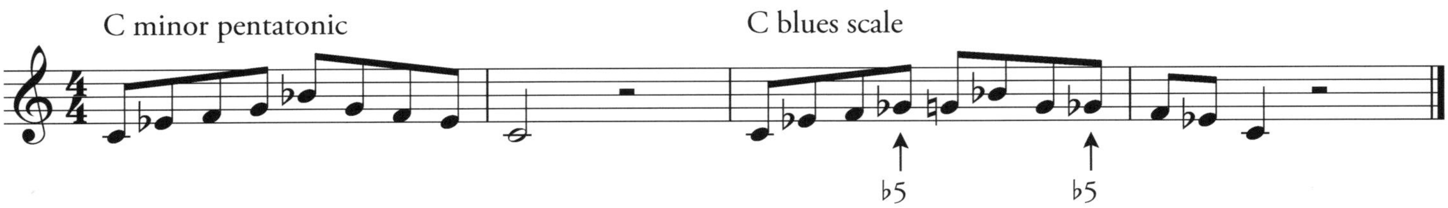

Here is a simple lick mixing up the two:

Fig 3.11 Minor Pentatonic / Blues Scale Lick

Whilst sounding OK, this lick feels a little awkward. The flattened fifth feels like it's been shoehorned into the phrase. Because pentatonic phrases rely so much on their rhythm, adding an extra note in the middle can upset the swing and make it feel a little unbalanced. A good way to remedy this is to make a triplet out of one of the pairs of quavers, this allows you to fit in an extra note and doesn't upset the rhythmic feel:

Fig 3.12 Triplet Feel

A great example of a tune that is based on the blues and pentatonics is 'Moanin''. Written by pianist **Bobby Timmons**, it is the title track of the 1958 album by legendary drummer **Art Blakey** and his band **The Jazz Messengers**. Have a listen to this tune and see if you can spot the blues touches in the head.

Triplets

Triplets occupy a vital place in jazz music – swung quavers are after all derived from triplets. If you are unsure how to fit them in, think of a three syllable word to get used to them. Clarinet is a good example:

Fig 3.13 Triplets

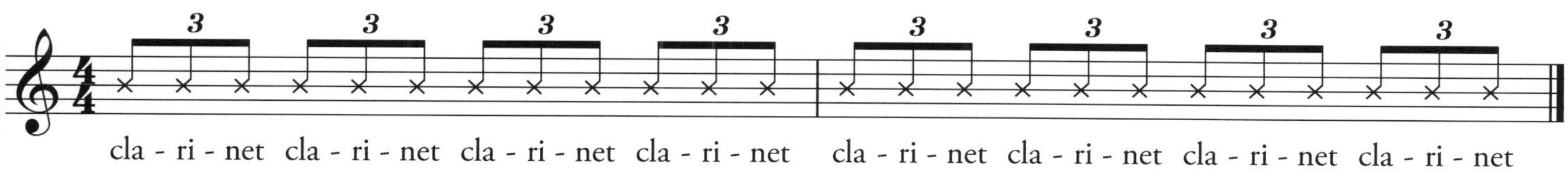

Here is a rhythmic variation based on our minor pentatonic pattern. Notice that whenever the flattened fifth appears, a triplet does a good job of making space for it, thus avoiding awkward, unswinging phrases.

Fig 3.14a

Fig 3.14b

Fig 3.14c

These bluesy triplet patterns really add interest to your pentatonic scales. Feel free to explore different combinations of flattened fifths and triplets. Just put on the backing tracks and play.

Miles Davis – Kind of Blue

In 1959, **Miles Davis** released *Kind of Blue*, an album that has gone on to be the best selling jazz album of all time. Assembled on the album are some of the greats of modern jazz including **Miles Davis** himself on trumpet, **John Coltrane** on tenor sax and **Julian 'Cannonball' Adderley** on alto.

The opening track of the album is called 'So What' and is based around two minor seventh chords – the musicians give a master class in minor chord improvisation, each gracing the tune with their own sound. This album was revolutionary in 1959 and retains its freshness and importance to this day.

Checkpoint

We have now covered the basics of the minor key and the minor seventh chord. By flattening the third of a major key, we can create a much sadder, moodier, sound world. You should now be able to recognize quickly major and minor tonalities and the resultant atmospheres they create.

We have also learned some interesting ways to solo over a minor seventh chord – using the Dorian scale, pentatonics and the blues scale. You will now be fluent in the minor vocabulary and be soloing with ease.

This tune is another 32-bar tune with an AABA form. The 'A' sections use one minor seventh chord, the tune then moves up a semitone for the 'B' section, then back down for the last 'A' section. I've included an intro of eight bars to set the mood (this happens only once and isn't part of the form).

Fig 3.15a **'So Far, So Good'**

12 2

Ollie Weston

* Piano chords written in the clarinet home key.

Assignments and Improvisation Tips

Passing Tones and Extensions

So far we have only numbered notes from one to eight, covering an octave. If we extend from eight upwards, we can repeat the scale but an octave higher (so the eighth degree is simply the root note but an octave higher). The second degree becomes the 9th, the third a 10th and so on. These higher notes are called 'extensions'; this is where the passing tones really become useful. Here is a minor seventh chord spelt out, and then with the passing tones up an octave and placed on top, becoming the 9th, 11th, and 13th (extensions) of the chord.

Fig 3.15b **Extensions**

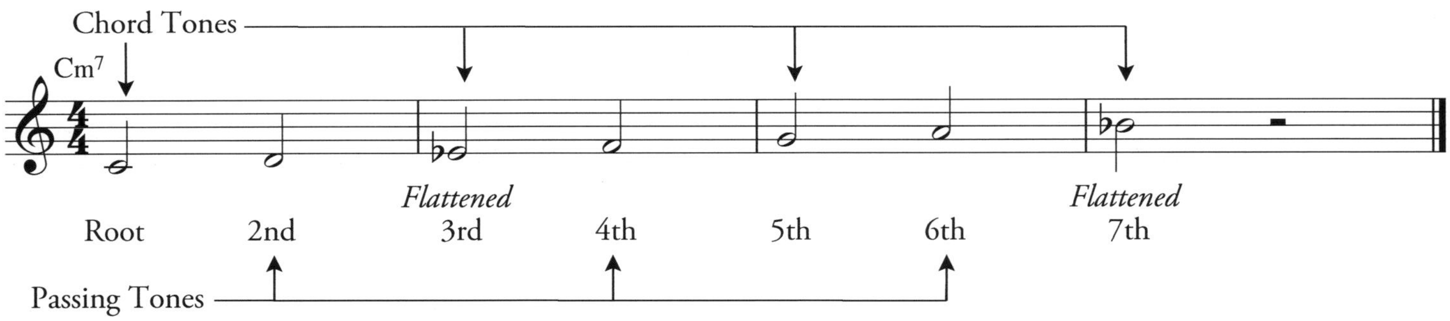

Fig 3.15c

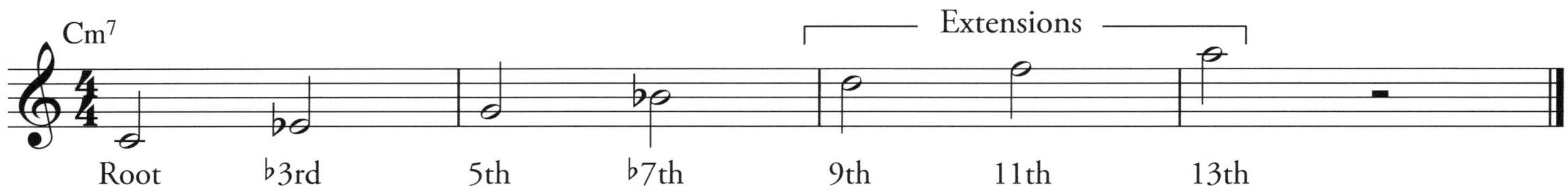

These notes can now be played as part of the chord if desired. Now the passing tones have been transposed up by an octave, it stops the notes clashing together and creates beautiful variations for chords containing root, third, fifth, and sevenths. (N.B. The original chord tones still need to be present; the extensions are harmonic luxuries rather than necessities). Look again at 'So Far, So Good,' in particular the first time bar – notice how the melody lands on the second, or as we will now call it the 9th. This non-chord tone adds a touch of colour to the melody and creates a more ambiguous end to the phrase.

Anticipating the Chord Progression

Have a look at the second time bar; you'll see that the melody anticipates the next chord by 2 beats. The phrase actually belongs to the chord in the 'B' section; the B♭ and C of the next chord have no place in the 'A' section. By playing them early we create a sense of tension that's then resolved as the chord progression catches up by bar 13. Try this in your solo – pick a note that belongs to the 'B' section and start to play it in the second time bar – don't worry when it clashes, the release that comes when the chord changes is worth it! Notice how this is achieved in bar 20 of the head.

Rhythmic Development

Rhythm is all-important in jazz – a solo that hits all the right notes but meanders rhythmically isn't as effective as a really punchy rhythmic statement. The sample solo here comprises one simple rhythmic motif (see below) which then gets developed to create rhythmic interest in Fig 3.16b.

Fig 3.16a **Rhythmic Motif**

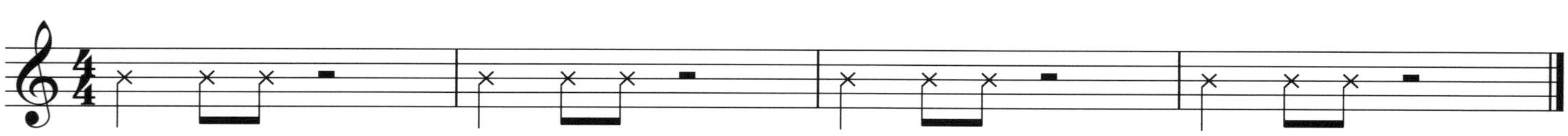

Every phrase has a two-bar gap for you to improvise in – try to make a sympathetic response to what has come before, using mp3 track 12.

Fig 3.16b Sample Solo

12

Here are some other simple rhythms to explore:

Fig 3.17 Additional Rhythmic Motifs

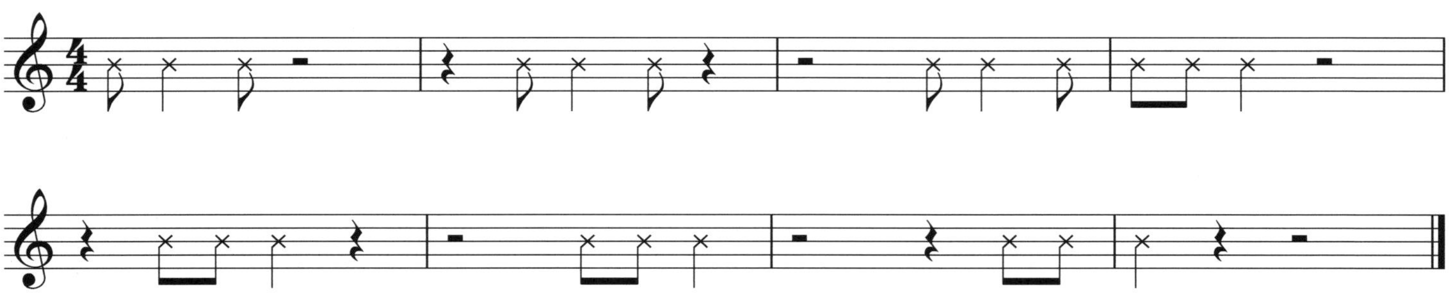

The crossed note heads indicate that no specific notes are to be played – the note choice is up to you. Initially you could use the pitches of the sample solo, but change the rhythms to the above alternatives – try to concentrate on making the rhythms really punchy. When you are comfortable with each separate rhythm, mix them up and solo freely.

Less is More

A good challenge is to limit yourself to a couple of notes per eight-bar section. You will then have to explore those notes thoroughly and think of different ways to maintain interest – this will really test you as a musician and an improviser. You'll be amazed at how creative you have become!

4: The Seventh Chord

Having covered major seventh (e.g. C^{maj7}) and minor seventh chords (e.g. Cm^7) in the last two chapters the next chord to study is the dominant seventh chord (e.g. C^7). Of all the chord types the dominant seventh is possibly the most evocative of the jazz sound – in fact it's so ubiquitous that it's often referred to as simply the 'seventh' chord. Once you unlock the sound of the seventh chord successfully, your improvising will develop further. This chapter will look at how to create a seventh chord, some of the scales that relate to it and its practical significance to the jazz musician.

Creating a Seventh Chord

So far you have built a major seventh chord from the major scale by using the root, major third, fifth and major seventh and then turned that into a minor seventh chord by flattening the third and the seventh notes. To create a seventh chord, leave the third as a major interval, but flatten the seventh. Here is a major seventh chord converted to a seventh chord:

Fig 4.1 Converting C^{maj7} to C^7

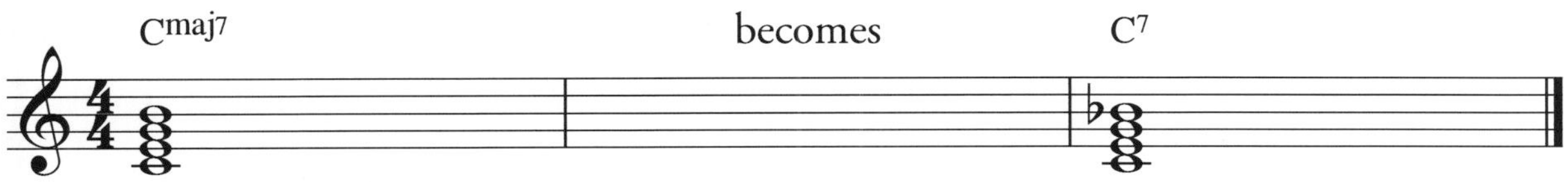

Changing just one note creates a totally different sounding chord – one that instantly conjures up the sound not only of jazz, but rock and pop music too. Here is the seventh chord built as a rising arpeggio.

Fig 4.2 C^7 Built up note-by-note

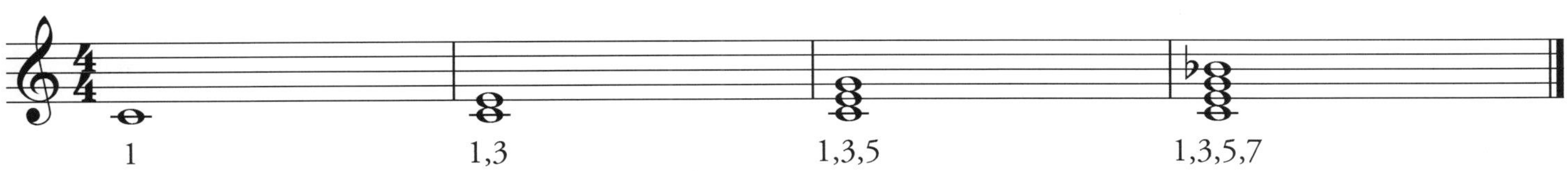

Adding one note at a time to build the chord clearly demonstrates its chord tones and lets the ear focus on one note at a time.

The Tritone Interval

The interest in the seventh chord is created by the clash between the third and seventh. The interval between these two notes is that of a 'tritone'. As the name suggests, this is an interval of three tones ('tri' meaing three).

Fig 4.3 The Tritone

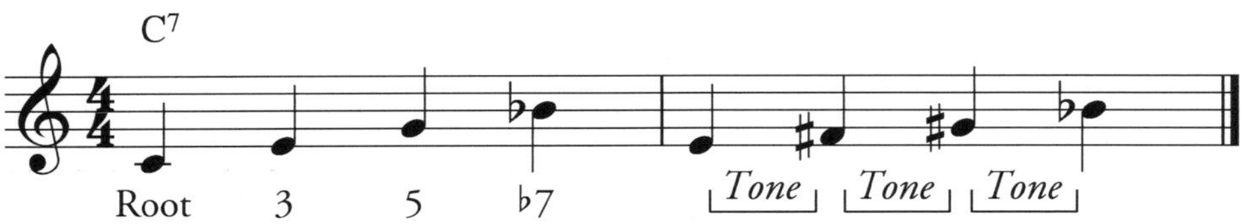

(Note that the F♯ and G♯ in this example form no part of the chord. They are there merely to demonstrate the three intervals of a tone that separate the third and seventh.)

A restless, unsettled interval, the tritone was considered an ugly dissonance by medieval composers and was avoided at all costs.

It was so frowned upon that it became known as the 'diabolus in musica' or the 'devil in music'. There is an interesting poetic parallel that can be drawn here between **Robert Johnson**'s alleged meeting with the devil and the significance of the 'devil in music' tritone interval in Johnson's music and also that which followed.

The Mixolydian Mode

The previous two chapters have explained the construction of chords and have then applied relevant scales to them. This relationship between chords and scales is of great importance to an improviser, providing a clear idea of where the chord tones and passing tones fall. You also have a starting point for your solos and a fail-safe fallback to help you avoid playing any really bad notes. Because of the seventh's unique sound, neither the major or minor scales will fit over it very well, so we must find a new scale that accurately spells out its main features – the major third and flattened seventh.

Because there is only one note difference between the major seventh and dominant seventh chords, it is necessary only to change one note of the scale – the seventh. This must be flattened, which creates the tritone interval with the third and so the distinctive 'crunch' of the chord.

Fig 4.4 The Mixolydian Mode

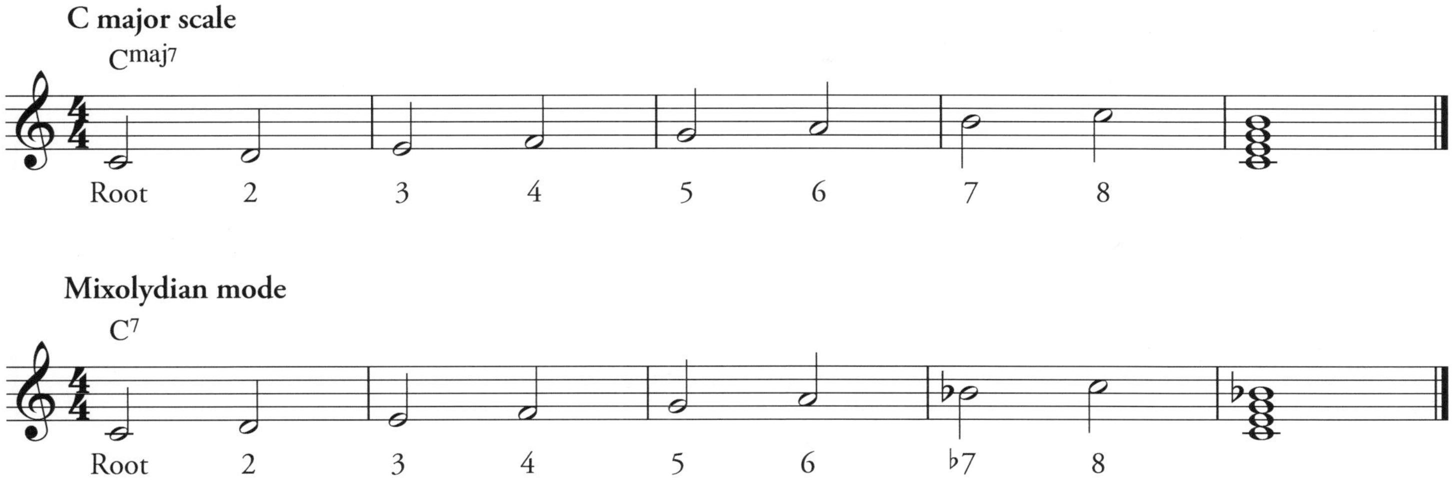

The root, third, fifth and the passing tones are the same in both scales – only the seventh is different. This new scale is another of the 'modes' and is called the 'Mixolydian mode'.

Checkpoint

You should now be familiar with the seventh chord and the Mixolydian mode. The tritone dissonance between the major third and the flattened seventh is a huge part of the jazz sound world and a vital one to explore.

Assignments and Improvisation Tips

Seventh Chord Workout

Play along with mp3 tracks 13, 14, and 15 to get to know your seventh chords. As in the major scale workout in chapter two and the minor workout in chapter three, you have both the scale and the chord tones (root, third, fifth, and seventh) laid out for you. They are organized as before with four keys per track. Try to familiarize yourself with the sound of the scales and the chord tones.

Fig 4.5a Mixolydian Workout

13

Fig 4.5b

14

Fig 4.5c

15

The differences and similarities between the three main chord types should now be clear to you. The three workouts on major, minor and seventh chords and their respective scales are a great exercise. Like an athlete, musicians need to stretch and warm up muscles before playing. The major seventh, minor seventh and seventh chord workouts provide a great technical warm up for you and your instrument. Pick one set of each of the chord types per practice session and really nail them – this way you will soon become fluent with the chords and the scales that go with them.

Another variation on these scale/chord tone exercises is to play the three chord types consecutively from the same root note. Here are the three chord/scale types arranged in the order that the notes change: the difference between the major seventh chord and the seventh chord is only one note (the seventh degree) and the difference between the seventh chord and the minor seventh chord is also only one note (the third degree). This gradual progression can be seen as a flattening process where each new chord type flattens another note, taking the bright, settled, major sound and darkening it. Playing the three scales from the same root reinforces the difference between them from a static point, making the subtle changes between each chord easy to hear.

As before, these are arranged into three groups of four keys. Use both the above scale exercises as warm ups. For space reasons only the major seventh versions of these exercises have been written ascending and descending, but apply the same principle to the other versions of the scales.

Fig 4.6a Main Chord Types from the Same Root

Fig 4.6b

Fig 4.6c

Using a Metronome

Exercise 4.6 doesn't have a backing track. You do however still need to play the exercises in steady time and with a good feel. Jazz musicians put a high price on good time and feel. A great lick played slightly out of time, or on the wrong beat of the bar, will sound awkward and lose its effect – play it in the right place and really lock with the rhythm section and the gig will be yours!

A metronome is an invaluable practice tool, it will keep the beat for you and allow you to work on building your technique and internal pulse (your own personal sense of where the beat is). For the price of a box of reeds, the metronome will really help you maximize your practice time.

Beats 2 and 4

For a swing feel (initially you should be playing these exercises with swung quavers) set the metronome to beat on the second and fourth beats (rather than the first and third beats). The second and fourth beats have a stronger rhythmic association with jazz. This goes back to jazz's African rhythmic roots and is an early form of syncopation.

Try clapping along with a jazz tune – one of the demo tracks on the CD would be fine. First clap on all four beats, then just the first and third beats. Lastly swap from the first and third to the second and fourth beats – the tune will seem to 'sit' better (feel more comfortable) with this method.

Fig 4.7 Beats 2 and 4

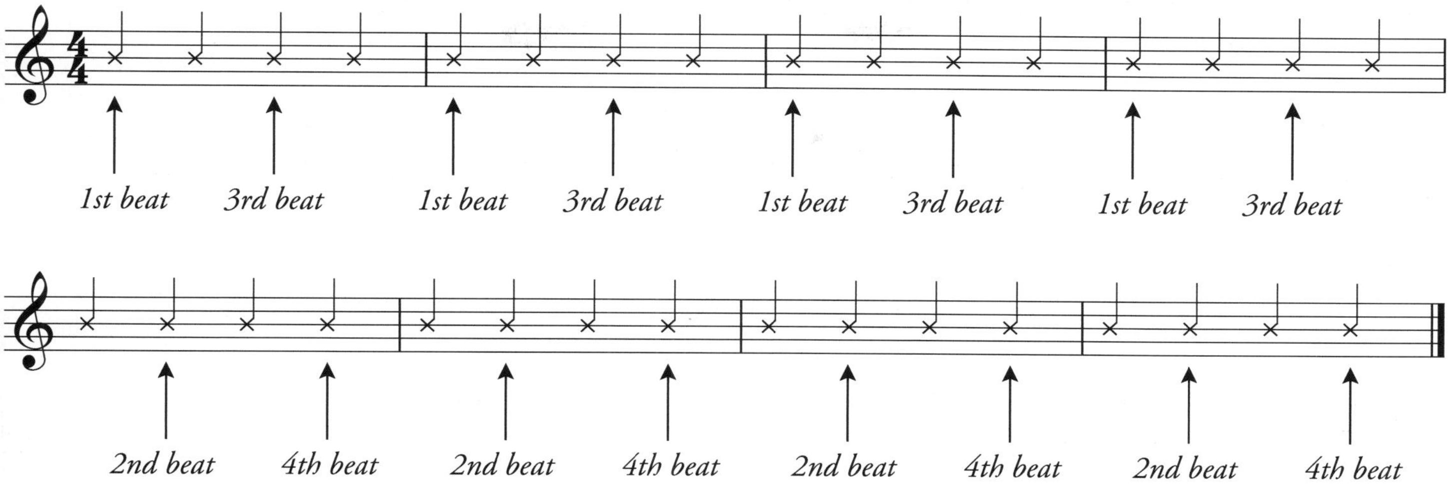

The second and fourth beats have a stronger rhythmic association with jazz and so are easier to groove with. The rhythmic emphasis on beats two and four is sometimes called a 'backbeat' and is present in much pop, blues and R&B music. Listen out for a strong emphasis (often on the snare drum) on the second and fourth beats in any of these styles of music.

The Seventh Chord in the 12-Bar Blues

Back in chapter one we looked at the 12-Bar blues – in particular, Fig 1.8 focused on the bass notes of the 12-Bar blues chord progression. This gave you an idea of the 'root movement' of the chords. This spells out where the root of each chord is going. However, a series of bass notes doesn't make a chord progression, so we're now going to fill in the gaps.

The standard 12-Bar blues is made up of three different seventh chords. The first chord is built on the first degree (root) of the scale and tells us the key of the tune (i.e. a 'G' blues begins with a chord of G^7). The other seventh chords used in the 12-Bar progression are built on the fourth degree (C^7 in this case) and the fifth (D^7). Here are the chords for a standard blues in G.

Fig 4.8 Chords of the 12-Bar blues in G

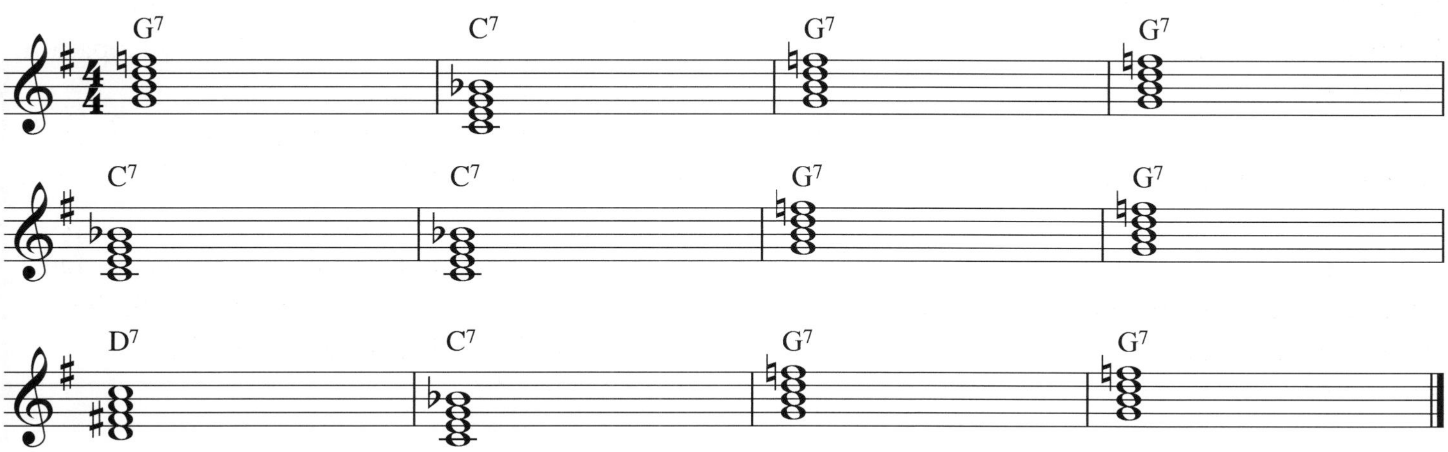

As we've seen, the really descriptive notes of the seventh chord are the third and the seventh – they create the tritone interval and the dissonance within the chord. The third and the seventh are also the only notes that change from chord to chord – look again at the process of changing C^{maj7} to Cm^7 or C^{maj7} to C^7: the root and the fifth are constant. The root and the fifth don't carry much information about the specific characteristics of the chord, it's the thirds and sevenths that make all the difference. Here are just the thirds and sevenths of the chords in the 12-Bar blues.

Fig 4.9 Thirds and Sevenths of the 12-Bar Blues

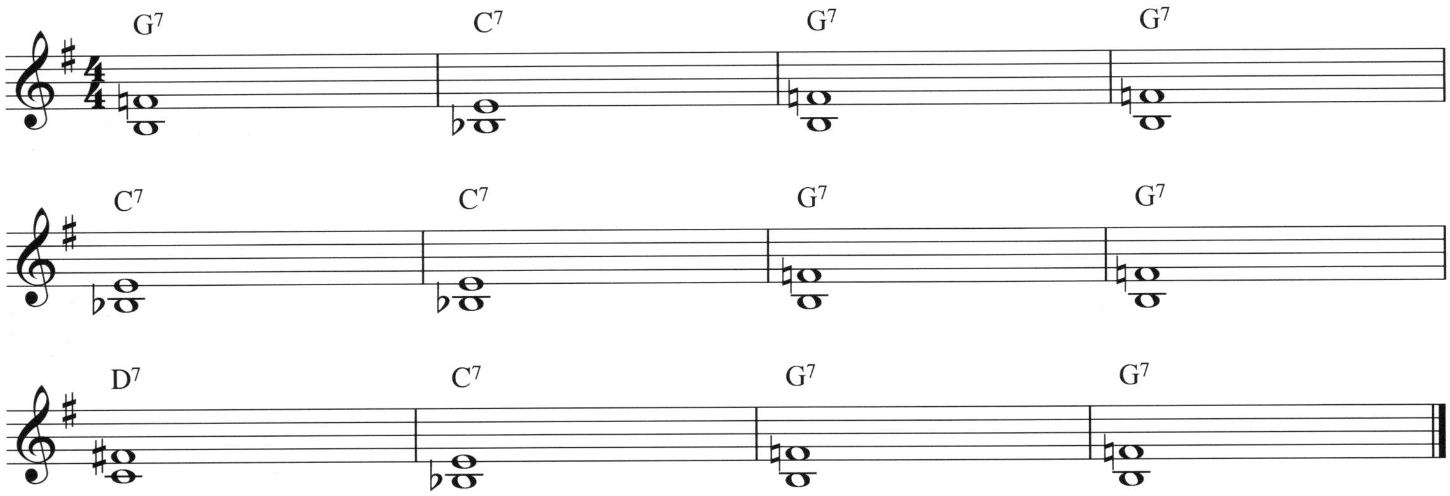

Notice how subtle the movements are between the chords – by only moving a semitone, the third of the G chord becomes the seventh of the C chord. Likewise the seventh of the G chord becomes the third of the C chord by moving a semitone. Knowing the inner workings of a chord progression is extremely helpful for an improviser as you can move effortlessly from chord to chord by making tiny adjustments. Here is the rhythmic motif from the blues root note exercise in chapter one (Fig 1.9) but now using only the thirds and sevenths of the chords to create two paths through the progression (the text beneath the stave denotes the chord tone of the chord above that note).

Fig 4.10 Moving Between Thirds and Sevenths

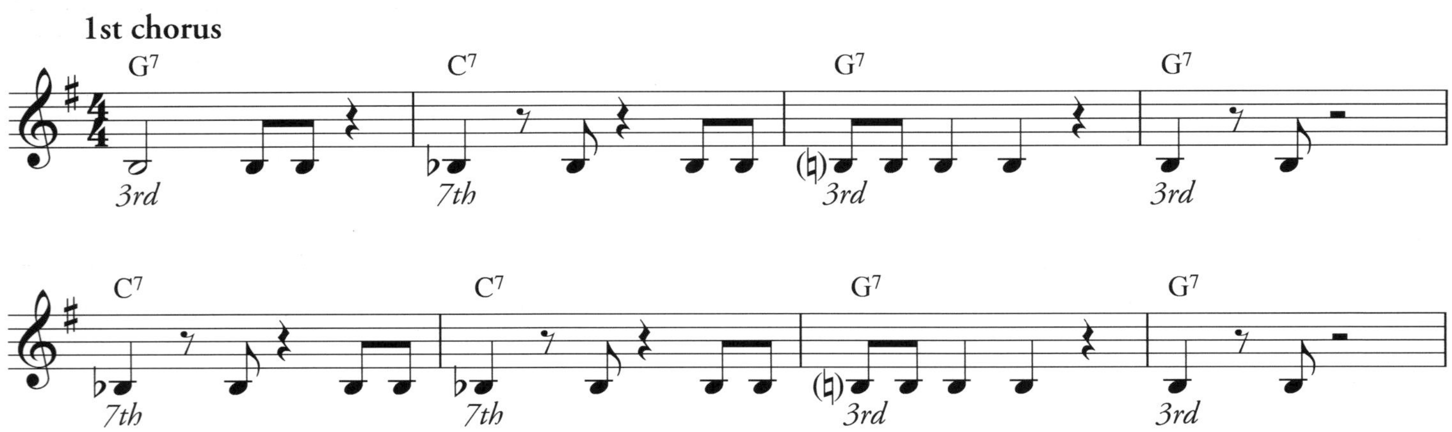

These two paths through the chord progression hint at the chords without playing the roots. Knowing these inner lines is extremely important to an improviser as you can then suggest chords and move freely between them in many different ways. Play Fig 4.10 with a metronome (on beats two and four of course!) and try to hear the roots of the chords you are playing and the effect of the thirds and sevenths against those. If you find it difficult to pitch them straight away in your head, replace one of the third or seventh lines with the root. Using a couple of root notes will help you get your bearings and hear the roots against the thirds and sevenths of the chords without upsetting the rhythmic pattern. The first four bars might look like this.

Fig 4.11 Thirds and Sevenths with the Root as a Reference

Eventually you'll be moving between the notes effortlessly without hitting the roots at all. Keep playing this exercise with the metronome and you will soon have the blues progression under your creative control, as well as safely under your fingers.

The Major Vs. Minor Third in the Blues

One of the first things covered in chapter one was the practice of substituting the major third with the minor third as part of the blues scale. This was looked at as a way of playing authentic sounding lines in a jazz/blues style. However, now that the seventh chord has been added to the mix there are more options. The seventh chord's effect on the ears relies on the tension created between the third and the seventh degrees of the scale, the major third and the flattened seventh. If a flattened third is imposed over this chord it cancels out the tritone interval and so lessens the effect of the seventh chord.

However it is possible to fit the minor third interval over the twelve bar progression:

Fig 4.12 Major or Minor Third Over Each Chord

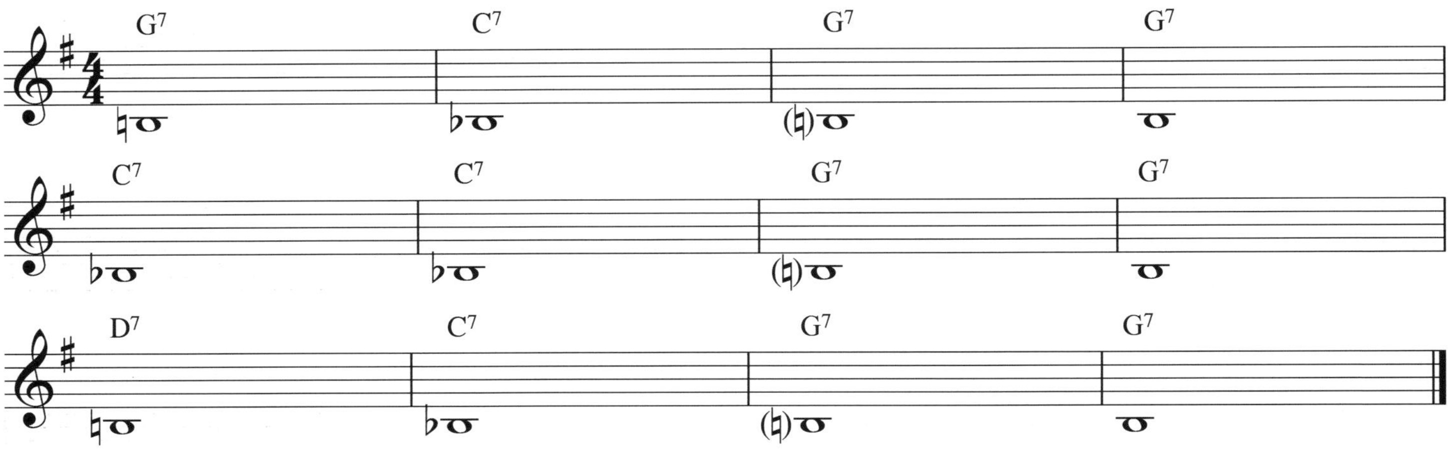

Here is the 12-Bar progression again but this time with the major or minor third of the tonic key (G) written for each chord. The note B over the tonic G^7 chord is the obvious choice – as the major third it's one of the chord tones and essential for the seventh chord sound. As seen in Fig 4.10, flattening this note by a semitone – to a B♭ – will land on a strong chord tone of the next chord which is the seventh of C^7. Whilst fitting the chord, the B♭ also lends a minor quality to the line as it's the minor third of the tonic key. (N.B. A change of chord isn't the same as a change of key. The key of G remains constant throughout this tune.) A big change is at bar five of the progression: this is the second line of the head, often melodically repeating this first line. Crucially though the chord has changed, so you can't necessarily play exactly the same pitches as you did on the first line. Be careful to change to a B♭ over the C^7 chord as a B♮ over it sounds pretty bad – to be avoided!

The only chord that has no B♭ or B♮ as one of its chord tones is D^7. A B♮ is the best choice as it is part of the D Mixolydian scale and also part of the key of the tune (G).

Fig 4.13 'Sonny's Blues'

16 3

Ollie Weston

This is a standard 12-Bar blues head – inspired by the great tenor saxophonist **Sonny Rollins**. Similar to 'Leavin' Town' in its three line structure, 'Sonny's Blues' is more jazz-based because of the new chords and harmony applied. Listen to mp3 track 16 for a recorded version and particularly listen out for the variety created by using the different scales and chord tones. Check out the jump of a tritone in bar eleven – the third jumping to the flattened seventh. The medieval musicians who so desperately avoided the 'Diabolus In Musica' would have winced, but for our purposes it sounds great.

Now play through the head and solo of 'Sonny's Blues' with the backing on CD track 3. Don't forget your rhythmic work – this tune needs to swing hard to be really effective!

Checkpoint

The 12-Bar blues should now be familiar to you in much more detail than it was in chapter one. The use of the seventh chords to spell out the harmonic progression gives you a larger palette of notes with which to express yourself. Navigating the subtle differences between the chords gives you options other than just the blues scale. Within the blues progression you have space to suggest both the major and minor key – the constant switching between major third over the root chord and flattened seventh over the IV chord allows you to create phrases that answer each other in subtly differing ways.

Major and Minor Third

The head of 'Sonny's Blues' has several examples of the different options available for the third: note the use of B♮ and B♭ and listen to their effect on the tune, and also how they fit over the chord progression. The big difference is at bar 5 when the initial melody is repeated but with the B♮ flattened to B♭ to make it fit over the C^7 chord (if you were to ignore these natural signs, the results would sound pretty terrible). Many blues heads use this technique to create a memorable repeated theme.

Another way to play off the major and minor thirds is to use the minor third as a passing tone to the major. Although not a part of the Mixolydian mode, the minor third can be used as a passing tone between the second and third notes (refer back to chapters two and three if in doubt). Look at bar six of the first solo chorus and notice how the B♭ becomes a B♮ as the chord changes back to G^7. The same technique is used in bar 10. Look through all four choruses of the solo and analyse the use of B♭s and B♮s and their relationship to both the chord they are a part of, and the overall key of the tune.

The Last Four Bars of the Progression

Another area to explore within the blues progression is the last four bars. The concluding line is different to the first two in that it's the first time the V chord is introduced. Using the thirds and sevenths as outlined in this chapter over the D^7 chord will produce an F♯. Fitting perfectly over the chord, this note produces another interesting major/minor clash with the key of the tune. Both the blues scale and the Mixolydian scale of our key (G) have an F♮ – so an F♯ would appear to be a note to be avoided as it would suggest the major seventh. Much like the use of the major and minor thirds earlier in the progression timing and placement are all-important.

Look at each of the sections of the sample solo where D^7 is followed by C^7 and you'll see that I've used an F♯ each time. In the second chorus the F♯ appears in bar eight – one bar before the D^7 chord will start in the rhythm section. This is an example of 'anticipating' the chords (as introduced in chapter three), the F♯ is still used as part of the D^7chord.

Another common approach is to play a parallel phrase over these two chords. If a phrase is strong over a D^7 chord it should be just as strong over a C^7 chord – but a tone lower. Listen to the recorded version of the solo (mp3 track 16) and listen to the last line of the second and third choruses: the same phrase is used in bars nine and ten, but a tone lower to make it fit the new chord. Jazz musicians love to repeat phrases in this way and incorporating it in your solos will enhance both your enjoyment and that of the audience.

Assignments and Improvisation Tips

Play Along with the Solo

To appreciate the subtle inflections and nuances of jazz it's important to listen closely to the music. Playing along with another clarinettist is essential if you are to pick out the subtleties of tone, vibrato and accents that are so redolent of the jazz style. The musical examples on the CD are a useful starting point: play along with these and try to copy the playing on the track exactly. This will help you develop a good tone and good feel.

Developing a Lick

Take a lick – either one of your own or a short line (two bars at the most) from the solo on 'Sonny's Blues' – that you've enjoyed playing and try to apply it to the 12-Bar blues. You should include some of the ideas looked at in this chapter, particularly the use of major and minor thirds over particular chords, and the movement between the V and IV chords at the end of the 12-Bar progression.

Play as much as possible!

The CD backing track 3 has a blues progression repeated so that you can try things out. You could just play the written solo and the head as a complete performance but this would only achieve some of the results that you're looking for. The sample solo exists to provide inspiration for you. The best way to develop is to improvise over the progression and discover the things that resonate with you and that you would like to explore further.

5: Putting It Together

You've now covered the three main chord types: the major seventh, minor seventh and seventh chords should now be under your fingers and equally importantly, in your ears. The tunes in the last three chapters have focused on one particular chord each and applied the principles covered in that chapter. In the real world tunes aren't constructed from just one chord type but a mixture of them all. The array of different colours and moods created by different chords is wide open for the composer and improviser to manipulate as they wish, different chord types will often sit next to each other in a tune. In the next chapter we're going to look at the way chord progressions are put together and the relationships between certain chord types. For now, look at each chord as a separate entity – aim to familiarize yourself and build fluency with each chord and its melodic or rhythmic possibilities.

'Pearly White'

This is a simple, melodic tune with a chord progression that mixes up major seventh, minor seventh and seventh chords. Inspired by **Kurt Weill**'s classic song 'Mack The Knife' it's a great vehicle to test out all that you've learned so far.

The tune has two eight-bar sections – 'A' and 'B' – and uses only four chords. There's nothing technically difficult about this tune, and it relies on feel for its effect, making it an ideal opportunity to put into practice the topics covered. The 'A' section is built of several short phrases whose notes are similar, but are subtly tailored to fit the different chords: notice in the third bar of the 'A' section that the F is the minor third of the Dm^7 chord. The F is then used again two bars later over the G^7 chord, where it has become the seventh. This use of the strong chord tones allows the simple melody to be effective in spelling out the chord progression. The 'B' section is a little busier note-wise, but the emphasis is still on simplicity and strong note choices. Listen to the recorded version (mp3 track 17) and pay attention to the relaxed mood of the tune. Try to reproduce this in your version.

Fig 5.1 **'Pearly White'**

17 4

Ollie Weston

Half-Time Feel

Listen to CD backing track 4 and pay particular attention to the bass and drums the first time the head is played. Previously in a swing feel tune, the bass has been playing quarter notes (crotchets), usually moving by step to the nearest available note of the scale. This is called a 'walking bass' – a defining characteristic of the swing feel. In the first chorus of 'Pearly White' the bass isn't walking, but playing half notes (minims) on beats one and three – this is called a 'half-time feel'.

Fig 5.2a **Half-Time Feel**

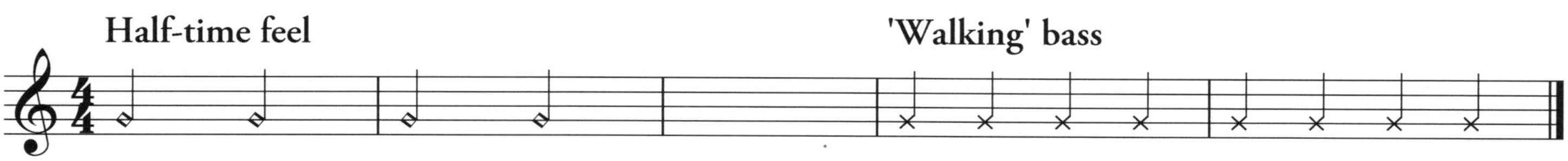

This gives the tune a more relaxed feel, so that when the swing section does start, it has greater impact.

The sample solo for 'Pearly White' is set out below – let's find out how it's been put together. The first chorus of this solo – like the head – is made up of short, simple phrases. By leaving gaps between each phrase the ideas have time to register with the listener and the solo builds at a slower pace – this can be preferable to going in with all guns blazing! Let the solo breathe, let your musical ideas have some freedom – take your time. Observe that each phrase ends on one of the chord tones – the F in bar three for example, is the third of the Dm^7 chord. The first chorus ends on an E – the third of the C^{maj7} chord. The E is also the third of the tonic key, therefore this also reaffirms the key of the tune.

The triplet decoration in bar six of this section is the only tricky part note-wise. The embellishment sounds great but remember not to let it interrupt the rhythmic flow. The important notes are the D and the B – the accents on these notes should remind you of this fact. Without these, the phrase won't work. The second two notes of the triplet are the decoration, the phrase doesn't rely on these for its direction.

The second chorus is more scale-based than the first chorus – the line in the fifth bar is simply a G Mixolydian scale. Starting on the third (a chord tone of the G^7 chord), it then lands on the E as the chord changes to C^{maj7}, giving a strong major third sound. Despite being a scale, this line still sounds good as it starts and ends on strong chord tones. A smooth delivery is also important.

The 'B' section uses the A minor pentatonic scale over the Am^7 chord. The F at the end of the second bar isn't part of this pentatonic, but belongs to the Dm^7 chord in the next bar – anticipating this chord change helps the swing.

The third chorus starts with a 'gear change' and builds intensity. The rhythm section feel has changed from half-time to swing and the release of tension creates a lift in the solo. This is mirrored in the solo by a more direct, emphatic style.
The accented quarter notes (crotchets) in the first two bars state the beat clearly and should be rhythmic and punchy.

The 'B' section continues the harder swinging feel of this chorus by introducing the blues scale. The E♭ in the second bar of the 'B' section is the flattened fifth (of Am) and so part of the blues scale of A. By waiting until the third chorus to introduce the blues scale it has a greater effect as the major tonality has been thoroughly explored before it's 'roughed up' by the blues.

The fourth chorus builds on the third chorus and takes the solo to its climax. The opening mixes up the blues ideas with the punchy, rhythmic quarter notes (crotchets). The bluesy grace note in the seventh bar also keeps the tension alive. The 'B' section is introduced a beat early by the solo and makes a rhythmic statement by picking up the backbeat (see chapter four – Fig 4.7). Make sure you come in strongly on this note – anticipated phrases need to be emphasized, otherwise they can sound uncertain. The last bar is left empty to allow you to play the pick-up, back into the head.

When playing this solo, try to build from a subtle, easy-going beginning, to a bluesy, swinging ending. I've explained how the notes achieve this but it relies on the performance as well. The example (mp3 track 17) demonstrates some of the tonal possibilities.

Fig 5.2b **'Pearly White' – Sample Solo**

Your Solo

As with previous tracks, the sample solo is meant to demonstrate some of the topics discussed in a practical setting. It's good for you to learn the solo and use it as a launch pad for your own ideas but you should be playing your own solos too. Using CD backing track 4, play the head and then four choruses of your own solo, then the head again making a gig-style performance of 'Pearly White'. Use the first two choruses to build up simple ideas, heading towards a more energetic approach for the last two. The rhythm section changing from a half-time feel to a swing feel at the third chorus is a great moment to change up a gear!

Jazz/Funk

The success of rock and pop music in the 1960s meant that jazz lost some of the mainstream popularity. Musicians sought ways to incorporate the music of **The Beatles**, **The Rolling Stones**, **Jimi Hendrix** etc. into their music. The resulting mix was 'jazz funk'. The main difference was the feel generated by the rhythm section: jazz was swung whereas the jazz/funk sound relied on a straighter groove. A steady 'backbeat' with astrong second and fourth beat became all-important. Quavers aren't swung but are played 'straight'.

'Down To It' is a simple funk tune based around minor seventh and seventh chords.

18 5

Fig 5.3 **'Down To It'**

Ollie Weston

* Piano chords written in the clarinet home key.

Ignoring the introduction (as this only happens once at the start), the form is made up of four sections, each four bars long, making sixteen bars in total. I've indicated these with the letters 'A', 'B', 'C' and 'D'. The tune is definitely not a swing tune – listen to the track (mp3 track 18) and notice the straight, punchy groove of the rhythm section and the straight eighths played by the clarinet.

The intro is written as four bars repeated twice. Intro sections are there to set the mood of a tune and establish the groove, pulse and tonality of the music. In a gig situation the intro can go on for as long as is required. The groove can build and settle to get the audience prepared for the head that follows. If a groove is repeated in this way it is often referred to as a 'vamp'. The first two notes in the clarinet part are the start of the melody and make it clear to the rhythm section that the head is to begin. In Classical music this would be known as an 'anacrusis' – the term 'pick-up' is more often used by jazz musicians. These two notes could be referred to as the pick-up into the 'A' section.

The 'A' section is constructed from a G minor pentatonic scale – the melody follows the rhythm section stating the strong rhythmic groove with a simple melody. Accent the off-beat eighth notes as marked: this will give them the syncopated funkiness of the genre. The fourth bar of the 'A' section has another pick-up into letter 'B'.

The 'B' section is the same rhythmically and melodically as the 'A' section. All that's changed is the underlying chord, which has moved from a Gm^7 to an $E\flat^7$. Here are the two chords and their scales written out.

Fig 5.4 Gm^7 and $E\flat^7$ Chords

Be aware of the differences but also the similarities between the two chords – both have a G and a B♭ as chord tones. The main differences are the note D (in the Gm^7) becoming a D♭ (in the $E\flat^7$), therefore implying the blues scale and the E natural becoming an E♭. (The A♮ also becomes flattened to fit the new chord but is of less importance as in both chords, the A is a passing tone.)

Another pick-up leads to the 'C' section: the 'C' section is very different to the 'A' and 'B' sections. The consistent groove that has built up from the intro has now changed to a looser groove. The repeated rhythmic figure holds the beat together but the pulse isn't as strongly stated. I've reflected this in the melody by having a single long note soaring over the rhythm section.

The change of chord also comes as a surprise – the Em^7 sounds very bright compared to the previous chords – notice particularly how the B♮ is used – this note would clash horribly with either the Gm^7 or the E♭^{7} chords but sounds great over an Em^7.

Fig 5.5 E minor 7th Scale / Chord

The now familiar pick-up brings the tune to the 'D' section and a return of the original groove. Similar to the intro, these four bars serve to settle us back into the groove before the head returns.

Now play 'Down To It' with mp3 track 18 or CD track 5. Play along with both the clarinet and backing track version and try to mirror the sound and the phrasing, particularly the accents and vibrato.

The Solo

This sample solo contains a mixture of some of the concepts explored in the first four chapters of this book. The solo contains blues-based ideas, pentatonic scales as well as using the chord and passing tones of each chord. The progression spends four bars on each chord so there is time to develop ideas and fluency over each one.

Fig 5.6 'Down To It' Sample Solo

A
2nd chorus
Gm7
3
3
B
E♭7
3
C
Em7
D
Gm7
A
3rd chorus
Gm7
B
E♭7
C
Em7
D
Gm7
A
4th chorus
Gm7
B
E♭7

First Chorus

The first chorus sticks closely to the shape and mood established by the head. The solo begins with a pick-up and uses the first line of the head as a starting point. Notice how the 'flattened' third (the B♭) and root (the G) are used as the focus of the phrase – these notes are also chord tones of the E♭^{7} chord. In bar five I've continued to develop these notes over this chord while changing other chord tones to fit the E♭^{7} chord. (Often bar numbers can become confusing if the first bar contains a pick-up. The convention is to call the bar that follows the pick-up bar, bar one.)

The semiquaver pick-up introduces the 'C' section and a change of texture. The smoother, less percussive, nature of this section is matched by the solo: instead of short punchy phrases it becomes more lyrical – the high A should really sing out.

The solo then resumes the mood of the theme established in the 'A' and 'B' sections as the main vamp returns. Notice the triplet embellishment in the second bar of the D section – this gives the phrase a funky twist à la **Cannonball Adderley** or **Dexter Gordon**.

Second Chorus

The second chorus develops the triplet embellishment by repeating it several times – try not to let the triplet upset the flow of the piece. As discussed in chapter two the note after the triplet is the important note and where you are aiming to 'land'. If in doubt, just play the C and the B♭ – add the triplet later.

Fig 5.7 **With and Without Triplet Embellishment**

This idea is repeated in the 'B' section of the second chorus with the D changing to a D♭, to fit the $E\flat^7$ chord. Notice also how the triplet idea is now on the third beat of the bar rather than the fourth.

The 'B' and 'C' sections of this chorus are more scale-based – study the use of the Mixolydian and Dorian modes over these sections.

Third Chorus

This chorus begins with a simple emphatic line that is repeated and developed over the 'A' and 'B' sections. The markings over the crotchets indicate that the notes are to be short and accented (sometimes called a 'hat'). If they are played legato, these notes will lose their effect.

In the third and fourth bars of the 'B' section I've transposed a phrase up a semitone. This is a similar trick to the parallel phrases introduced in the sample solo on 'Sonny's Blues' in chapter four. The transposed phrase also anticipates the chord in the following 'C' section.

Fourth Chorus

The pick-up to the fourth chorus is a pentatonic scale shape that sets the style for the rest of the chorus. Notice that the D♭ in the fourth bar of the 'A' section anticipates the change of chord. Remember that pentatonic shapes have more effect if they are percussive as well as melodic. Try to lock with the rhythm section on the CD. The faster parts will be an excellent technical workout too.

Letter 'B' uses the Mixolydian mode. Be sure you accent the crotchet on beat two of the third bar – make it short and punchy!

Letter 'C' is pentatonic-based and like those in the 'A' section these patterns need to be rhythmic and technically secure.

Your Solo

The CD backing track 5 has eight choruses of the progression for you to play along with. Initially, learn the written solo. It's more challenging than some of the others in the book and will benefit your playing. Focus on sections that you particularly like and analyse them – is it the rhythm that you like particularly? Or a certain run of notes?

Play the head as written, then improvise your own solo – this is where you will put everything you've learned into place and develop your jazz style. Don't be afraid to try new ideas – when it comes off it sounds amazing and these adventurous, inspired solos are what jazz musicians and audiences live for!

beyerdynamic

6: Modes of the Major Scale

So far our study of chords has involved looking at each chord as a separate entity – its own sound world – unrelated to the previous or next chord in a progression. This has allowed you to gain understanding of both the sound and the mood of each chord as well as some technical fluency and jazz ideas specific to your instrument.

However, jazz isn't always constructed from unrelated chords. The relationships between chords and the manipulation of these allow both composers and improvisers to create the huge range of emotions conveyed by music. In this chapter we will look at a set of chords that are derived from the major scale and some of the practical uses for these.

Diatonic and Chromatic

If a note belongs to a key it is said to be 'diatonic' to that key. For example the notes C, D, E, F, G, A and B are diatonic to the key of C major. Any other note doesn't belong to the key of C and is said to be 'chromatic'. An F♯ for example would be a non-diatonic or 'chromatic' note. It is always important to know which key you are playing in, and this can be established by observing the key signature and the tonic chord. This will help you to make good note choices and give you a better understanding of the bigger picture of the tune and its overall direction.

Modes of the Major Scale

Dating back as far as the ancient Greeks, the modes have been used for centuries as a source of musical invention. The names of the modes are taken from different peoples of the ancient Greek society (the Ionians, Aeolians and the Dorians) or areas of Greece (Locris becoming the Locrian mode). The two most exotic sounding modes, 'Lydian' and 'Phrygian', were adopted from neighbouring regions. The philosopher Plato suggested that playing music in a particular mode would inspire a particular emotion associated with that mode. Some modes were used to inspire fortitude and bravery before battle, others suggested peace and love.

The modes were also used in medieval church music, where a system with similar names was used. Collectively these church modes are called the 'Gregorian modes'. Crucially this set of modes includes the Mixolydian mode (see chapter three) that existed in Greek times but in a different form to the one we now know, and was little used.

The easiest way to introduce the modes is to see them as derivatives of a 'parent' scale. Each degree of the parent scale becomes the starting point for one of the modes. The pattern of tones and semitones – as established in the major scale (see chapter one) – is different for each mode but each still contains five intervals of a tone and two intervals of a semitone. It is the re-ordering of these intervals that creates a new set of scales – each with its own unique sound.

Here are the modes of F major with the tone and semitone intervals marked.

Fig 6.1 **The Modes of F Major**

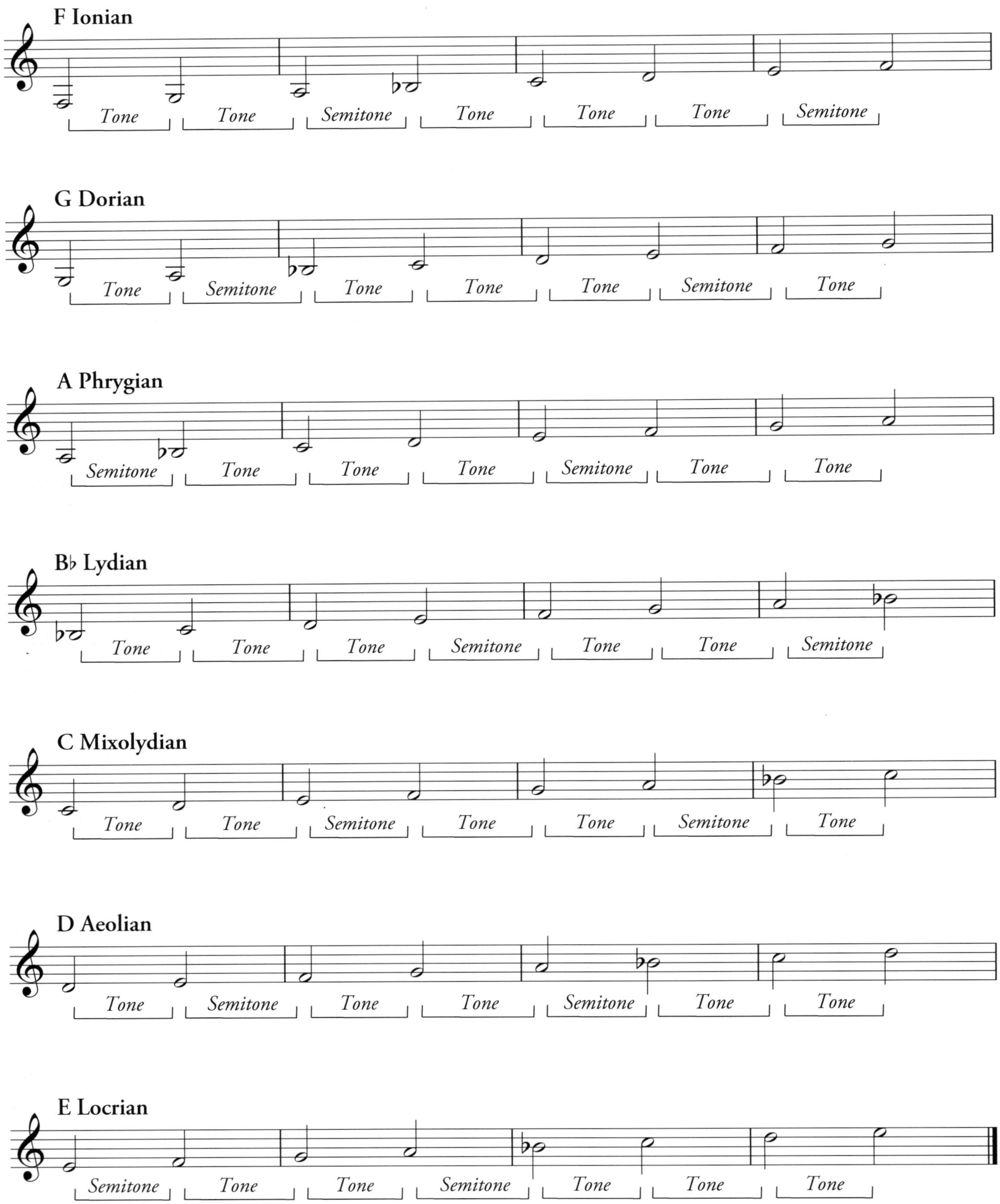

Be aware that each mode is named after its own root note, not the parent scale (e.g.) the second mode of F major is **G** Dorian and not F Dorian. The fifth mode of F is **C** Mixolydian, not F Mixolydian. When referring to modes the root note and the name of the mode are all that is needed to describe it – the parent scale merely shows the source of the notes and need not be referred to.

These seven scales are diatonic to the key of F major as they contain only the notes of the F major scale. If we treat the starting note of each new mode as a root, we can then create a varied palette of notes and chords. Here are the modes again with the notes numbered from the root and a chord built from the root, third, fifth and seventh.

Fig 6.2 Chord / Passing Tones of F Major Modes

Major, minor and seventh type chords can be constructed from each mode to produce a set of 'diatonic' chords for the key, but there is another chord type to explore. If we take the root, third, fifth and seventh of the Locrian mode, we get an interesting result. It is similar to a minor seventh chord but also has the fifth flattened – a tritone is created between the root and flattened fifth resulting in a dark, unsettled chord. This type of chord is written as, for example $Em^{7(\flat 5)}$.

Modal Workout

Play along with mp3 track 19 and try to get a feel for each of the modes. The track moves through the modes of F major and as discussed, each is diatonic to the key of F. Therefore the only notes you will need are all derived from the scale of F major. Try to explore the different qualities of each mode and see how much inspiration can be derived from a simple F major scale.

Fig 6.3 **Modal Workout**

19

D Aeolian

E Locrian

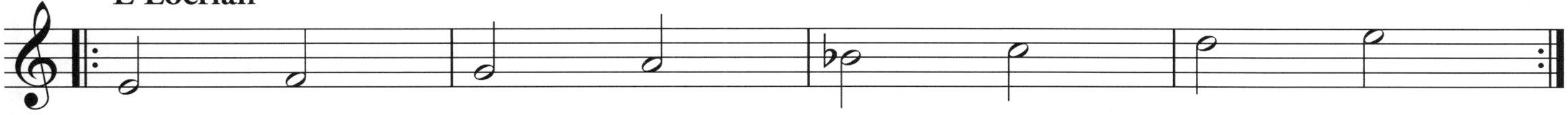

As you play through the modes try to associate each with a major or minor tonality. Identify also any unique features of each mode. The Phrygian mode for example has a flattened second (between the first and second degree) which evokes a Spanish type of sound.

Fig 6.3 deals with the modes diatonic to F major and this is a good way to organise the modes within a key. If you know the major scale of a particular key you will also know the seven modes of that major scale. This is great as it means that you don't have to learn a whole new set of scales, you merely change the starting note.

By knowing the relationship of the modes to the parent scale, you can work backwards to the source and find the parent scale relevant to your mode. For example – we know that Dorian is the second mode of the major scale and is built on the second degree. To find the parent scale of G Dorian, ask yourself which scale has G as the second degree? The answer in this case is F major. Similarly to find the parent scale of A Mixolydian, work out which key has A as its fifth degree, the answer therefore is D major. By knowing the relationship of the mode to its parent scale you will have a safe palette of notes to use in a new modal context.

Here's a checklist of the degree of the scale each mode is based on:

Ionian – First mode of major scale.

Dorian – Always built on the **second** degree of the major scale.

Phrygian – Always built on the **third** degree of the major scale.

Lydian – Always built on the **fourth** degree of the major scale.

Mixolydian – Always built on the **fifth** degree of the major scale.

Aeolian – Always built on the **sixth** degree of the major scale.

Locrian – Always built on the **seventh** degree of the major scale.

Modes from a Static Root

Another way to organise the modes and gain a different perspective is to keep a static root note and play each of the modes from that same point. This will give you a better understanding of the transitional process the modes go through from the softest, brightest mode (Lydian) to the most sombre and dissonant (Locrian). This progression starts with the Lydian mode – the sharpened fourth makes it even brighter than the major scale.

Fig 6.4 Modal Progression from a Static Root

20

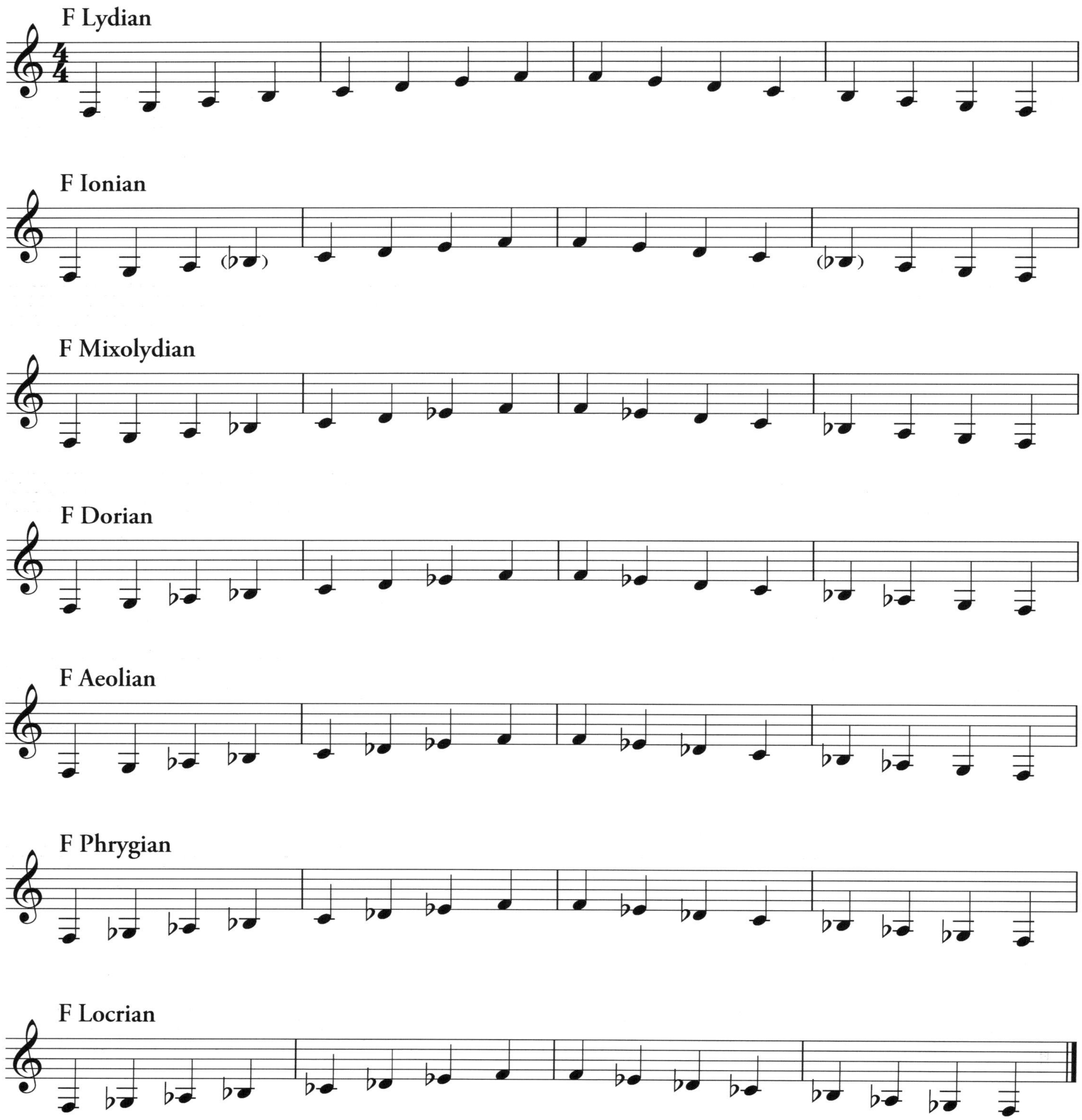

The static root serves as a good point from which to compare the gradual changing of the modes, here they have been arranged in an order from very major (Lydian) to very minor (Locrian). Notice that each mode is similar to the preceding one but with one note flattened – to turn a mode from Lydian to Ionian – you flatten the fourth. To turn the Ionian into a Mixolydian mode you retain the flattened fourth and flatten the seventh. If we continue in the same manner, the Dorian mode introduces a flattened third to the previous mode, the Aeolian a flattened sixth, the Phrygian a flattened second and the Locrian a flattened fifth. By viewing the modes in this progression each can be said to have a characteristic note that separates it from its predecessor.

Fig 6.5 **Static Root Modes with Characteristic Notes Highlighted**

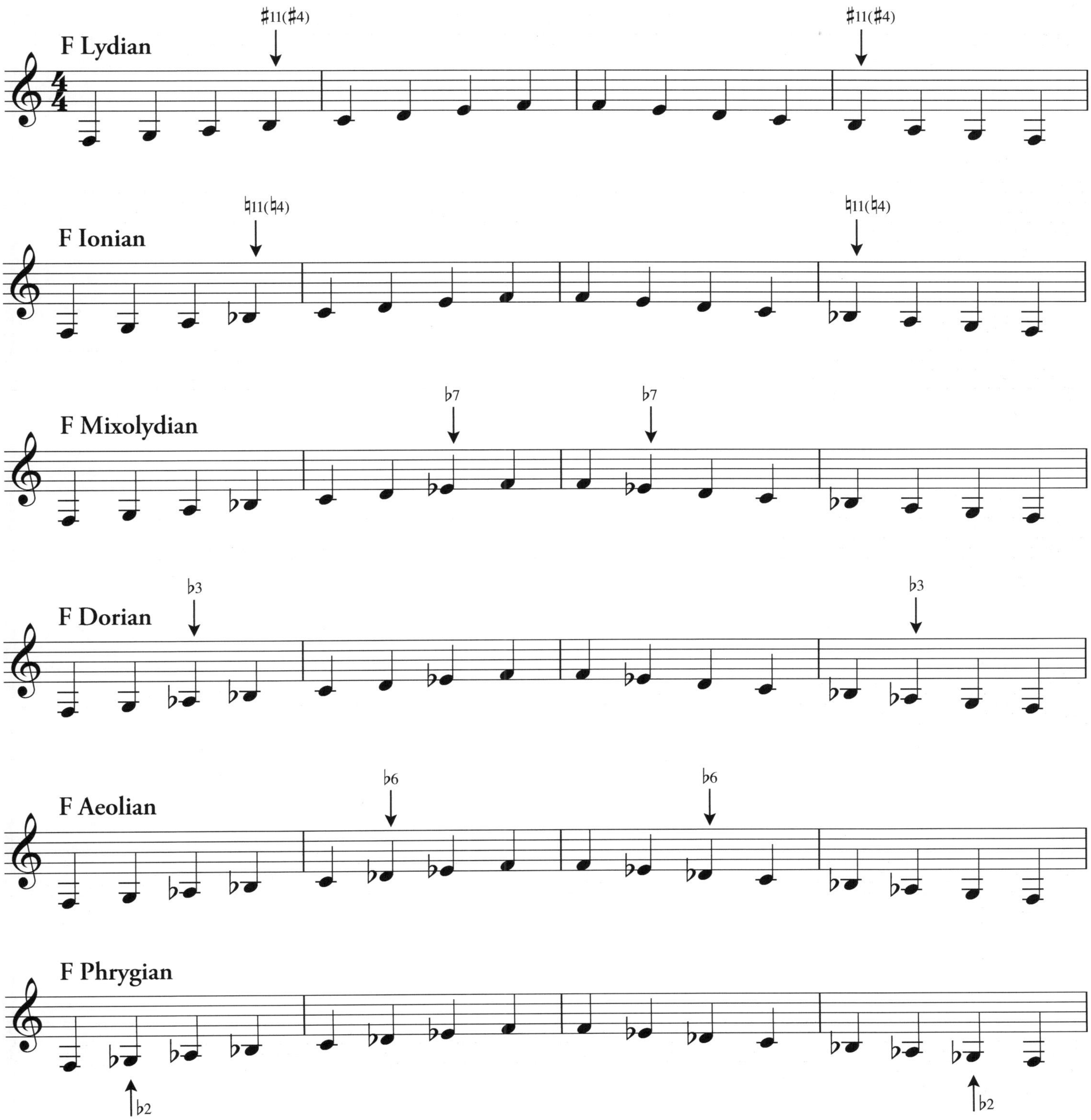

By knowing the characteristic note of each mode you can focus on the specific mood of that mode and so draw out the particular sound required.

Checkpoint

You should now be familiar with the modes of the major scale. The Ionian (identical to the major scale and usually just called major), Dorian and Mixolydian modes are already familiar to us from earlier chapters and are the most commonly used in major keys. The other modes have valuable uses and the colours they add can be useful additions to your options as an improviser.

Assignments and Improvisation Tips

Here is a simple line based on an F Lydian scale. After each four bars the mode is going to change and gradually make its transition from Lydian to Locrian via all seven of the major scale's modes.

Fig 6.6 Lydian Line Through a Modal Progression

F Dorian

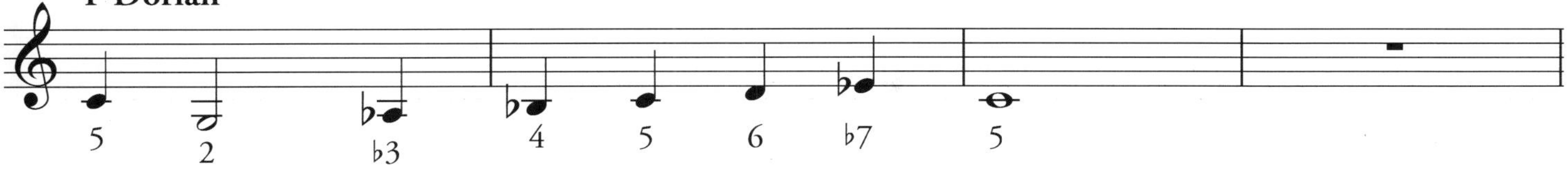

F Aeolian

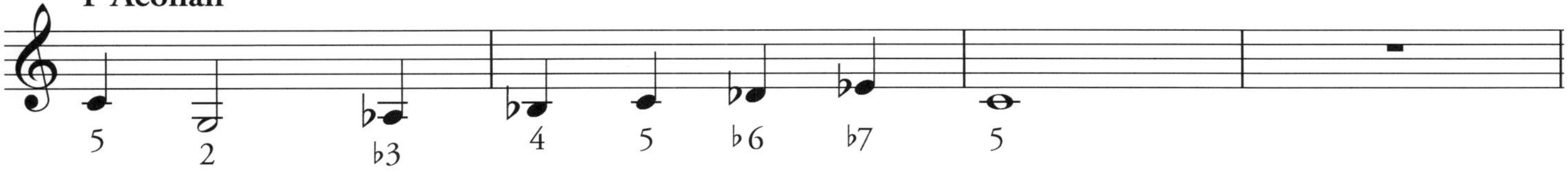

F Phrygian

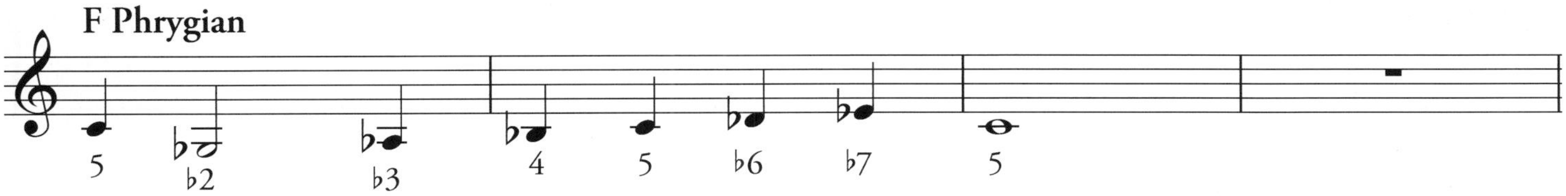

F Locrian

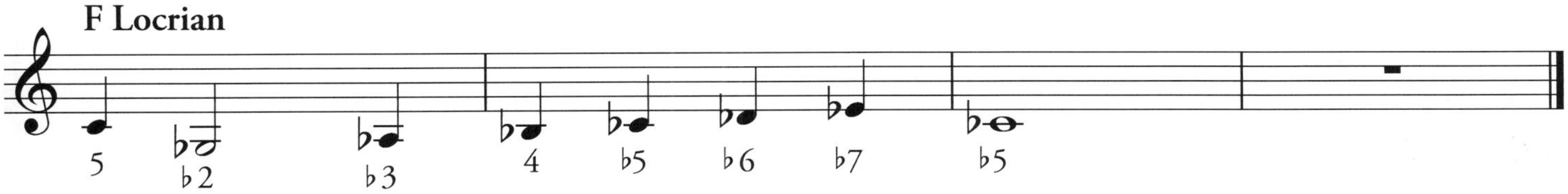

Play through this exercise with mp3 backing track 20 and listen to the darkening process of the progression. The line works as a bright Lydian lick but as the notes are flattened the lick sounds more minor and evokes a darker mood.

Here's another Lydian line, try to transfer this to each of the modes. Analyse the lick in its original form and then make the adjustments necessary for it to fit the other modes – so when it changes from the Lydian mode to the Ionian (major) scale, the characteristic Lydian sharpened fourth needs to be flattened to become the fourth of the major scale.

Fig 6.7 Another Lydian Line Through a Modal Progression

F Lydian

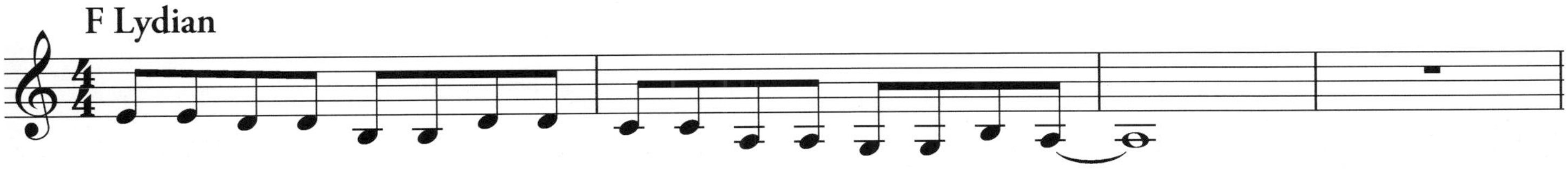

F Major

F Mixolydian

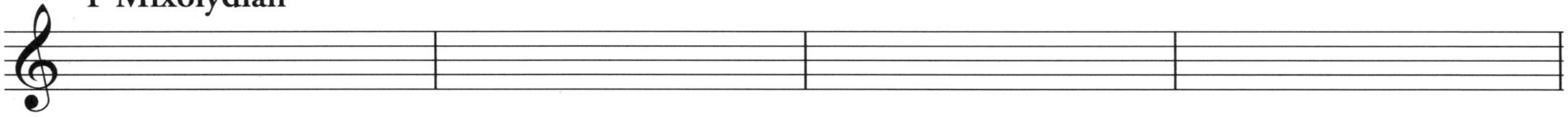

F Dorian

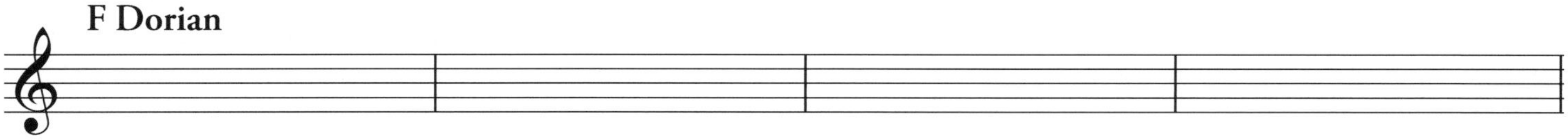

F Aeolian

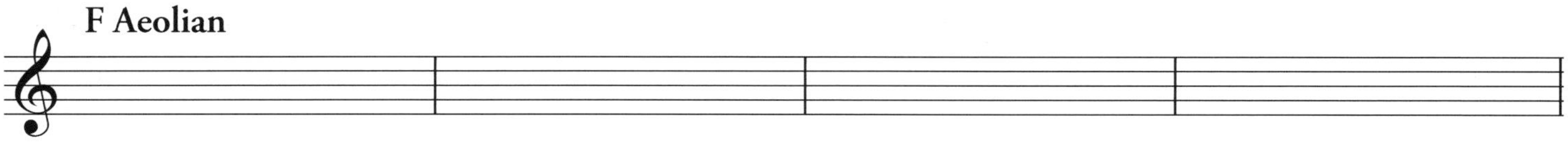

F Phrygian

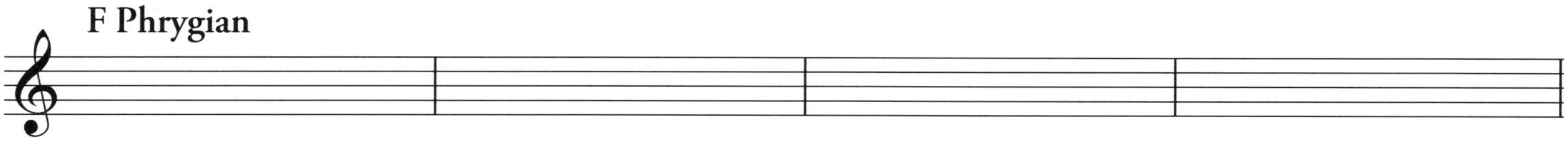

F Locrian

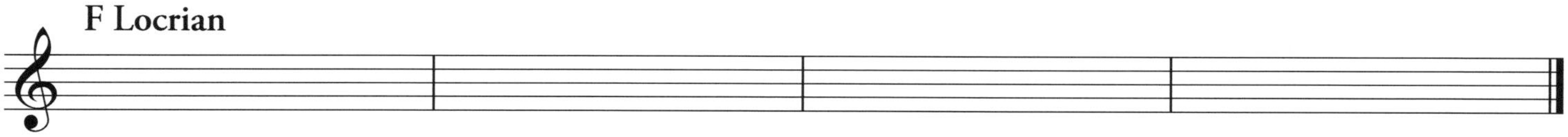

Use of Modes in Jazz and Popular Music

For each of the modes there are a few examples below of how it has been used in a famous pop or jazz tune. Listen to the originals and try to play them yourself.

Ionian – **Harold Arlen**'s 'Somewhere Over The Rainbow' is a beautiful melody in a major key – try to work it out in G major. When you are comfortable with the melody in this key transfer it to less familiar ones.

Dorian – The Dorian mode is often used in folk music – the natural sixth adds brightness and a touch of optimism to the minor key. 'Scarborough Fair' is in the Dorian mode. The third syllable of the word 'rose-ma-ry' picks out the natural sixth making this melody unmistakably Dorian. Try to play this melody using an A Dorian scale.

'So What' by **Miles Davis** (see chapter three) is a famous example of a jazz tune in the Dorian mode. The tune is built around the two scales of D Dorian and E♭ Dorian. The prominent bass line in the head also clearly spells out the Dorian mode.

Phrygian – The flattened second degree of the Phrygian mode gives it a dark sinister sound. This has been used frequently to create a tense mood in music – the bass line of 'Deeper Underground' by **Jamiroquai** is built on the Phrygian mode. 'Hunter' by **Bjork** is also in the Phrygian mode.

'My Favourite Things' by **Rogers and Hammerstein** features the Phrygian mode as part of the melody – the line 'these are a few of my favourite…' runs up a Phrygian scale.

Lydian – The sharpened fourth of the Lydian mode is often used to brighten up melodies and add a touch of mystery. The verse of 'Every Little Thing She Does Is Magic' by the **Police** is in the Lydian mode. Listen to the four note bass line as it ascends a Lydian scale – the fourth note being the characteristic sharpened fourth of the mode. **Sting**'s vocal in the verse is derived from the Lydian mode.

The theme to 'The Simpsons' is also based on the Lydian mode. Try to play this starting on a C – notice how the third note of the tune needs to be an F♯ to give the tune its quirkiness. Try playing this as an Ionian melody (replacing the F♯ with an F♮) and listen to how different this sounds.

Mixolydian – The Mixolydian mode should already be familiar to you from studying seventh chords in chapter four. The flattened seventh characteristic of the Mixolydian mode is synonymous with the jazz and blues sound. The vamp section of 'All Blues' by **Miles Davis** is based on the Mixolydian mode. Play along with this tune and pick out the notes of the vamp – the fifth, sixth and seventh (E, F♯ and G on the clarinet) are very descriptive of the Mixolydian mode and its distinctive flattened seventh.

Aeolian – This mode is similar to the Dorian but with the sixth degree flattened. The Aeolian mode is the same as the descending melodic minor scale and is sometimes referred to as the 'natural minor'.

'Blue Bossa' by trumpeter **Kenny Dorham** is a good example of a tune in the Aeolian mode. The first note of the third bar of the head is the flattened sixth of the Aeolian mode (B♭ for clarinet).

The flattened sixth of the Aeolian mode is also used frequently in descending bass lines. This is a common minor 'vamp'.

Fig 6.8 Descending Minor Vamp in F Minor

This vamp in F uses the root, flattened seventh, flattened sixth and the fifth of the key – it is therefore using the F Aeolian mode.

With added syncopation it sounds more authentic and could be the basis of a minor vamp.

Fig 6.8b Descending Minor Vamp with Syncopation

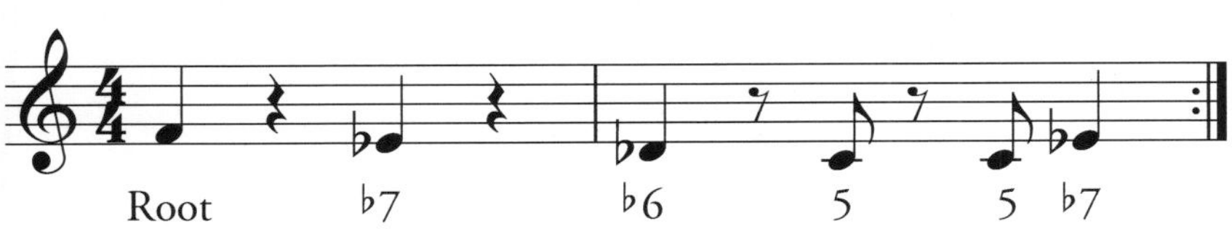

Locrian – Historically the Locrian mode was considered unworkable as a melodic source as it is the most dissonant of the modes. The slightly awkward arrangement of intervals and in particular the flattened fifth (the tritone) make any melodies derived from this mode potentially problematic. It is seldom used as a mode in its own right, but the Locrian scale and the chord derived from it – the m7(♭5) chord does have its uses. We will explore these later in the minor keys section of the book. This is a simple modal tune using a 32 AABA form.

The tune has a straight quaver feel indicated at the start, so don't swing the quavers. Listen to mp3 track 21 and pay attention to the relaxed floating feel produced by the repeated bass rhythm and the gentle cymbals – these provide a textural accompaniment rather than a really driving rhythm, allowing the melody to float over the rhythm section. This is a similar feel to 'Maiden Voyage' by **Herbie Hancock** or 'Phase Dance' by guitar giant **Pat Metheny**.

Fig 6.9 **'First Impression'**

21 6

Ollie Weston

Based around G major this tune uses a mixture of modes that aren't necessarily diatonic to G major.

Let's look at each chord from bar five onwards together with its mode and then relate it back to its parent major scale.

Fig 6.10a G Major 7

The first mode (Ionian) of G major. The familiar major scale sets the tonality of the tune.

Fig 6.10b G^7

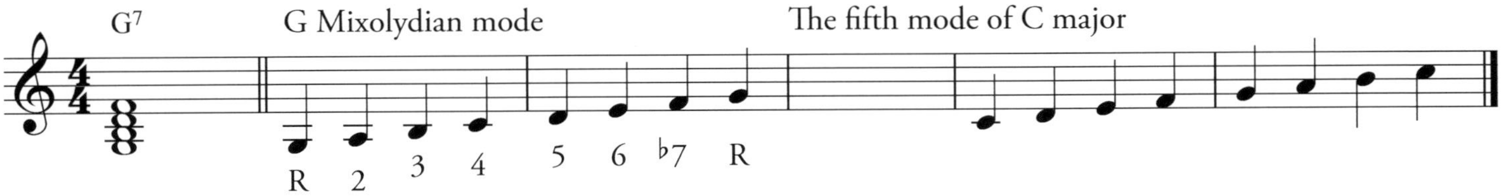

A seventh chord requires the Mixolydian mode, so we shall use G Mixolydian here. We know that the Mixolydian mode starts on the fifth degree of a major scale, so when we count backwards from G, we will find the parent scale of C major.

Fig 6.10c $E\flat^{maj7(\sharp 11)}$

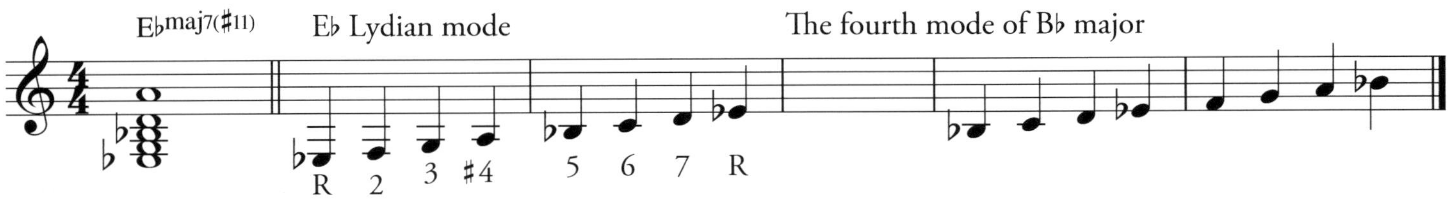

This is the same chord as $E\flat^{maj7(\#4)}$. The sharp eleventh is the same as the sharpened fourth but an octave higher (see the section on extensions in chapter three, Fig 3.15). Played in the lower octave, the sharpened fourth would clash with the fifth as they are too close together. With nearly an octave between the fifth and sharpened eleventh, the lush sound of this interval is much clearer. For this reason the sharpened fourth is nearly always referred to as the sharpened eleventh.

The sharp eleventh (or fourth) is the character note of the Lydian mode. The Lydian mode is always built on the fourth degree of the major scale. To find the parent major scale of the $E\flat^{maj7(\sharp 11)}$ chord establish which major scale has E♭ as its fourth. Counting back four steps from E♭ brings us to B♭ major – the parent major scale of E♭ Lydian.

Fig 6.10d A Minor 7th

Minor chords in modal tunes open up a number of options: three modes of the major scale that can be described by the m7 symbol – Dorian, Aeolian and Phrygian. When you have a clear idea of the key you are in, you can relate the different minor modes to their parent scale more easily. The first chord of this tune is a G major chord.

Although the following chords aren't diatonic to G major the 'A' section does begin and end with a G major chord. This establishes a G major tonality as the tune moves to the 'B' section. By relating A minor 7 to the modes of G major it can be seen as the second mode and therefore A Dorian would be a good choice of scale.

Fig 6.10e A♭$^{maj7(\sharp 11)}$

The sharp eleventh tells us that this is another Lydian sounding chord. To find the parent scale, establish which major scale has A♭ as its fourth degree – in this case it's E♭ major.

Checkpoint

The whole subject of modes is surrounded with mystery and misunderstanding. You should now be aware of the sound of each mode on its own and its characteristics in terms of flattened/sharpened interval combinations that don't appear anywhere else. It's also important to remember that each mode is only a major scale played from a different starting point – this allows you quickly to refer the mode back to its parent scale and avoid uncertainty over the accidentals.

'First Impression' explores a variety of modes that aren't necessarily related by parent scale or key but that simply sound good when played together.

Your Solo

Now play your own version of 'First Impression' with CD track 6. There are four choruses in total so open with the head, then play two choruses of solo and the head again to finish. Explore each mode thoroughly and aim to create smooth melodic lines over the rhythm section.

Improvisation Tips

Although each mode is different and derived from a different parent major scale, there are similarities between the modes – for example the difference between the chords G^{maj7} and the G^{7} in the 'A' section is only that of one note – the F♯ becoming an F♮. Notice that the two chords in the bridge share a common third and seventh. The chords Am^{7} and the A♭^{maj7} both have C and G as their thirds and sevenths. Holding either of these notes as the chord changes underneath will sound really effective.

By understanding the different qualities of each mode you will be able to unlock a variety of new sounds and chords. It's important to remember that each mode is derived from a major scale, meaning that you don't have a whole new set of scales to learn – just new ways to use the existing scales. The modes also offer a variety of options for playing over minor chords – different options are available for the non-chord tones, namely the flattened sixth and second, which further extends the range of your melodic opportunities.

Modal improvising in jazz has led to some exquisite and evocative music, such as **Herbie Hancock**'s album 'Maiden Voyage' which features five modal compositions about the mystery and beauty of the sea. **Wayne Shorter** is another exponent of modal harmony, notably on the album 'Speak No Evil', in which he explores the dark subjects of sorcery and witchcraft.

7: The II-V-I Progression

This chapter will explore the different chord types studied so far, and their uses for creating chord progressions and for moving between keys. It will investigate the 'perfect cadence' of classical music and its counterpart in jazz. Certain progressions of chords occur frequently in music and by recognizing these, you will be able to play fluently and intuitively over them.

Music – like any other language – is comprised of short sections that when put together make a larger body of work. Imagine a book that reads as a constant stream of words and ideas without any gaps or division into smaller sections – it would be unreadable, as there would be no time or space for the reader to pause and digest the words, before moving onto the next section. Written language is divided into paragraphs and sentences, with punctuation, to allow the overall message to be delivered in smaller, clearer sections. In the same way a piece of music can also be divided up into smaller sections. Chapter one introduced some common musical forms used in pop and jazz (the 12-Bar blues and AABA form are the two most used so far). Each of the sections of these forms could be thought of as a paragraph or sentence of its own. This chapter will look at ways to use chords to create resolution within these sections and thus make them work as self-contained musical sections.

The Perfect Cadence

A cadence is a way of drawing a musical phrase to a close. To continue the grammatical analogy, the cadence is the equivalent of the comma or full stop in written text. Some cadences are very final and conclude a piece, others serve merely as a pause, and herald the start of another section.

Cadences are defined by particular chords and the movement between them, rather than any melodic content. It is important to be aware of the difference between the melodic and harmonic properties of music when discussing cadences: the **melodic** properties of music are those concerning melody – the tune! This is usually the top line of the music and is the most memorable aspect of it – most people will whistle the tune rather than the harmony or bass part. The **harmonic** properties of music are the aspects that take place underneath the melody – the chords and bass part. These make up the foundations of the music and give the melody its context. It is well worth devoting a significant amount of time to the study of these harmonic aspects, as using them in different ways can create many variations in mood and context. A simple way to distinguish these two aspects is to think of the melodic properties as moving in a horizontal plane across the page and the harmonic properties moving in a vertical plane – underneath the melody.

The most commonly used cadence is the 'perfect cadence'. This cadence has the greatest sense of resolution and finality. A perfect cadence is created when the fifth chord of the key is followed by the root (tonic) chord. As we are dealing with a diatonic progression (see chapter six – the modes of the major scale), the chords will be those diatonic to the key of the piece. This means that a V-I progression in F major will be a seventh chord on the fifth degree of the scale (C^7) moving to a major chord on the tonic (F) – Roman numerals are used to signify the movement of the root notes of the chords, for a perfect cadence you would use V and I.

Fig 7.1 C^7 to F Major

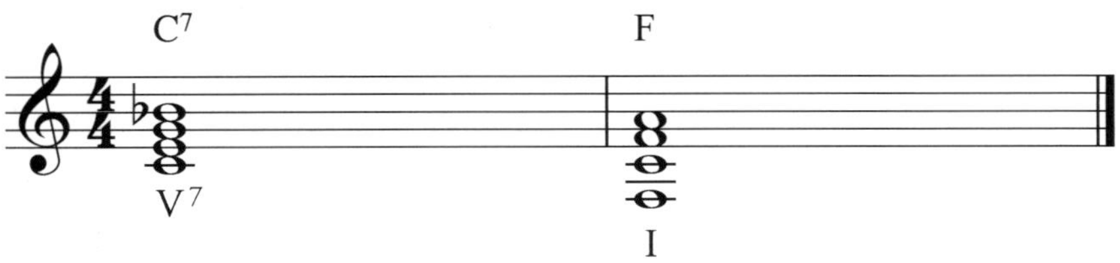

Composers have used the perfect cadence for centuries as a means of creating a definite and satisfying conclusion to a section of music or for the overall ending of a piece. Classical composers such as **Mozart** and **Haydn** would draw out the perfect cadence for some time, building the music up over repeated V-I cadences before the final 'full stop' at the end. The perfect cadence works so well because it creates an element of dissonance that is then resolved to produce a stable ending. The dissonance is created by the tritone interval in the seventh chord (the tritone was introduced in chapter four as the interval that gives the seventh chord its distinct sound, with the interval between the major third and flattened seventh clashing with each other).

Here is the perfect cadence again but this time with only the tritone and its resolution.

Fig 7.2 Tritone Within a 7th Chord

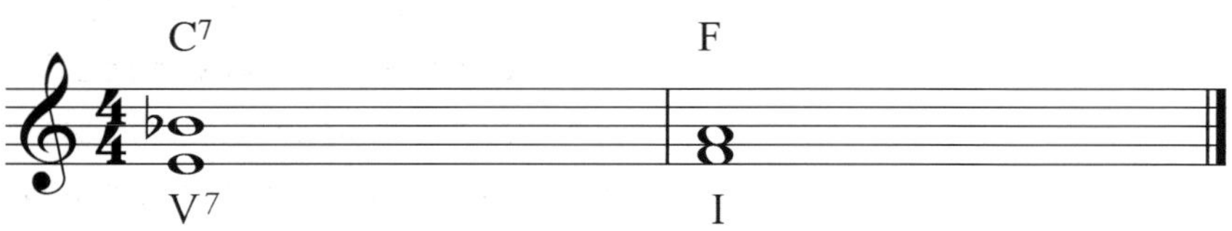

By playing just the tritone interval, the essential content of a perfect cadence is highlighted – the interval on its own has an unresolved, tense feel that wouldn't make a satisfactory conclusion to a piece. By resolving the E and B♭ (the third and seventh of the C^7 chord) to F and A we create a perfect cadence and a stable harmonic conclusion.

Here is a famous phrase that we will leave 'hanging' at the seventh chord. Listen to mp3 track 22.

Fig 7.3a Unresolved Ending 22

Fig 7.3b Resolved Ending 23

The melody note contributes to the tension, as it is one of the notes from the tritone. If a piece of music ended in this way you would feel that it had stopped early. Now look at Fig 7.3b and listen to mp3 track 23. This version resolves the tension created in the seventh chord and the phrase ends on a stable, conclusive I chord (in this case F major). The melody line also follows this pattern – with the E resolving to an F (the third of the C^7 chord resolving to the root of the tonic chord).

When a seventh chord is used to create a cadence, it is called a '**dominant seventh**' chord. It is so called because it is the most dominant and descriptive chord of the key. The strong pull towards the root chord that the dominant seventh chord produces (the ear wanting to resolve the tritone) is a very clear way to define a key. As it is the only seventh type chord in the set of diatonic modes (the others being either major seventh or minor seventh variations) a seventh chord is an unmistakable road-sign within a chord progression. For the most part a seventh chord is acting as a dominant seventh chord and so is the fifth chord of the key.

The Cycle of Fifths

The cycle of fifths is a method for arranging the keys in a cyclic form. It contains much of the knowledge and theory behind western music in terms of keys, cadences and resolutions. It's also a handy tool for remembering key signatures and the order of sharps and flats. In short the cycle of fifths contains most of the fundamental musical logic that you'll need!

Starting with C at the top, the cycle of fifths arranges the twelve keys by their root notes, each one followed by a key five tones higher. To find the next key on from C you need to establish which note is the fifth of C – it's G. In the same manner D is the fifth of G, A the fifth of D and so on. By continuing this pattern the progression will eventually come back round to C. The method of arranging these into a circle and the fact that there are twelve keys means that the cycle of fifths can be visually laid out like a clock. C is usually used to start the sequence at twelve o'clock, for no other reason than that C major has no sharps or flats and so is a sensible place to start. The cycle can be started from any point as all the keys have equal importance within it.

Fig 7.4 The Cycle of Fifths

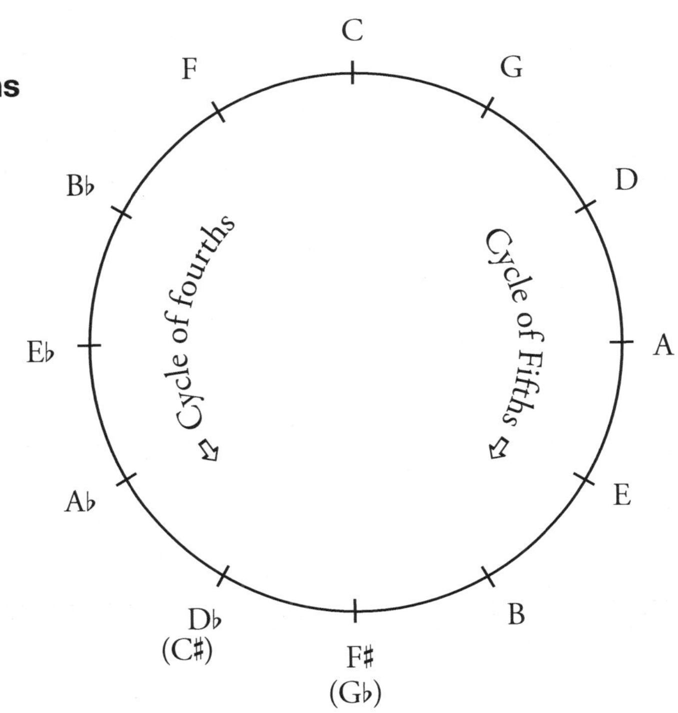

Going clockwise around the cycle of fifths is a 'sharpening' process with each new key adding another sharp to the previous key. The sharps come in a particular order – the phrase 'Father Charles Goes Down And Ends Battle' is a useful line to remember the order of the sharps.

G major – one sharp (**F**ather)
D major – two sharps (**F**ather **C**harles)
A major – three sharps (**F**ather **C**harles **G**oes)
E major – four sharps (**F**ather **C**harles **G**oes **D**own)
B major – five sharps (**F**ather **C**harles **G**oes **D**own **A**nd)
F sharp major – six sharps (**F**ather **C**harles **G**oes **D**own **A**nd **E**nds)

The bottom of the circle is where sharps and flats crossover. G flat major is 'enharmonically' (the pitches sound the same but are spelt differently) the same as F sharp major.

The flats also occur in a certain order. Each key has the same number of flats as the mirror opposite sharp key on the clock face. The sentence is also mirrored – said in reverse it is 'Battle Ends And Down Goes Charles' Father'

F major – one flat (**B**attle)
B flat major – two flats (**B**attle **E**nds)
G flat major – six flats (**B**attle **E**nds **A**nd **D**own **G**oes **C**harles **F**ather)

NB the sharps and flats always come in this order. You will never see a key signature with only an A flat for example. For **A** flat to exist in a key signature there must also be a **B** flat and an **E** flat. Similarly, **D** sharp would never appear in a key signature without **F**, **C**, and **G** sharps. If a note is flattened or sharpened for effect and is not a usual part of the key, it is called an 'accidental'.

Interestingly if you travel in an anticlockwise direction around the cycle of fifths you will notice that a cycle of fourths is created.

Dominant Seventh Chords Within the Cycle of Fifths

As established above, each note in the cycle is the fifth degree of the scale of the previous key.

Fig 7.5 **Dominant Seventh Chords Within the Cycle of Fifths**

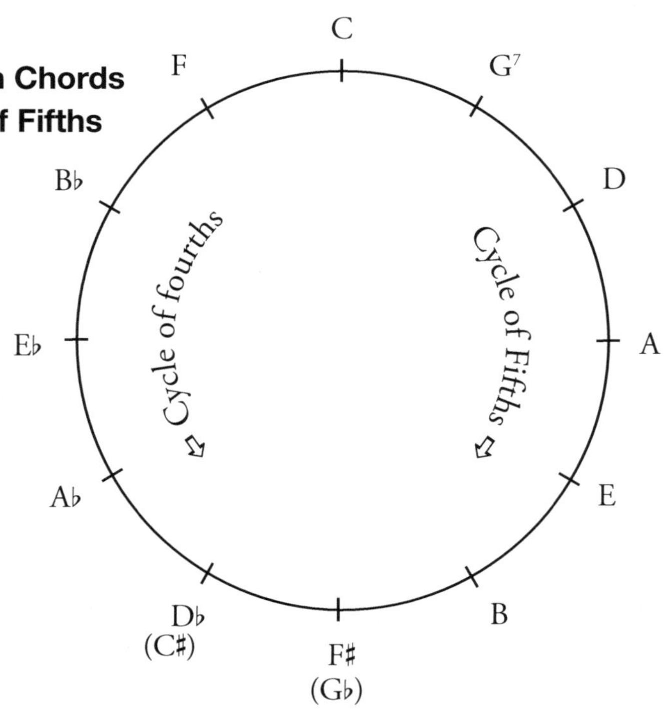

By adding the seventh to each chord on the cycle of fifths, an endless series of dominant sevenths is created, each leading to the next. In this example we have made the G into G^7, thus creating the dominant seventh chord of C major.

The result is a progression that is constantly changing to a new key as each new chord arrives.

The cycle of fifths is often used in chord progressions but usually only in short sections of three or four consecutive seventh chords. You would seldom move through all twelve keys as the constant harmonic movement can be frustrating on the ear – to break the cycle a resolution is needed in the shape of a root (I) chord to complete the cadence and resolve the harmonic movement.

Checkpoint

Having familiarized yourself with chords on their own and dealt with them within a modal framework, we are now starting to put them into a harmonic context. The harmony of jazz and western tonal music in general relies on the establishment of a key and the movement within that key of chords and harmonies. Understanding the perfect cadence and the use of the dominant seventh chord within it is the starting point for exploring the relationships within keys and the possible movement to other keys. The use of harmony in this way is called 'functional' harmony – each chord is there for a reason and to perform a 'function'. This is opposite to the modal harmony explored in chapter six where chords are used purely because they sound good!

Assignments and Improvisation Tips

Thirds and Sevenths Around the Cycle of Fifths

To get used to the sound and function of the dominant seventh chord it's important to focus on the third and seventh notes of these chords. The interval between these notes is the tritone and is the essential element of the perfect cadence. Fig. 7.6 has the cycle of fifths written out with the third and seventh of each chord (starting at F on the cycle).

Fig 7.6 Third and Seventh Notes of each Dominant Chord

24

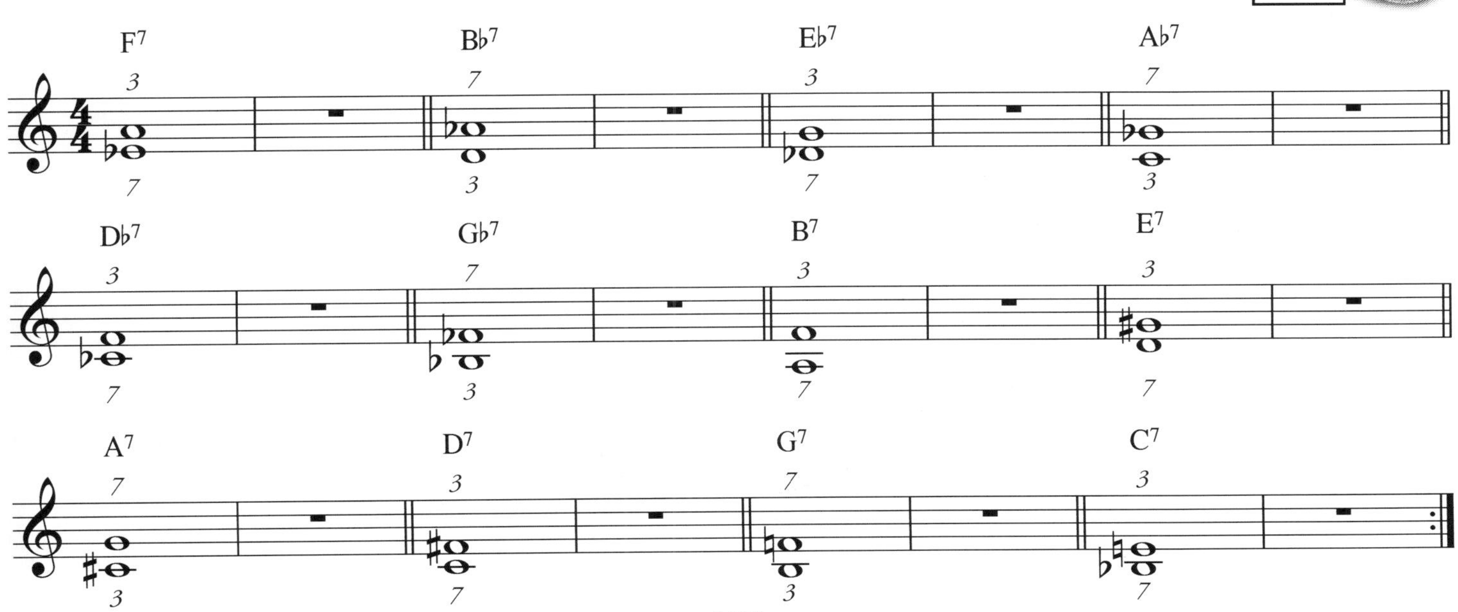

Notice that the two lines in Fig 7.6 are just two descending chromatic scales on top of one another. Play just the top line of the exercise – the A is the third of the F^7 moving down a semitone to A♭ to become the seventh of the $B\flat^7$. It moves down a semitone to G and becomes the third of the $E\flat^7$ chord. This line continues chromatically downwards alternating between being the third and seventh of each new chord.

The bottom line starts on an E♭ and is the seventh of the F^7 chord. This line is the same as the first in that it moves chromatically downwards and each note alternates between being the third and the seventh of each new chord.

The thirds and the sevenths tell us all we need to know about the chords by using the fewest notes – they are often called the '**guide tones**' within a chord progression and spell out the harmony. Knowing how to move between chords using the guide tone thirds and sevenths is an important skill for successful improvising – if you can only play one note at a time on your instrument it makes sense to try to convey as much information about the chord as possible.

Now play the two guide tone lines using the following rhythmic figures. The first one (Fig 7.6b) starts on the top line whereas Fig 7.6c starts on the bottom line. The accents over the crotchets mean that they are to be short and accented. Play these lines with a punchy swing feel.

Fig 7.6b Rhythmic Ideas for Guide-Tone Lines (starting on the third)

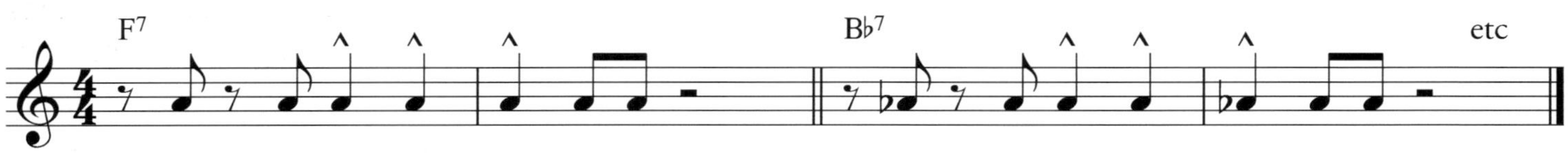

Fig 7.6c Rhythmic Ideas for Guide-Tone Lines (starting on the seventh)

Fig 7.7 mixes up the guide tones over another rhythmic figure. Using both the third and seventh in a melodic line highlights the tritone interval between them. Frowned upon in early music (see the section on the tritone in chapter four) it can add a bright, quirky sound to the line.

Each chord also contains its root at some point in the phrase – this is to help you get your 'harmonic bearings' and relate the thirds and sevenths to the root of the chord. Play this exercise along with the mp3 backing track 24.

Fig 7.7 Guide-Tone Line with Swing Rhythm

24

'I Got Rhythm' by **George** and **Ira Gershwin** is a famous example of the use of the cycle of fifths. The song uses the AABA form with the 'B' (the bridge) section using four chords from the cycle of fifths.

Try to take the melody we have given you for this section and continue it by progressing through the cycle of fifths – the first line is done for you, play along with mp3 track 24.

Fig 7.8 'Rhythm Changes' Bridge

24

Although the original melody only uses the cycle of fifths for eight bars, continuing it through the progression gives you a sense of the constant movement of the harmony through the progression.

The Perfect Cadence in Jazz

Jazz uses the perfect cadence in a very similar way to Classical music. The only difference with a jazz cadence is that it is rarely referred to as a perfect cadence. Jazz musicians tend to name chords and chord progressions by their numerical relationship to the root. A perfect cadence in jazz terms is a V-I, meaning chord five followed by chord one. The quality of the chords as major, minor or seventh is taken for granted as you know that a chord built on the fifth degree of the major scale is a seventh and chord one is major.

The other difference between a jazz and Classical cadence is that the jazz progression often prepares the dominant seventh chord with a minor seventh chord built on the second degree of the scale (II). This means that chords are often moving more quickly and makes a walking bass line easier to produce.

II-V-I

The most common progression in jazz, the II-V-I, features in countless jazz standards. Recognizing the II-V-I in different keys will unlock the jazz standard repertoire and allow you to build your own jazz vocabulary that will be usable in a variety of situations. All serious jazz musicians have spent time learning patterns and licks in all twelve keys that will work over II-V-I progressions.

The II-V-I is created by building a chord on the second, fifth and root positions of the key. Our study of modes in chapter six illustrated that a chord for the second (Dorian) mode (II) would be a minor seventh. The chord for the fifth mode (Mixolydian) would be a seventh (dominant seventh to use classical terminology) and a major seventh on the first (Ionian) mode.

Fig 7.8a **II-V-I in F Major**

Because this progression of chords is diatonic to F major, the scales for each use the same parent scale (F major). The context differs in each – chord II uses the G Dorian scale, chord V the C Mixolydian scale and chord I the F major scale.

Here is the same II-V-I progression with just the guide-tones (third and seventh) on top of the root of each chord.

Fig 7.8b II-V-I Guide Tones

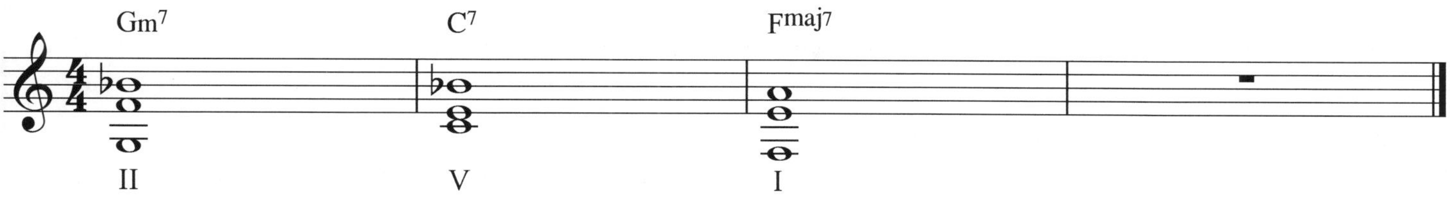

II-V-I Licks

Purists will tell you that licks (pre-rehearsed musical ideas) are a bad thing and are against the spirit of jazz as an improvised art form – no one wants to listen to a set of licks being systematically repeated on a gig. However, using licks as a way to navigate a chord progression is an essential part of the learning process all jazz musicians go through. Licks are the musical equivalent of vocabulary in verbal language. They can act as useful building blocks and staging posts in an improvised solo.

Here are some II-V-I lines in the style of some of the great jazz players to get you started.

Fig 7.9a II-V-I Ideas John Coltrane

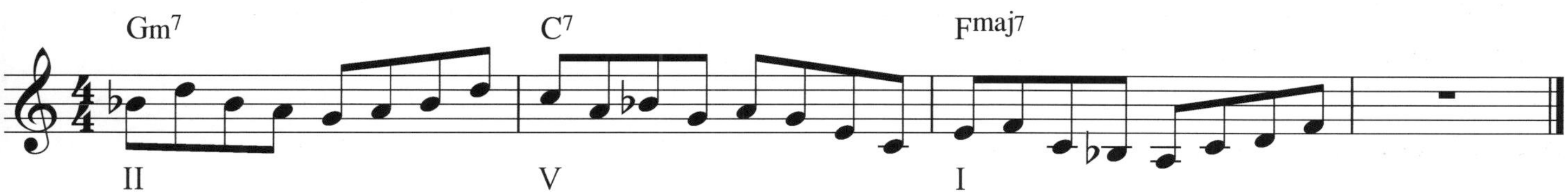

Fig 7.9b II-V-I Ideas Charlie Parker

Fig 7.9c II-V-I Ideas Cannonball Adderley

Each of these three licks is diatonic to the key (F in these examples) and so uses only the notes of the F major scale. Analyse each lick and see how the guide tones and the mode for each chord are used to describe the chord individually within the bigger context of the key.

Licks in All Keys

Eventually you will want to be fluent with this II-V-I language in all twelve keys – if you understand how a phrase works in one key, you can use it in all twelve. The barrier is a technical one on your instrument and can be overcome with patient practice.

Mp3 track 25 has the rhythm section backing for a II-V-I progression in all twelve keys. This follows the cycle of fifths from F, so each new key is another step round the cycle, have a listen and notice how it could keep going and going. This track takes you through the entire progression twice.

25 26

Fig 7.10a II-V-I in Twelve Keys

The first three II-V-Is (in F, B♭ and E♭ major) have the three sample licks written out in these three keys. Eventually try to replicate these in all twelve keys, but remember that it's better to cover a few keys really thoroughly than bluff through all twelve. Take your time with the transposition – this is a difficult exercise.

Mp3 track 26 also has the II-V-I progression in all twelve keys but this time starting with B major. This allows you to start at a different point in the cycle and approach the harder keys first.

This is a 32 bar AABA tune which pays homage to **Duke Ellington**'s 'Satin Doll'. Listen to the demonstration of the tune (mp3 track 27) and see if you can hear the II-V-Is within it.

27 7

Fig 7.11a 'Dancing With Duke' (Head)

Ollie Weston

Checkpoint

There is no arguing with the importance of the II-V-I in jazz. From jazz standards such as 'Autumn Leaves' and 'All The Things You Are', and bebop compositions such as 'Joy Spring' and 'Donna Lee', to **John Coltrane**'s groundbreaking 'Giant Steps', the II-V-I progression is used to establish a key and to modulate to other keys.

By playing the sample licks along with the rhythm section you will have played in the style of some of the great musicians. Try to come up with some licks of your own and transfer them to different keys, eventually working up to all twelve – remember to spell out the chords as effectively as possible using the guide tones.

Assignments and Improvisation Tips

Play 'Dancing With Duke' without the clarinet demonstration (CD track 7). The tune has lots of II-V progressions, some that resolve to chord I, others that do not. This is a common trick in jazz chord progressions, the II and the V chords are often repeated implying a perfect cadence, but delaying the satisfying resolution. Look for the key centre of each II-V and work out where it would resolve to and therefore identify the parent major scale.

The 'A' section of 'Dancing With Duke' starts with repeated II-V's in F major but doesn't resolve to chord I. In the third bar the chord progression moves up a tone using the II-V chords of G major, but similarly chord I isn't stated. The last four bars are a longer II-V-I in F major where the harmony moves at one chord per bar. This is the first time we hear the tonic chord (F) and it works as a musical full stop – a satisfying end to the phrase both in terms of melody and harmony.

The first four bars of the bridge (the 'B' section) are a II-V-I progression in another key. The clues for this are the types of chords used. Cm^7 isn't a diatonic chord of F major, neither is F^7. These are chords II and V of B♭ major. To identify the new key, look for the seventh chord – it nearly always acts as a dominant chord and so is the fifth (V) of the key. The E♭ in the melody also points to a new key, as the E♭ isn't present in F major. The bridge has '**modulated**' (changed key) to B♭ major.

The second four bars of the bridge start with another unresolved II-V progression. The Dm^7 and G^7 are chords II and V of C major. Although the cadence is never resolved, the parent scale C major will fit over both of these chords. The melody again is a clue to the key – the B♮ isn't part of the original key of F major or the modulated key of B♭ major.

The bridge finishes by leading back to the last 'A' section by using another II-V in the tonic key – F major.

The sample solo for 'Dancing With Duke' is written as a swing style solo using lots of II-V-I style language. Notice how the phrases fit the chords, usually incorporating the guide tones of the chords and landing on a chord tone each time. Try to analyse the phrases you like – as always, number their relationship to the root and try to explain what each note is doing.

Fig 7.11b 'Dancing With Duke' Sample Solo

2nd Chorus
A
Gm7 C7 Gm7 C7 Am7 D7 Am7 D7
Gm7 C7 Fmaj7
3
A
Gm7 C7 Gm7 C7 Am7 D7 Am7 D7
Gm7 C7 Fmaj7
B
Cm7 F7 B♭maj7
Dm7 G7 Gm7 C7
A
Gm7 C7 Gm7 C7 Am7 D7 Am7 D7
Gm7 C7 Fmaj7

Notice that the **Cannonball Adderley** style lick appears in the first 'B' section, it has been transposed to fit the II-V-I in B♭ major. The **John Coltrane** style lick is used to finish the first chorus, this time in its original key of F.

Listen to the recorded version of the solo and try to copy the feel and tone of the solo. For it to swing hard it needs to be relaxed and warm, aim for a sweet lyrical approach.

Now play your own version of 'Dancing With Duke'. CD backing track 7 has four choruses of the progression. For the solo section Fig 7.11c has the guide tones for each chord written.

Play the head then two choruses of your own solo, then a final head. Try to incorporate the II-V-I language we've looked at in this chapter. Another challenge is to slot the licks you've learned into your solo – harder than it sounds but great when it works!

Fig 7.11c **'Dancing With Duke' Guide Tones**

This chapter has explained the perfect cadence and its importance as a means of punctuating a series of musical phrases. Every composer from **Bach** to **Basie** to the **Beatles** has used perfect cadences frequently in their compositions. In jazz the standard V^7-I of the perfect cadence is expanded by the addition of chord II to create the progression II-V-I – the 'jazz perfect cadence'. By learning about the II-V-I and different ways to play over it you are learning to use one of the fundamental building blocks of jazz. Jazz musicians are always referring to II-V-I progressions and discussing licks that fit well over them. Becoming fluent with this progression will allow you to be party to those discussions, and to unlock literally hundreds of standard jazz tunes.

8: The Minor II-V-I

Chapter seven explored the II-V-I progression. Understanding the II-V-I and being able to improvise fluently over it is an essential part of your development – a large part of a jazz musician's practice is invested in learning II-V-I patterns in a variety of keys. These are then at your disposal and can be slotted into your solos.

This chapter will look at the minor keys and some of the relationships between major and minor harmonies. We will also look at the minor version of the II-V-I progression and some practical approaches for improvisation in minor keys.

Relative Major and Minor

Anyone with a smattering of music theory knowledge knows about major scales and their relative minor versions. So, the good news is that each major key has a minor key that it is related to. They share a key signature and are described as the 'relative' major/minor of each other.

This means that if you know the major key signatures you also know the minors. The relative minor key of a major key is found by counting down three semitones from the root. For example the relative minor of F major is D minor, as illustrated below.

Fig 8.1 F to D by Semitones

If you play the F major scale from this new starting point you will be playing the A Aeolian mode as introduced in chapter six. The Aeolian mode is sometimes referred to as the 'natural' minor as it is the literal relative minor scale – it shares the same key signature and the exact same set of notes with no added accidentals.

Fig 8.2 F Major – D Aeolian

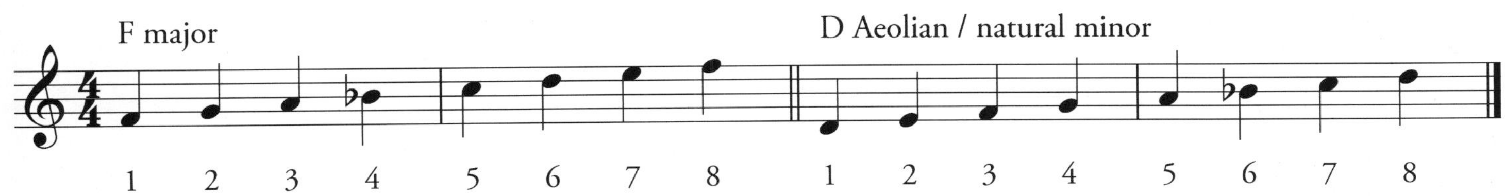

Understanding the link between the major key and its relative minor is essential for improvising in minor keys. Here is the cycle of fifths again, this time with the relative minor of each key next to it. Try to familiarize yourself with the relationship between each major key and its relative minor.

Fig 8.3 **Cycle of Fifths with Relative Minor Keys**

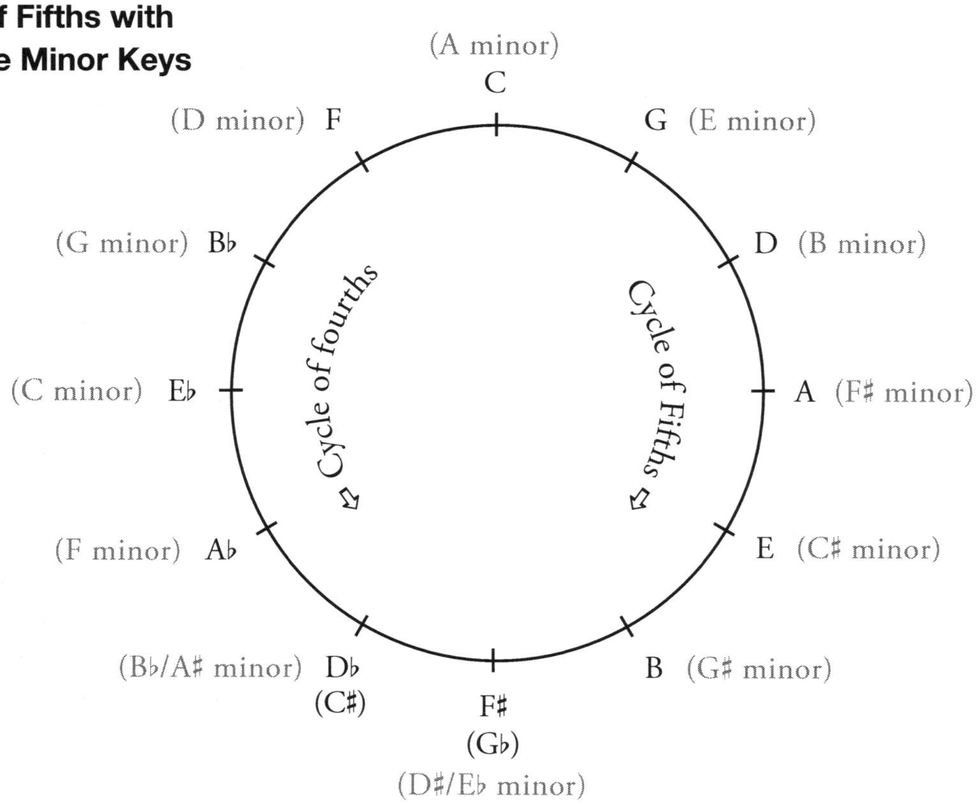

Just like the major keys we looked at in previous chapters minor keys also have natural resolution points which we call cadences. The Aeolian/natural minor scale will fit perfectly over a minor cadence, and like the Dorian mode sounds great over static minor seventh chords. There are however other options that enable you to make the most of the tension and resolution possible in minor cadences.

Melodic and Harmonic Minor

Classical music generally focuses on two types of minor scale – the 'melodic' minor and the 'harmonic' minor. As the name suggests, the melodic minor deals with the melodic aspects of the music – the tune. The harmonic minor is concerned with outlining the harmonic content of the minor key and in particular a minor cadence.

Here are the melodic and harmonic minor scales in the key of D minor:

Fig 8.4 **D Melodic and Harmonic Minor**

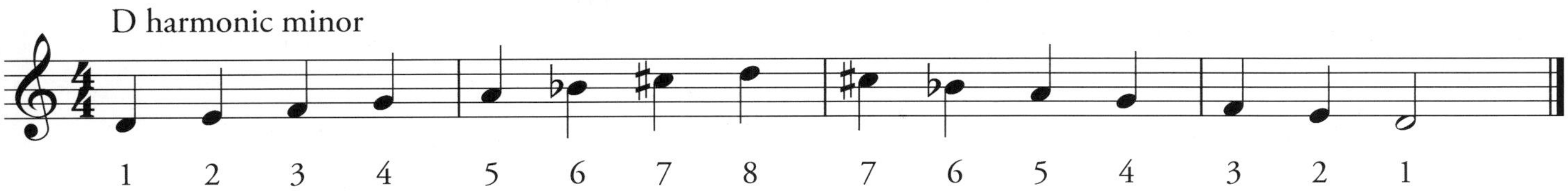

Notice that the melodic minor is different in its ascending and descending forms. The ascending version of the melodic minor scale has only one note different from the D major scale – the third. This needs to be flattened for the scale to qualify as a minor. The seventh note of the scale is a major seventh – like that of a major scale and the major seventh chord. This use of the major seventh is the notable difference between the melodic/harmonic minor scales and the Aeolian/Dorian modes. The Aeolian and Dorian modes have a flattened seventh and so fit the minor seventh chord perfectly. However, a minor cadence (II-V-I) can be made more effective by using the major seventh.

When listened to in the context of functional tonality, that is to say a system of harmony based on the functional relationship between chords of a given key and the 'pull' of a cadence in a certain harmonic direction, the major seventh has a strong 'pull' up to the root. Play the scale of D melodic minor and stop at the seventh note – the C♯ creates a tension if it is left unresolved and is best resolved by playing a D (the root). The harmonic minor scale also has a major seventh and the resultant pull towards the root note. This tension is similar to those discussed in the perfect cadences explored in chapter seven.

The term 'leading note' is used to describe a note that is a semitone below the tonic – it 'leads you' towards the tonic note – the seventh degree of the major scale or harmonic minor scale can be named as a leading note.

Fig 8.5 Minor Scales Stopping at the Leading Note

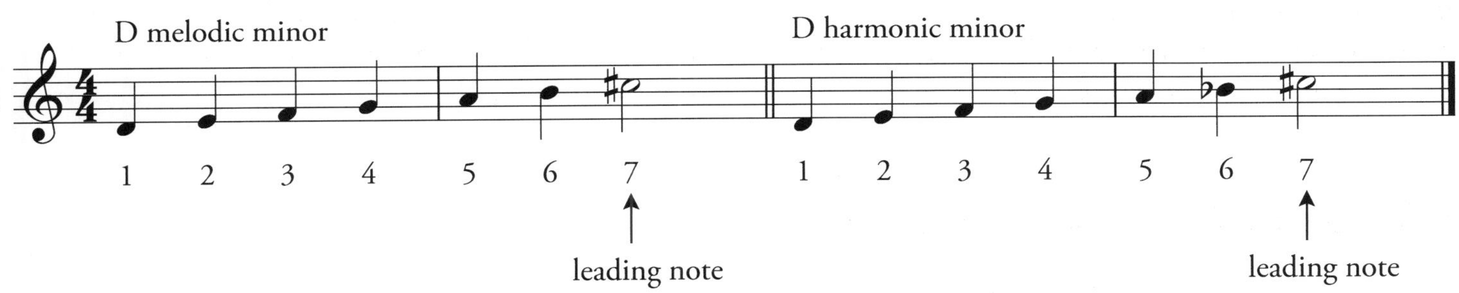

Because the leading note has such a strong pull towards the root note of the key, composers of tonal music found it difficult to write descending melodies using the harmonic minor pattern, as any use of the leading note would always tend to lead the music back to the root. The descending melodic minor has a flattened sixth and seventh to cancel out the strong pull of the leading note and so make descending melodies easier to write. The descending version of the melodic minor is the same as the Aeolian/natural minor scale. Here is a short phrase in D minor using the leading note (Fig 8.6a) and then a flattened seventh (Fig 8.6b).

Fig 8.6 Leading-Note Lick

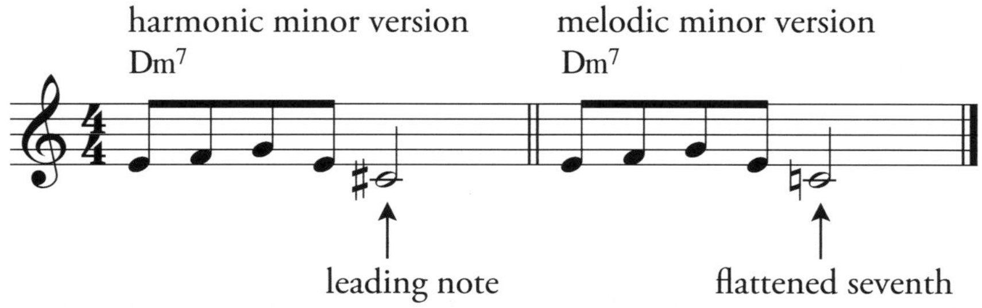

Notice that the harmonic minor version leaves the leading note 'hanging' and so creates tension, as it wants to resolve to the D. The flattened seventh (C♮) in the melodic minor version is much more settled and less bound to the root, this opens up more melodic possibilities. Play this second version again and try to continue the phrase using the descending D melodic minor scale – here is one possibility:

Fig 8.7 Descending Melodic-Minor Line

Use of the leading note creates the expectancy of a cadence. This an important part of music making and in an improvisation can be used to great effect to bring sections of a tune to a satisfying conclusion.

The Leading Note within the Dominant Seventh Chord

The perfect cadence in the minor key follows exactly the same chord pattern as a perfect cadence in a major key. The dominant seventh chord (V^7) resolving to the tonic chord (I) is exactly the same – the only difference is that the tonic chord is minor rather than major. We can denote minor chords in Roman numerals by using an 'm' for minor.

Fig 8.8 Perfect Cadence in D Minor

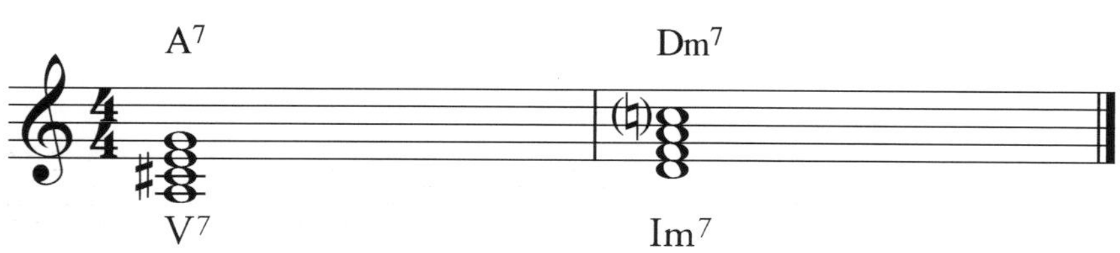

We established in the previous chapter that the essential element of the perfect cadence is the unstable tritone interval between the third and the seventh degrees of the dominant chord (V^7). The same is the case in minor cadences – here is the same V^7-Im^7 cadence but with only the tritone and its resolution.

Fig 8.9 Tritone and Resolution within a Minor Cadence

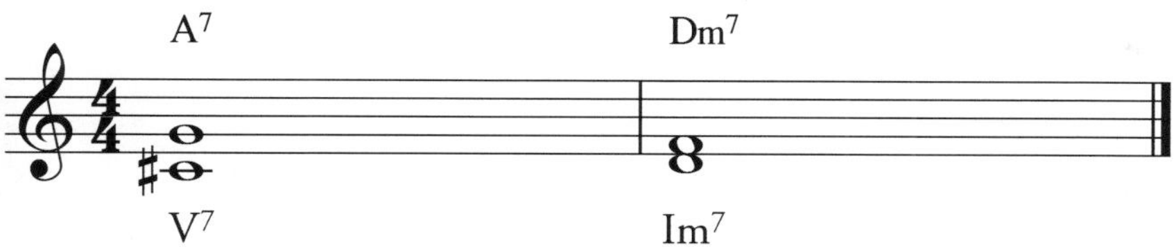

Importantly the leading note is present in this cadence. The third of the dominant seventh chord is the leading note of the tonic scale – in our examples the third of the A^7 chord (C♯) is the leading note of the D minor scale. The strong pull towards the root exerted by the leading note is an essential part of a minor cadence.

The Harmonic Minor Scale in Minor Cadences

The harmonic minor scale is a great starting point for capturing the sound of a minor key. The leading note in the scale fits the dominant seventh chord and creates the tension required for the cadence.

Fig 8.10 Harmonic Minor Scale over Minor V^7-Im^7

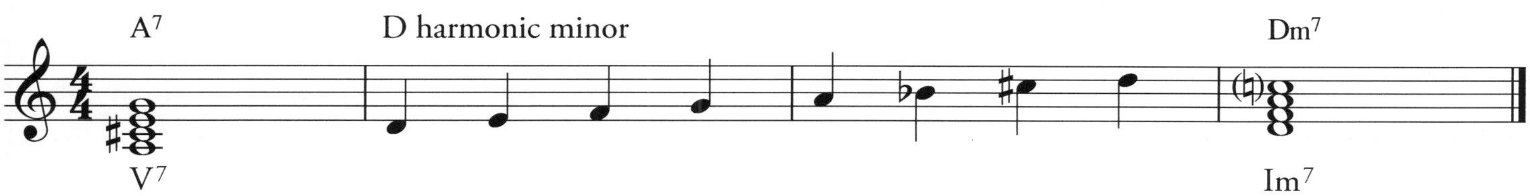

Play the chord tones of the A^7 chord (the root, third, fifth and seventh) and then play the chord tones of Dm^7 – this will outline our perfect cadence in D minor. Now play the D harmonic minor scale – all the chord tones of the A^7 chord are contained in the scale including the all-important leading note (C♯ in this example). Starting the scale on the root sounds a little awkward over the dominant chord as the end of the cadence (the resolution to the D) is given away too early – here is the same example but this time starting the D harmonic minor scale on its fifth degree.

Fig 8.11 Harmonic Minor Scale from the Fifth Degree

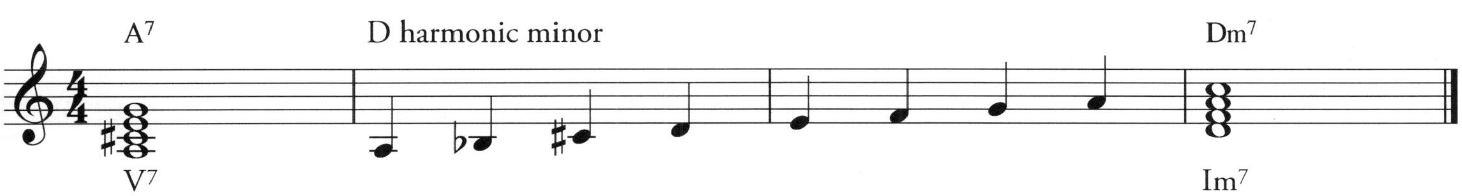

By playing the scale starting on the fifth degree you are effectively creating a variant on the Mixolydian scale previously used on seventh chords. However, because we are using the seventh chord to point towards a minor conclusion (remember the progression here is a II-V-I in a minor key) the Mixolydian mode would sound too bright. The B♭ from the D harmonic minor scale gives the dominant seventh (A^7) chord a flattened second – usually referred to as a flattened ninth (this is the same note but an octave higher). Because the B♭ is also present in the key we are heading to (D minor) it is effective over the dominant seventh chord of that key too.

Fig 8.12 **Harmonic Minor and Dominant Seven, Flat Nine**

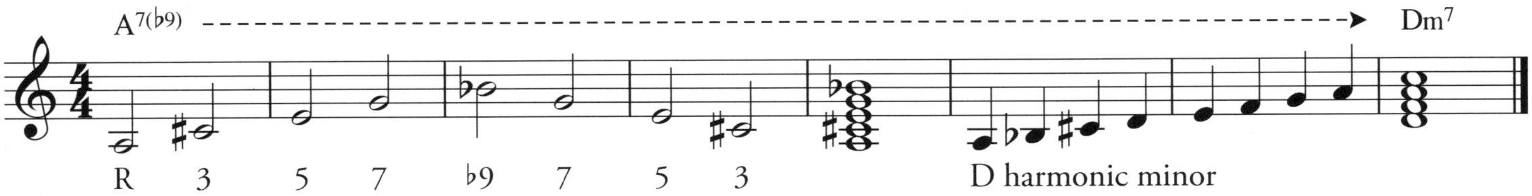

This example contains the chord tones of an $A^{7(\flat 9)}$ chord as well as its parent scale – D harmonic minor. The first seven bars of this example deal with the V^7 chord where the tension is created by the presence of the C♯ (the leading note of the key of D minor and the third of the A^7 chord). Only when this has resolved to the D in the Dm^7 chord will the cadence be finished (bar eight) – the phrase ends on a static minor seventh chord.

Checkpoint

You should now be familiar with the idea of a minor cadence. In the same way as a major cadence (II-V-I), the minor cadence uses the tritone interval between the third and the seventh degree of the dominant seventh chord. The main difference is the use of the major seventh note, and the strength of the semitonal 'pull' between it and the tonic note. As the major seventh is already present in the major key (think of B♮ in a C major scale) the leading note in a major key doesn't have the same power as its minor key counterpart.

A major seventh note in a minor key isn't part of the key itself – C♯ doesn't appear in the key signature of D minor – because the key of D minor allows for both the C♮ (in the descending melodic version of the scale) and the C♯ (in the harmonic version and in the ascending melodic one). Therefore, when the seventh degree of the scale is raised the leading note really stands out, making the cadence more effective.

Minor V^7-Im^7 Exercise

The mp3 track 28 has a minor V^7-Im^7 cadence in all twelve keys. Over the V^7 chord the tonic key's harmonic minor scale is written. Over the root chord I have used the Aeolian mode – this isn't the only option for static minor chords (previously we've used the Dorian mode) but to 'spell out' the minor key clearly, the natural minor (Aeolian) is a good scale choice.

Fig 8.13 Minor V^7-I in Twelve Keys

28 29

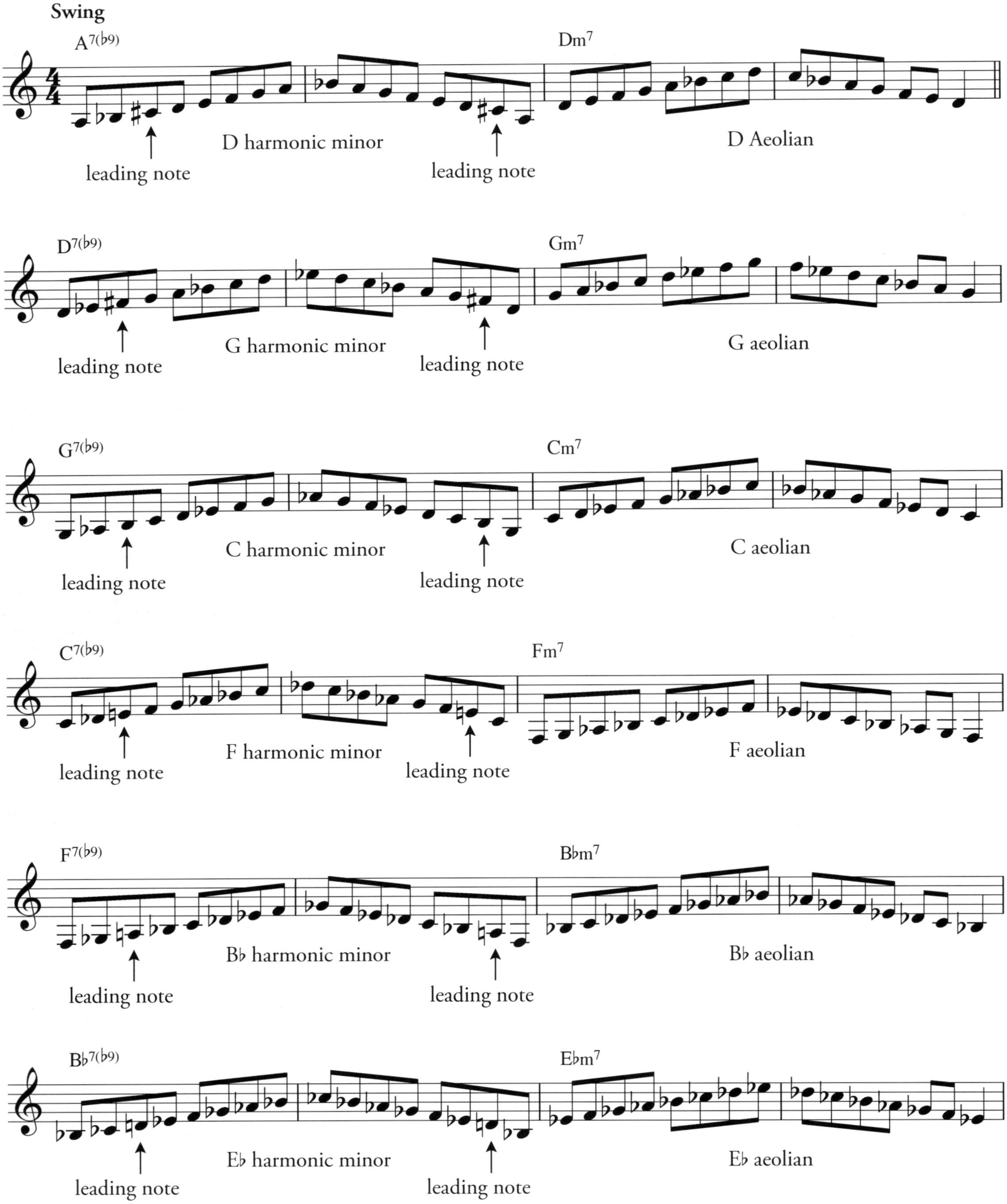

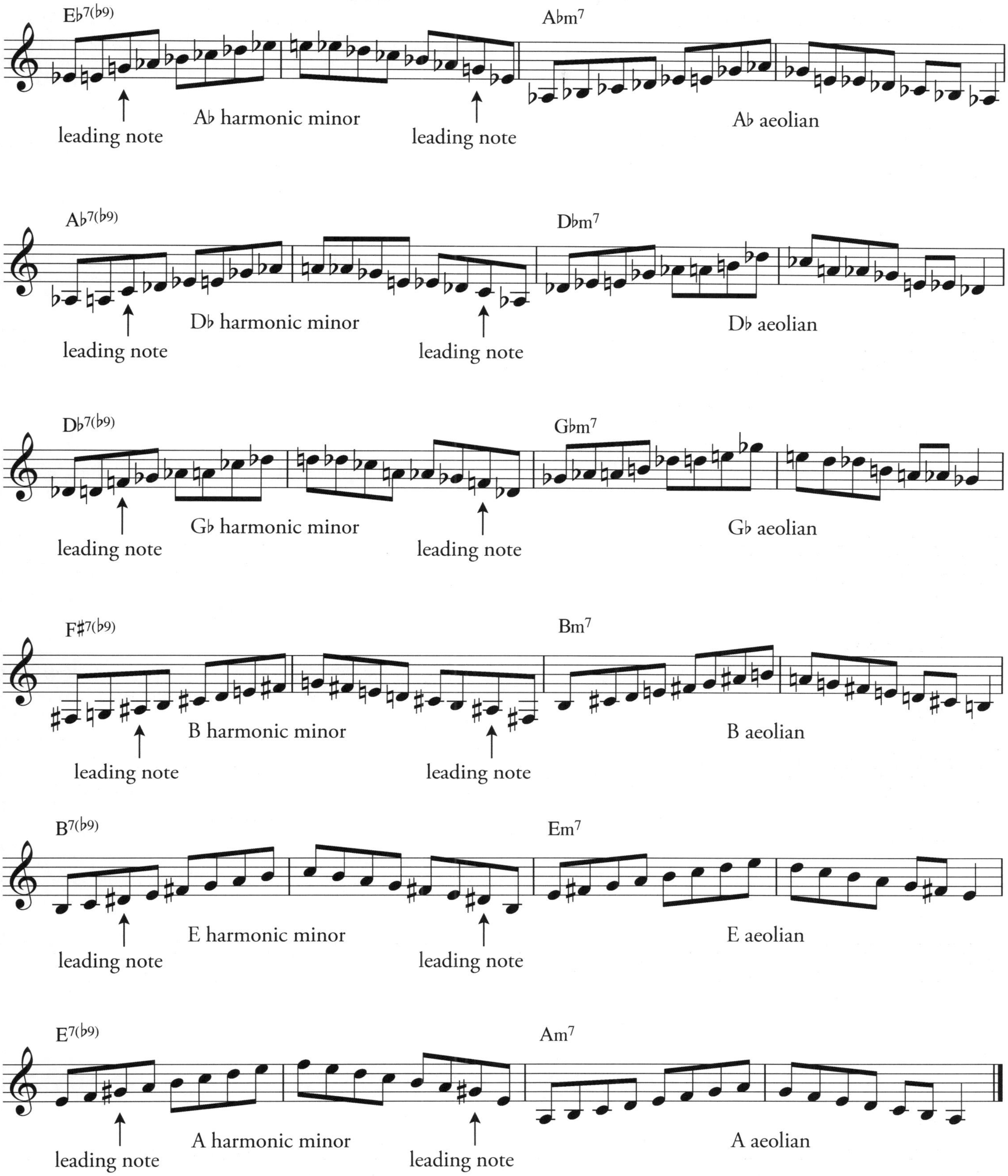

This exercise will familiarize you with the minor scales you can use over the minor V^7-I progression. The leading note is highlighted over each seventh chord to help you recognize the dissonant sound it creates. The harmonic minor scale sets up the cadence by using the leading note, and the use of the Aeolian confirms the minor key as the chord changes from dominant seventh to tonic.

Why do we switch to the Aeolian mode at this point? When the cadence is resolved on the tonic chord (I) there is no need for the leading note as the harmonic 'event' – the move from V^7 to I – has already happened. This is why the Aeolian mode is suggested for the static chord.

These exercises have been arranged to go round the cycle of fifths. Mp3 track 28 starts with D minor and moves through the twelve keys. Mp3 track 29 has the same progression but starts in the middle of the cycle with the perfect cadence in A♭ minor. This means you can start the progression in a different place and familiarize yourself with the other side of the cycle. As always, take your time with the transpositions – learning patterns in all keys takes time, and you won't learn all twelve harmonic minors properly in one go. Concentrate on a few at a time and let the sound sink in.

Minor V^7-I Lick

Here is a short jazz lick for a minor V^7-I progression. The first three keys are written for you. Try to work out the lick for the rest of the keys. Use mp3 tracks 28 and 29 as the accompaniment:

Fig 8.14 Minor V^7-Im^7 Lick 28 29

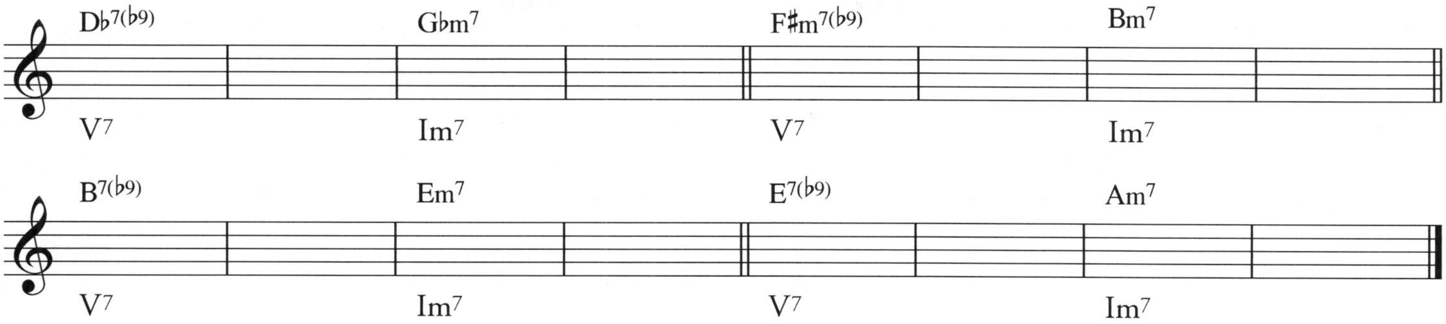

Notice the use of the leading note on the dominant chord and then the flattened seventh on chord I – in the first example this is the C♯ and then the C♮. This reflects the move from the harmonic minor to the Aeolian mode as outlined above.

Now try some ideas of your own over the progression. Use the harmonic minor of the tonic chord and you won't go far wrong. Once you've navigated the V^7 part of the progression and are on to the resolved chord I, try some minor seventh chord language. I've introduced the Aeolian mode as an option for you but the pentatonic, Dorian or blues scales will also fit the tonic chords of each key.

Minor Cadences in Jazz Progressions

Although many jazz tunes are written in minor keys the example above starts in a major key and then modulates to the minor. Understanding this modulation will help clarify the function of a minor cadence and relate it to the key of the tune.

Fig 8.15 Diatonic Chord Progression in C Major

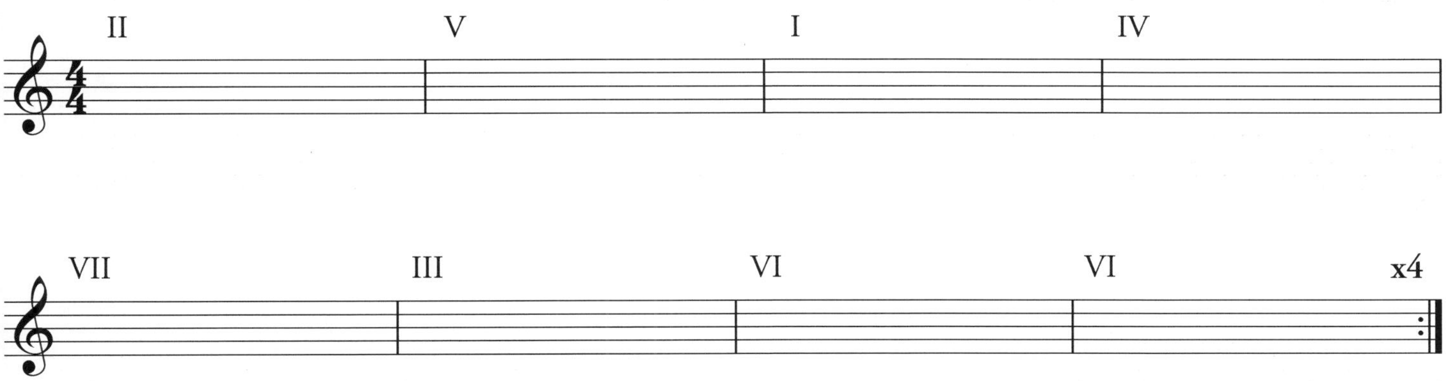

This eight bar chord progression uses the chords and modes of C major. They are named by their roman numerical relationships to the root. Knowing these diatonic relationships and knowing that we are in C major means that you can fill in the information required for each chord – the root note and the quality (major seventh, minor seventh, seventh) of each chord. If in doubt refer back to chapter six and review the modes and their specific chord types (Ionian (I) – major seventh, Dorian (II) – minor seventh, Mixolydian (V) – seventh etc). Try to complete the eight-bar progression in Fig 8.15 by writing in the chord symbols for each bar.

Here is the progression again but with the mode and the chord type written (remember that the progression is diatonic to C major and so the 'parent' scale of each mode is C major).

All seven of the modes are used here – D Dorian (II), G Mixolydian (V), C Ionian (I), F Lydian (IV), B Locrian (VII), E Phrygian (III) and A Aeolian (VI).

Fig 8.16 Diatonic Chord Progression with Chord Types and Guide Tones

30

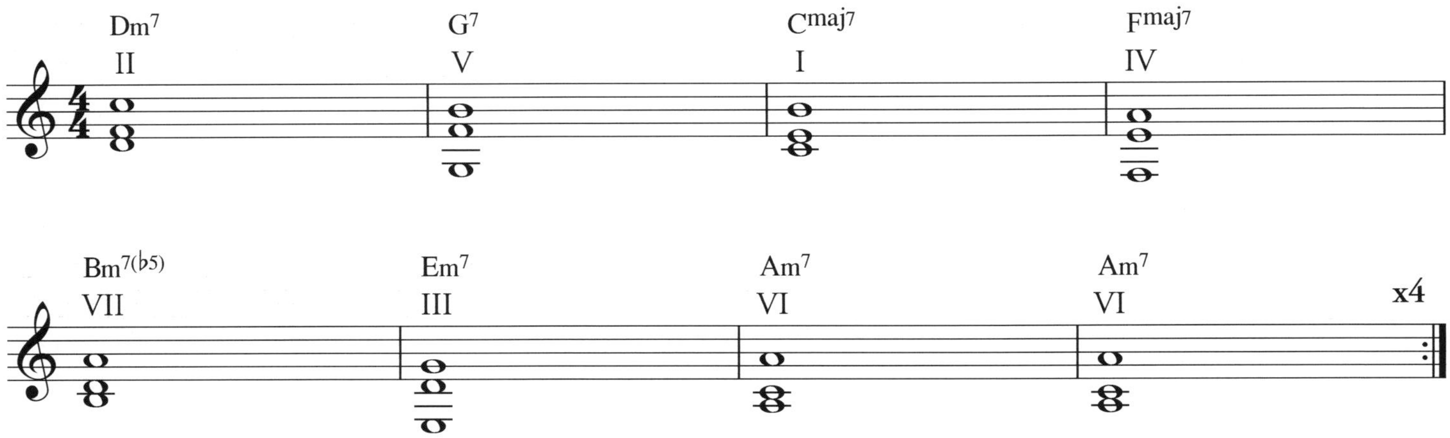

Play along with the progression (mp3 track 30) using only the C major scale. Try to apply the major II-V-I ideas from chapter seven to the first three bars then explore the different contexts of the C major scale over the last three chords. Limit yourself to C major only – this will challenge you to be creative with only a set palette of notes. The guide tones written will help you pick the strong notes for each chord.

Playing diatonically over this works perfectly well, however to bring it to life and add more interest both for the improviser and the audience we can add a minor cadence to the progression. The A minor seventh chord in bars seven and eight could be seen as the sixth chord / mode of C major and treated as a diatonic chord – but in this case there has been a modulation to A minor and so the last two bars have become chord I in this new key. This progression has therefore modulated to its relative minor key.

To make the minor cadence really obvious and effective we can turn the Em^7 chord in bar six into a dominant seventh. This will make a strong V^7-Im^7 progression in A minor. This can be achieved by raising the third of the Em^7 chord by a semitone to G♯ – the chord can now be named E^7 – this G♯ introduces the leading note to the progression and so clearly states the cadence in A minor. The G♯ leading note isn't part of the key signature of C major or A minor but is an accidental that exists to make the modulation more effective.

By making this subtle transformation the scale choice for this chord changes from E Phrygian to A harmonic minor – a change of only one note, but it can totally alter the sound and musical effect of the progression.

Fig 8.17 Phrygian to Harmonic Minor

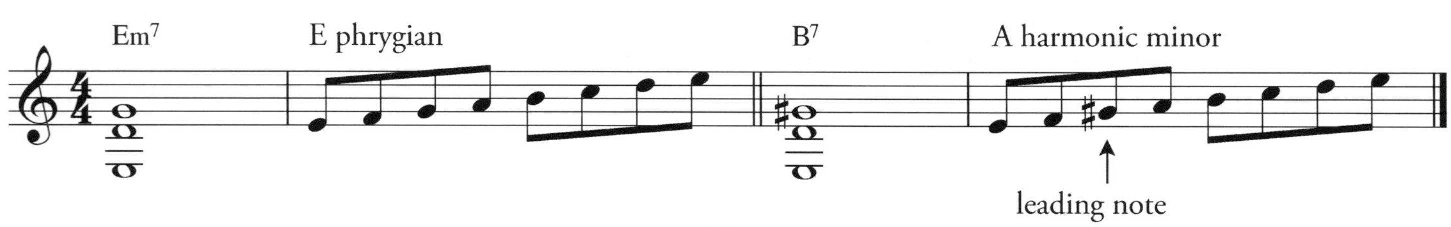

Therefore the E minor seventh chord has been replaced by an E^7 chord. The minor cadence (II-V-I) chords are written underneath the stave.

Fig 8.18 Diatonic Progression with Minor V^7-I

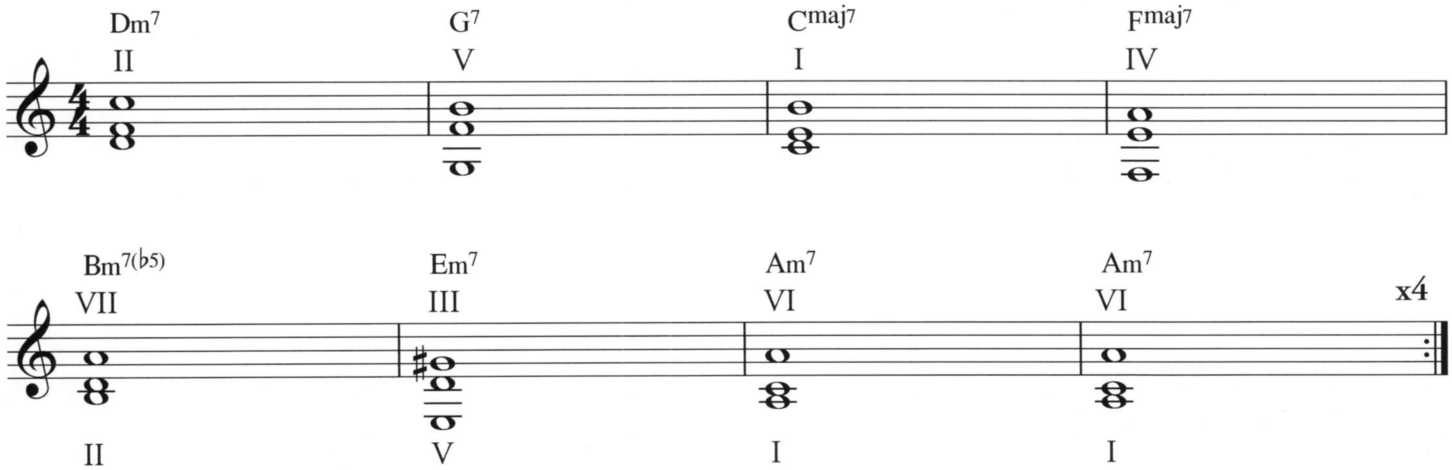

The Minor Seven Flat Five Chord

So far minor cadences have only been described as a V^7-Im^7 progression. Chapter seven introduced the chord II as part of the jazz perfect cadence (II-V-I). In the same way, minor keys also make use of chord II and can have a II-V-I cadence.

The seventh mode (Locrian) has been seldom used up until now, as its primary purpose is to act as chord II in minor cadences. Look again at the progression in Fig 8.18 to see the chords VII-III-VI in C major written as II-V-I in A minor. To build a chord from the Locrian mode take the root, third, fifth and seventh of the mode.

Fig 8.19 Locrian Mode / m7(♭5) Chord

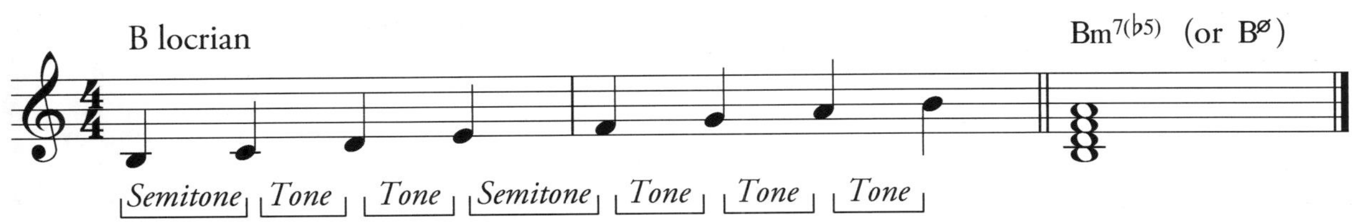

The semitone interval between the fourth and fifth degrees of the Locrian mode produce a flattened fifth giving both the scale and its chord a dark sound. In the examples above, the flattened fifth of the $Bm^{7(\flat 5)}$ chord is an F which is diatonic to both the major and relative minor keys (C major and A minor in this case).

NB The m7(♭5) chord is sometimes referred to as a half-diminished chord and denoted by a small circle with a line through it (as in Fig 8.19). This is simply another term for the same thing – don't treat it any differently if you see a chord written as half diminished.

Fig 8.20 **'Autumn Sun'**

31 8

Ollie Weston

This tune is inspired by the famous jazz standard 'Autumn Leaves' by **Joseph Kosma** and **Johnny Mercer**. Although this tune is a typical 32 bars in length, the form is slightly different from the AABA form that has previously been used. The two eight bar 'A' sections are a familiar length but the 'B' section is longer – sixteen bars – meaning that there is no final 'A' section. So the form is AAB.

The chord progression is one of the most commonly used in jazz and 'Autumn Leaves' is often played at jam sessions and on gigs. It moves between two keys – the tonic key of C major and its relative minor – A minor. The head has the keys highlighted to make it easy to spot the II-V-Is in both keys. Listen to the head and sample solo of the track (mp3 track 31) and look out for the shifts between major and minor.

Checkpoint

You should now be familiar with the minor II-V-I. The root movement is exactly the same as the major II-V-I but the content of the chords is slightly different. The minor seven flat five chord on the II derived from the Locrian mode is darker than the Dorian mode used in the major II-V-I.

The dominant seventh chord also is darker than its Mixolydian counterpart in the major key. The flattened ninth on the dominant chord is an important pointer towards the minor key. These differences in the chords are essential if the chords are to remain diatonic to the minor key and its key signature.

Assignments and Improvisation Tips

Play through 'Autumn Sun' using the accompaniment track (CD track 8). Both the head and the solo are written to demonstrate a practical use of the II-V-I ideas covered in the last two chapters. Notice that the only non-diatonic notes (i.e. those not naturally present in the key signature) in the head are the G♯s. These appear each time there is a cadence between an E^7 chord and Am^7. The G♯ is the leading note of the A minor key and makes the modulation all the more effective.

Feel and Swing

Play this solo with a relaxed swing – don't make the second quaver of each pair too short as this will make your playing sound choppy. Similarly, use soft tonguing to articulate the quavers lightly rather than playing everything staccato.

The accented notes in the second and fourth bars of the head should be separate but also not too short. If you are in doubt about how to articulate this tune listen to mp3 demonstration track 31 and play along with it.

Fig 8.21 **Sample Solo**

A
2nd chorus
Dm7 G7 Cmaj7 Fmaj7
Bm7(♭5) E7(♭9) Am7 Am7
A
Dm7 G7 Cmaj7 Fmaj7
Bm7(♭5) E7(♭9) Am7 Am7
B
Bm7(♭5) E7(♭9) Am7 Am7
Dm7 G7 Cmaj7 Fmaj7
Bm7(♭5) E7(♭9) Am7 Am7
Fmaj7 E7(♭9) Am7 Am7
(Back to the Head)

Similar to the head, the sample solo for 'Autumn Sun' demonstrates some effective II-V-I language in both the major key (C major) and the relative minor (A minor). The minor II-V-I ideas discussed in this chapter are explored in greater detail in this solo – analyse the minor II-V-Is in this solo and look at the use of the A harmonic minor scale over each of the E^7 chords. The F naturals and G sharps are particularly descriptive of the minor cadence. Bar six of the solo is a good example of this – the run from the G♯ to the C is a typical minor lick effectively spelling out the dominant seventh chord but also landing on a strong chord tone.

Using the Dorian Mode on Root Minor Seventh Chords

To play diatonically over this progression we have already established that the Aeolian mode is the correct choice for the static minor seventh chords – chord I of any minor key. As the harmonic event has already happened (the II-V) the chord I can be treated to some decoration. Chapter two dealt with static minor chords and used the Dorian mode exclusively. Any ideas you've used over Dorian chords can now be applied to the root minor chords in this tune – any Am^7 chord. Look at bars 15 and 16 of the second chorus of the solo to hear this effect – the F sharps suggest using A Dorian rather than A Aeolian, which used throughout this chapter. Using the Dorian mode in this way adds a bright, funky touch to your solos and is a trick used by many top jazz musicians.

The only other non-diatonic notes in this solo are the E flats in the 'B' sections of the first and second choruses – these add a shot of blues to the solo by incorporating the bluesy flattened fifth.

Play Your Own Version

The backing track (CD track 8) has four choruses of the tune (head, two choruses of solo and the head again). Play many times through the progression and try to apply some of the minor II-V-I language explored in this chapter as well as the major II-V-I language from chapter seven. Using the harmonic minor scale to bring out the tension created by the leading note and its resolution to the root will enable you to play authentic jazz lines and improvise with greater awareness of the passing harmony and the direction the music is heading in.

By the time you complete this chapter you will have learned some useful chord to scale theory that will help you navigate your way around all minor keys. As ever, make sure you are equally fluent in all keys with all of these exercises.

9: Songs and Standards

Jazz 'standards' are frequently played tunes that have become an essential part of the jazz repertoire. The original standards were popular songs taken from films and musicals from the 1920s onwards. The catchy melodies coupled with established structures and logical chord progressions provided ideal vehicles for improvising musicians to use as a base. The classic tunes composed by **George Gershwin**, **Richard Rodgers**, **Cole Porter**, **Jerome Kern** and many others are still replayed and re-interpreted today. Without having met beforehand, jazz musicians can play standards together through a shared knowledge and understanding of these great tunes – often with little or no rehearsal! Knowing a few standards from memory means that you can 'jam' with other players without music and without having to explain compositions in great detail. There is no one definitive set of standards, although several good editions are commonly available. Most jazz musicians will have a stock of tunes that they know well and can improvise comfortably with.

This chapter features several standard type tunes and investigates some traits common to many standards. You will see how to analyse a song quickly and apply your own ideas to it thereby making the tune your own – no two people play standards in the same way and forging your own style is an important part of your development as a player. Much of the work you've done on II-V-I language is relevant to standards. This chapter is where you put it all together.

'Among the Stars' is thirty-two bars in length but instead of being split into the commonly-found format of four eight-bar sections (AABA), this tune is split into two sections of sixteen bars (A and B). It is a tune inspired by the standard 'Fly Me To The Moon' by **Bart Howard** and immortalised by **Frank Sinatra** and **Count Basie** on the album *Sinatra At The Sands*.

Listen to the head and sample solo (mp3 track 32).

Fig 9.1 **'Among the Stars'**

Ollie Weston

Half-time feel
A
Chorus 1
Dm7 Gm7 C7 Fmaj7
B♭maj7 Em7(♭5) A7(♭9) Dm7
Gm7 C7 Am7 D7(♭9)
Gm7 3 C7 3 Fmaj7 A7(♭9)
B
Dm7 Gm7 C7 Fmaj7
B♭maj7 Em7(♭5) A7(♭9) Dm7
Gm7 3 C7 Am7 3 D7(♭9)
Gm7 C7 Fmaj7 A7(♭9)

Swing
Chorus 2
A
Dm7 Gm7 C7 Fmaj7
B♭maj7 Em7(♭5) A7(♭9) Dm7
Gm7 C7 Am7 D7(♭9)
Gm7 C7 Fmaj7 A7(♭9)
B
Dm7 Gm7 C7 Fmaj7
B♭maj7 Em7(♭5) 3 A7(♭9) Dm7
Gm7 C7 Am7 3 D7(♭9)
Gm7 C7 Fmaj7 A7(♭9)

A
Last Head
Dm7 Gm7 C7 Fmaj7
B♭maj7 Em7(♭5) A7(♭9) Dm7
Gm7 C7 Am7 D7(♭9)
Gm7 C7 Fmaj7 A7(♭9)
B
Dm7 Gm7 C7 Fmaj7
B♭maj7 Em7(♭5) A7(♭9) Dm7
Gm7 C7 Am7
3
D7(♭9) Gm7 C7

The Head

Play the head of the tune without the recorded clarinet (CD track 9). As with all medium swing tunes try to capture the relaxed mood. Don't over-articulate as a staccato approach to the tune will impair the swing – tongue lightly to separate the notes without making the phrase jerky. Notice the offbeat quavers (eighth notes) at the end of the first bar of the 'A' and 'B' sections – these can really add swing and bounce to the phrase, so be sure to observe the quaver rest at the start of the second bar as the silence will sound great. The crotchets (quarters) in bar five can be interpreted in different ways. Try them staccato, then legato. Which feels most natural to you?

The harmony of the head isn't dissimilar to 'Autumn Sun' (chapter eight) in that it is based around a major key (F major in this case) and its relative minor (D minor). Notice the modulation to D minor in bars six and seven is sign-posted by the use of the leading note C♯ and the $A^{7(\flat9)}$ chord. This is the same modulation to the relative minor as in 'Autumn Sun'. The $A^{7(\flat9)}$ chord breaks the pattern of diatonic chords established by the VI-II-V-I-IV of the first five bars and creates a modulation to the relative minor.

Uses of Chords III and VI

Having established that 'Among the Stars' is in F major it follows that chords III and VI are minor seventh chords (derived from the Phrygian and Aeolian modes respectively). To add interest and authenticity to your solos it's important to start to notice the inner workings of the chord progression and in particular the smaller cadence points. For the purposes of this discussion I will call these harmonic transitions 'mini-modulations', and for them to happen chords will perform slightly different functions at certain points within a progression. For example, in one context a chord may be acting as the tonic chord, but in another as the dominant of a fleeting, transitional tonal centre. Don't worry if this seems confusing when described in written text – it soon becomes apparent how this works when you start to play and hear the music.

Chapter eight looked at minor II-V-I progressions and the creation of a leading note to suggest a minor key. In this tune this means changing the chord based on A from the diatonic Am^7 (Phrygian mode) to A^7 and so modulating to D minor. Whenever the harmonic progression arrives at D minor the A^7 chord sets up the modulation.

Harmonically the modulations will work equally well with the simplified chord of A^7, but the flattened ninth of $A^{7(\flat9)}$ adds colour and depth.

Chord VI of the key (the chord of D minor) can be treated in exactly the same way and turned from a minor seventh chord into a seventh chord to create another harmonic twist to the progression.

III-VI-II-V-I Progression

Here the VI chord (Dm^7) is turned into a dominant seventh chord (D^7) and so creates another cadence – this time into G minor (again for interest the flattened ninth is used on this dominant seventh – $D^{7(\flat9)}$). The F♯ in bar twelve is the leading note of G minor and so creates a strong pull towards G minor and a 'mini-modulation' to G minor before the final II-V-I cadence in F major.

Here are the guide tones for the progression using chords III-VI-II-V-I in F major both diatonically (with chord VI as minor) and with chord VI as a dominant seventh (creating a cadence to G minor).

Fig 9.1a Roots and Guide Tones for III-VI (minor)-II-V-I in F Major

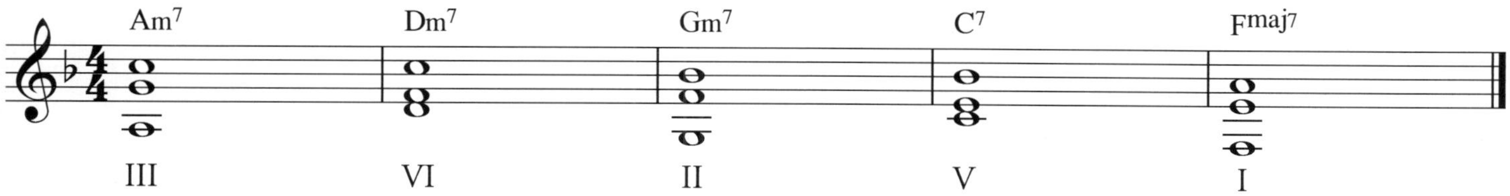

Fig 9.1b Roots and Guide Tones for III-VI (major)-II-V-I in F Major

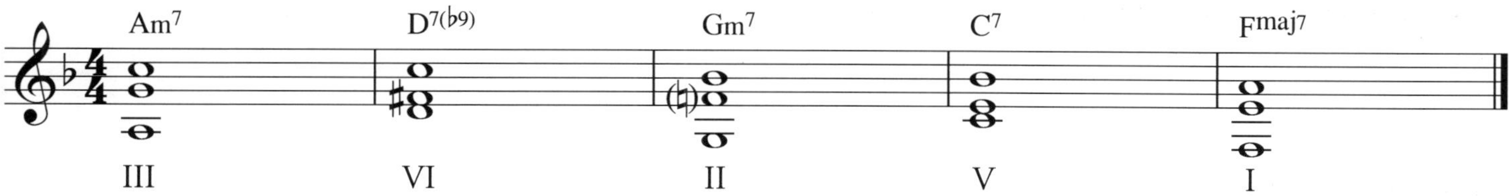

Effectively the III-VI-II-V-I is two II-V-I progressions joined together – a minor II-V to chord II followed by a major II-V to the root.

Adding diversity to chord progressions by creating extra dissonances and resolutions is a common practice in jazz – the F♯ added to chord VI of the III-VI-II-V-I creates interest by adding another punctuation mark in the harmonic phrase.

In this way, any minor chord can be prepared by its leading note and so a dissonance and resolution implied. The A^7 chord at the end of the 'A' section is a good example of this – the 'B' section starts on a D minor chord and so can be prepared by its dominant seventh (A^7). The C♯ in the melody is the leading note and so pulls the music towards D minor. This guides the music towards the next section rather than concluding on the tonic chord.

The Solo

The sample solo on 'Among the Stars' starts with a 'solo break'. This is where the rhythm section drops out and the soloist plays the opening of the solo totally unaccompanied. The sudden break in the texture can be exciting as the listener isn't expecting it. Solo breaks can be a great addition to a performance and are often used for a virtuosic flurry of notes – check out **Charlie Parker**'s famous break on 'A Night In Tunisia' (Dial Records) – an awesome four-bar break entirely of coruscating, rapid-fire semiquavers!

Without the rhythm section you are the only person keeping the time; make sure you are playing with a strong pulse so that when the rhythm section comes back in, you all agree where the first beat of the bar is! In 'Among the Stars' the harmony of the solo break starts by confirming the tonic key of F major in the first bar (the G♯ is just a blue note), the second bar uses the D harmonic minor scale over the $A^{7(\flat 9)}$ chord to lead the harmony to the D minor chord at the start of the progression. The C♯ and B♭ in particular spell out the $A^{7(\flat 9)}$ chord.

Chorus One

The first chorus of the sample solo picks up where the head left off in terms of mood and style. Concentrate on the relaxed easy swing – just as you did in the head, make sure the swung quavers aren't too short. In particular, the second quaver of each pair shouldn't be too short or it will upset the swing.

The solo starts with short groups of quavers, the last quaver of each bar anticipating the chord in the next bar. The B♭ at the end of the first bar is a chord tone of the G minor chord, while the B♭ at the end of the fourth bar anticipates the B♭ major seven chord.

The first chorus sticks closely to the chord tones and is effective because it spells out the harmony by using the thirds and sevenths of the chords. The progression is largely diatonic but notice the use of C sharps and F sharps as the leading notes of D minor and G minor respectively (see bars seven and twelve). There are also E flats on some of the D^7 chords to emphasize the flattened ninth and the resolution to G minor using the G harmonic minor scale. Try to establish what each accidental is there for – these non-diatonic notes help to underline the subtle modulations, and give the progression more depth and character.

Chorus Two

The second chorus builds the intensity from the first – listen to the change in the rhythm section as the feel changes from a light half-time feel to full on swing. Try to mirror this change in intensity in your playing. The offbeat quavers in the first bar should be strongly accented as this will capture the change in mood. The quavers in bars three and five might need some practice but will sound great at speed.

The Dm^7 and Gm^7 at the start of the 'B' section both use their leading notes for colour. The C♯ in the first bar of 'B' isn't technically part of a D minor chord but suggests the harmonic minor scale and creates interest. The F♯ in the next bar does exactly the same thing within the G minor chord.

The rest of the chorus shouldn't contain anything you can't now explain. Always analyse the notes for their melodic (horizontal) content as well as their harmonic (vertical) content.

The Ending

In much the same way as the rhythm section dropped out in the head to make space for the solo break, the ending has exactly the same stop but this time without the solo break. An emphatic 'dead stop' like this sounds great and gives the impression that you've been rehearsing for weeks!

Your Solo

Now use the backing track (CD track 9) of 'Among the Stars' to work on your own version of this tune. There are four sections in total – a head, two choruses of solo and a last head. Make sure you're ready for the solo break in the head. Remember the old adage 'less is more' in the first chorus, and leave lots of space. The best players seem to do this effortlessly – their solos seem to grow organically, and in the early stages their solo ideas seem to have plenty of room to breathe. When the swing kicks in at the second chorus you can shift up a gear. Always try to spell out the subtleties of the chord progression when you are soloing. Playing purely in F major will sound fine but the more you hit the subtle chromatically altered notes outlined in this chapter, the more accomplished your solos will sound. Here is a chord sheet for the progression with the II-V-Is marked. Use this as a 'route-map' when you are soloing – it will help you to identify the guide tones for each chord and nail the changes for this tune.

Fig 9.2 'Among the Stars' Chord Sheet

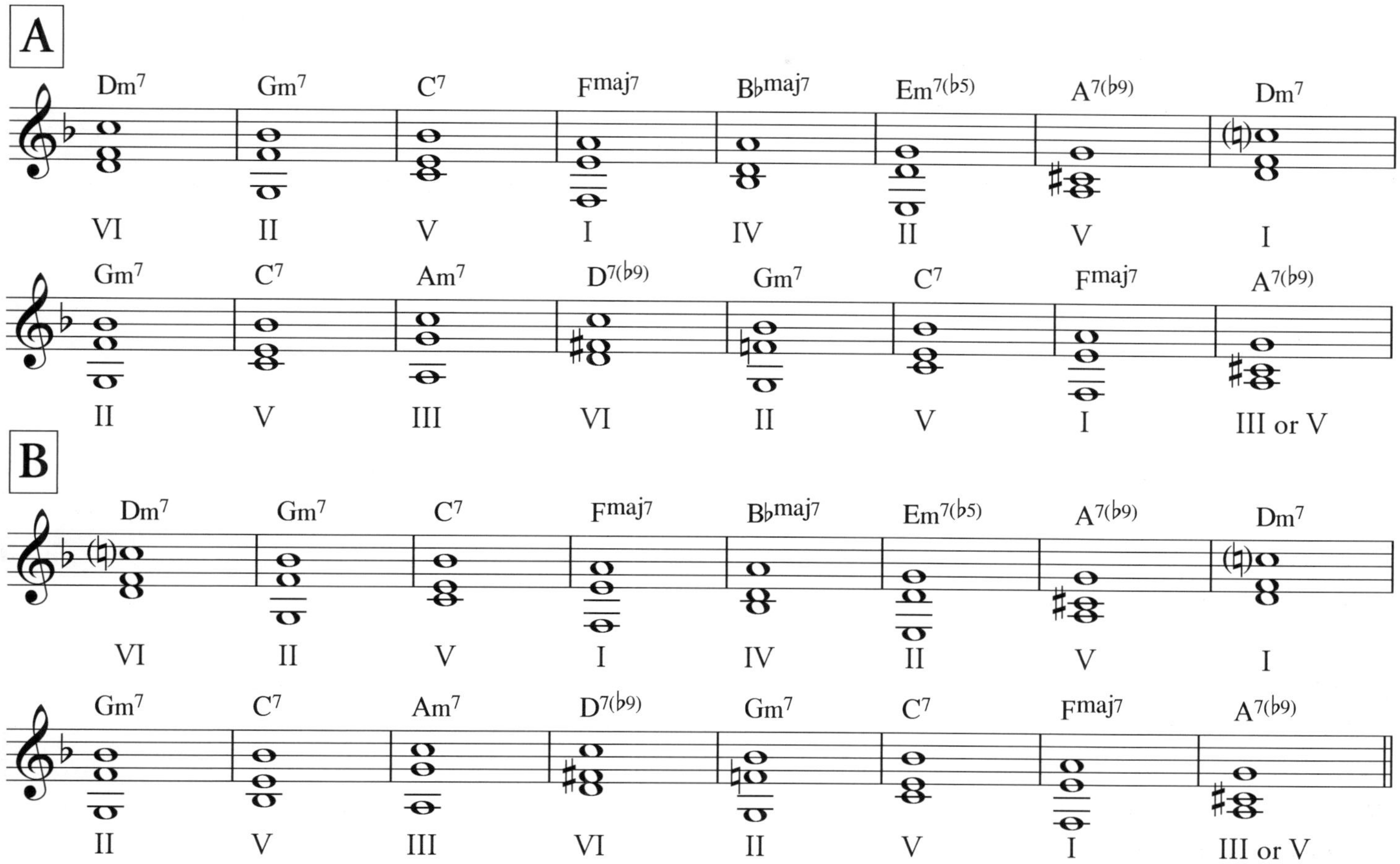

Expanding a Chord Progression

The last few chapters have dealt with recognizing chord progressions and key centres by the types of chords used and their numerical relationship to the key – a chord on the second degree of the key (chord II) has been treated as a minor seventh chord to make it diatonic to the major key. Similarly a seventh chord (e.g. G^7, A^7, D^7 etc.) is nearly always the dominant seventh of the key, or of a locally altered tonal centre, and so is recognized as chord V of that key or locally altered tonal centre. When you get to know these chord types, you start to recognize them as 'markers' within a progression, and this is particularly helpful and important to you as an improviser. Playing through groups of chords and relating them to a key centre is a very effective way to improvise, and allows you to play the harmonic progression of the tune as a whole, rather than as a series of unrelated chords.

The II-V-I progression is the most common way to resolve the 'A' section of music by establishing the key and providing a stable end to a musical phrase. The inevitability of the II-V-I (like the perfect cadence in classical music) is an all-important part of music. The inevitability of it is anticipated by the listener's brain, setting up an expectation that is satisfied by the resolution to the tonic chord and its related scale.

You can use this sense of anticipation in the listener to your advantage when soloing, by teasing the audience with a subtle delay to the final resolution. Just like any happily anticipated event, the experience of it can be enhanced by being made to wait. So an ending can be more satisfying if we are made to wait longer for it. Delaying the cadence builds the anticipation and so makes the cadence all the more rewarding when it does happen. There are various ways to delay the arrival of the tonic chord. Here is the first 'A' section of a tune called 'Undying Love' which we will then alter to delay the resolution.

Fig 9.3a **'A' Section of 'Undying Love'**

33

Ollie Weston

Listen to the recording of this section (mp3 track 33), particularly to the movement of the harmony – the resolution in the harmony part anticipates the resolution in the melody by a bar. This makes the phrase sound awkward because the melody and harmony are not resolving simultaneously. Landing on the tonic (I) chord in bar seven resolves the phrase a bit too early – delaying the arrival of the tonic chord extends the phrase and makes the resolution to the tonic chord all the more satisfying. Because the progression starts with a tonic chord, the resolution can be delayed until bar nine – where the 'A' section will be repeated. One way to achieve this delay is to alter the chord in bar five to a seventh chord:

Fig 9.3b **'A' Section of 'Undying Love' with II^7 Chord**

34

Ollie Weston

The II^7 Chord

Sometimes called a 'secondary dominant' a seventh chord on the second degree of the key is frequently used to 'hold up' the harmony (it is called this because it is the dominant seventh of the dominant seventh – e.g. D^7 is the dominant seventh of G^7 which is the dominant seventh of C). By landing on this chord for two bars the harmonic movement and resolution to chord I is delayed. Listen to mp3 track 34 and the effect the II^7 (D^7) chord has on the resolution of both the melody and the harmony.

Listen for the chords III and VI in bars three and four – these function as chords II and V into the D minor seventh chord whether it is a normal II (minor seventh) or a II^7 (seventh / secondary dominant). The D harmonic minor spells out the progression to this chord.

Here is the whole head of 'Undying Love' – the chord progression is similar to that of 'There Is No Greater Love' by **Marty Symes** and **Isham Jones**.

Fig 9.4 'Undying Love' – Head

10

Ollie Weston

Notice that in the second 'A' section the melody resolves to the root note – C in this tune. This concludes the second 'A' section and creates a static point – a musical full stop. The harmony concludes at this earlier point also, and there is no use of the II⁷ chord in the second 'A' section. This means that both the melody and harmony have resolved at the end of the second 'A' section, finishing with a musical full stop and allowing the 'B' section to take the music to another key (the relative minor in this case). The 'A' section after the bridge is the same as the second 'A' section. This means that the piece concludes on the I chord and like the second 'A' section ends with a clear cadence.

Here is the progression for 'Undying Love' with the guide tones and II-V-Is marked. Play along with CD track 10 which has four choruses. Look out for the III-VI-II-V-I progression as explored in 'Among the Stars'. Notice that the II^7 chord has only one note different to the IIm^7 – the F♯. This note therefore is quite important in spelling out the harmony of the first 'A' section:

Fig 9.5 Guide Tones / II-V-I Progressions for 'Undying Love'

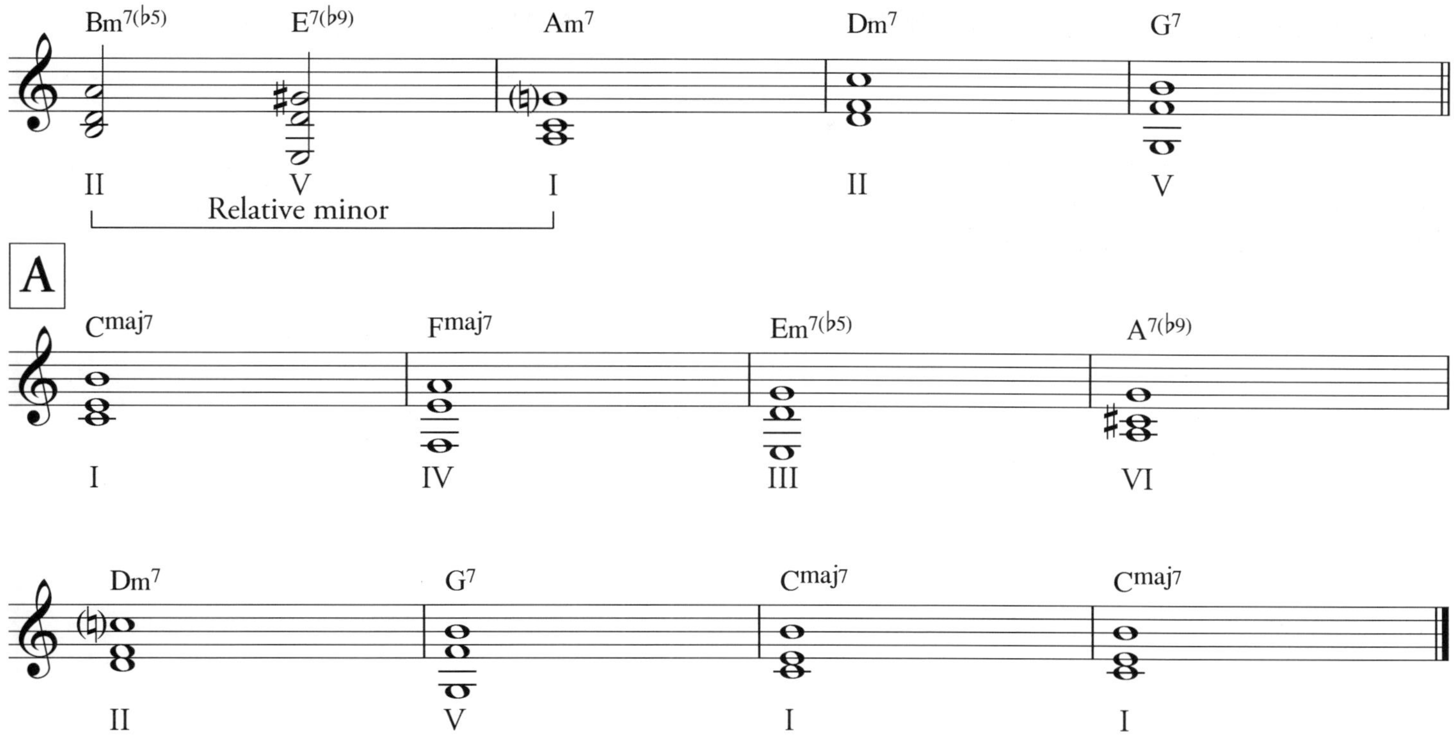

Assignments and Improvisation Tips

A good way to learn a chord progression and test your improvisation skills and speed of thought is to force yourself to improvise with a smaller palette of notes or rhythms. Here is a four-note rhythm repeated in each bar of the progression – the rhythm stays the same, but the notes change to fit the chord progression. The first eight bars are done for you – try to play along with the track (CD track 10) using only this rhythm, the choice of notes is up to you.

Fig 9.6 Rhythmic Exercise

Having this short rhythm to play will force you to be creative with the melodic aspect of what you play – make sure your melodies are spelling out the chords effectively.

When you are comfortable with this rhythm and improvising freely with it, try making some short rhythmic motifs of your own.

Turnarounds

A turnaround is a short progression of chords that can serve to keep the harmony moving at an otherwise static point. Usually a turnaround occurs at the end of an 'A' or 'B' section and either leads the music to a new section or 'turns it around' back to the beginning. Jazz musicians don't like to spend too long on one chord when playing standards as the interest and excitement is often created by the movements between chords. Turnarounds are therefore useful to give the harmony some movement without actually changing the harmonic direction of the piece.

Let's have a look turnarounds with this next tune 'Take the Express Train' inspired by **Duke Ellington**'s 'Take The A Train'. Listen to mp3 track 35.

Fig 9.7a 'Take the Express Train' 'A' Section

35

Ollie Weston

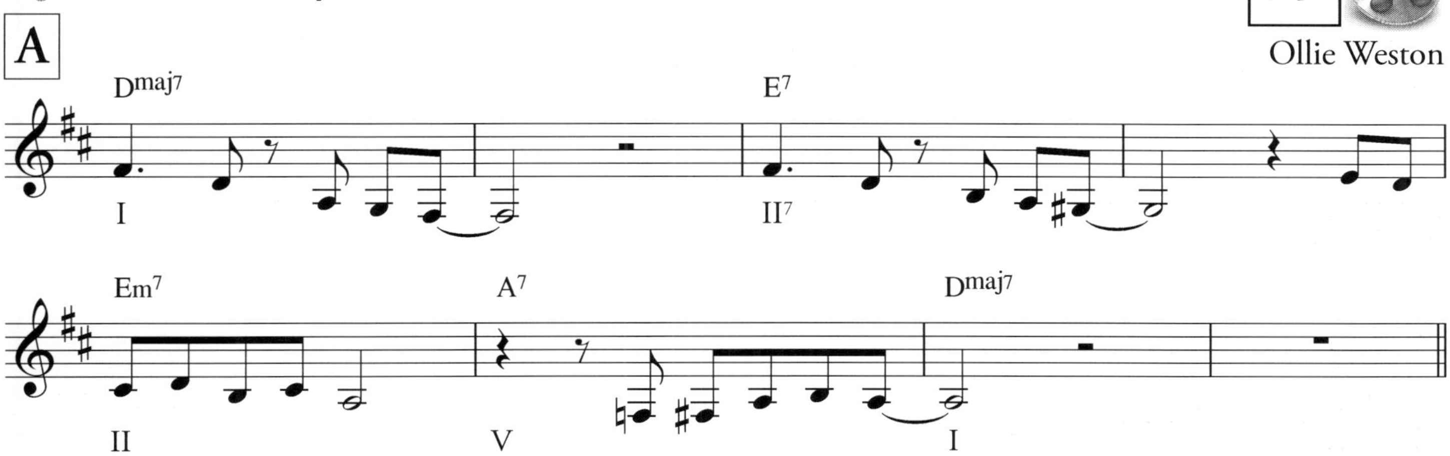

This is the chord progression at its most basic and functional. Using only four chords – D^{maj7} (I), D^7 (II^7 or secondary dominant), Em^7 (II) and A^7 (V) – it is easily possible to play a great sounding solo over this tune. However to add interest to the progression and give the improviser some more options, you can add a turnaround to the last two bars. The most common turnaround uses chords I-VI-II-V. Listen to the second version (mp3 track 36) and pay attention to the turnaround in the last two bars of the 'A' section:

Fig 9.7b 'Take the Express Train' expanded progression

36

Ollie Weston

As explored earlier in this chapter chord VI can be treated as either a minor seventh chord (the diatonic version) or as a seventh chord (acting as the dominant of chord II).

A variation on the I-VI-II-V turnaround is to swap the I chord with a III and create a III-VI-II-V progression as used in 'Among the Stars' earlier in the chapter. This is also a very effective turnaround as it delays the arrival of chord I until the second 'A' section – this makes the resolution all the more satisfying as it has taken longer to be delivered.

Listen to mp3 track 37.

Fig 9.7c III-VI-II-V-I

37

Ollie Weston

Here is the head and the guide tones for 'Take the Express Train':

Fig 9.8a 'Take the Express Train' – Head

11

Fig 9.8b 'Take the Express Train' Guide Tones

The form of this tune is AABA – often the two 'A' sections are written as a repeat. The only differences between the two sections are the first and second time bars so it's more economical to write it this way than two separate eight-bar sections.

Modulation to Chord Four

A modulation to chord IV is one of the most common modulations for the bridge of tunes. Moving from D to G in this case is one step round the cycle of fifths and so sounds logical to the ear. The difference between the key signatures of D major and G major is only one sharp (C♯ becoming C♮). Look at the C♮ in the second time bar – this note turns the chord from D^{maj7} to D^7 (chord V of G) and so creates a perfect cadence in G. Although chord II isn't present this still functions as a cadence. Chord II is usually used to extend the progression so isn't really needed in a one bar cadence.

Modulating to chord IV is a common feature of tunes in all styles, for example, 'Hey Jude' by the Beatles contains an obvious modulation to chord IV at the end of the verse as it goes to the bridge.

Your Solo

The CD track 11 has four choruses of the progression for you to practise with. For a performance you would play the head at the beginning and the end with two choruses of solo in the middle. For practice purposes though, don't feel you need to play the head every time – use all four choruses to try out your improvisation ideas. Figures 9.9a and 9.9b are two licks you can use at the turnaround in the first time bar – the first is a I-VI-II-V, the second a III-VI-II-V progression. The difference between the two is slight so you could use either lick over either turnaround type.

The most important note in this turnaround is the D♯ (the third of the B^7 chord and the leading note of Em). As the only non-diatonic note in the turnaround it's crucial that you include this note to make the turnaround really effective.

Fig 9.9a **Turnaround Lick (I-VI-II-V)**

Fig 9.9b **Turnaround Lick (III-VI-II-V)**

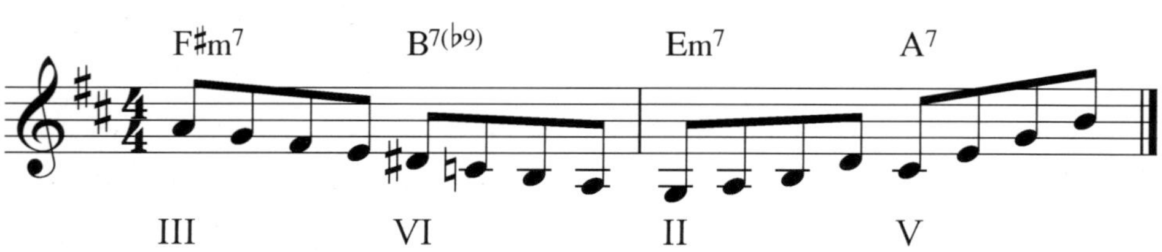

When you practise this tune try to put one of these licks into each first time bar – interrupting your own solo to play a prescribed idea is a good way to familiarize yourself with the progression.

Rhythmic Exercise

Here are two more rhythmic patterns to help you practise this chord progression – each has the pattern written and then a four-bar example over the first four bars. As with the 'Undying Love' idea in Fig 9.6, keep the rhythm the same but tailor the notes to fit the passing changes.

Fig 9.10a **Rhythmic Pattern 1**

Fig 9.10b **Rhythmic Pattern 2**

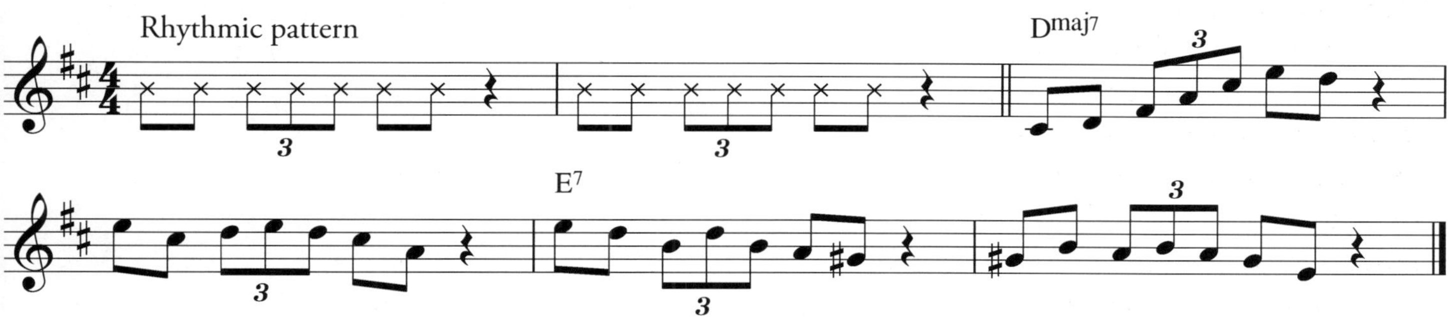

These are harder patterns than the earlier ones but once you have these under your fingers you will have this chord progression nailed. Practise at a slower tempo with the metronome before playing with the backing if it's more comfortable.

Checkpoint

Standards are an important part of jazz repertoire. These great tunes have been played and re-interpreted by everybody who's ever played jazz, and learning the workings of them is an essential part of the process of becoming an accomplished improviser for all jazz musicians. The good news is that the harmonic and structural language of standards is easily transferable between tunes. Major and minor II-V-Is, secondary dominant (II^7) chords and turnarounds appear in hundreds of tunes. Learning to navigate these changes on one tune will mean you have lots of ideas for many other tunes too. Once you can recognize these common features of the 'jazz standard' language you quickly decipher a set of chords and play fluently over them. A modulation to chord IV at the 'B' section isn't unique to 'Take The A Train', neither is the modulation to the relative minor in the 'B' section of 'There Is No Greater Love'. These popular modulations appear throughout the jazz and pop repertoire. For further repertoire refer to the listening lists throughout the book.

10: Bebop

In the early 1940s jazz moved in a new direction. The swing era of the thirties characterised by the good time music of the big bands of **Count Basie** and **Bennie Goodman** gave way to a new sound – 'bebop'. Improvisation had always been a part of the swing era but bebop and its musicians made improvisation the most important aspect of the music rather than the highly structured arrangements and shorter solo sections of the big band music. The world in the 1940s was in conflict and the larger swing bands and orchestras that had been so successful in the 1930s were finding work harder to come by. As a result of this many of the fifteen- to twenty-piece big bands were scaled down to much smaller units – usually a quintet consisting of a trumpet, saxophone, piano (or guitar), bass and drums. This has become the standard quintet format for jazz ever since.

Bebop reworked the tunes and standards of the swing era to produce highly syncopated and harmonically advanced music. The word 'bebop' itself is an onomatopoeic description of the sound used in this style of playing – this becomes most obvious when you hear jazz vocalists performing the 'scat' style of singing – where instead of words, short syllabic sounds are used to articulate the music. Bebop is characterised by blistering tempos and virtuosic improvisation and therefore isn't for the faint-hearted – challenging for both the performer and the audience. Alto saxophonist **Charlie Parker** and trumpeter **Dizzy Gillespie** are credited with developing the bebop sound through their legendary quintet, revolutionizing jazz and paving the way musically for much of what has followed. Many of the tunes they composed are staples of the present day bebop repertoire such as 'Billies Bounce', 'Anthropology', and 'A Night In Tunisia'.

In the same way that early jazz is associated with New Orleans, bebop is synonymous with New York. The legendary clubs of 52nd street including 'The Downbeat' and 'The Three Deuces' hosted the bands of **Charlie Parker**, **Dizzy Gillespie** and other bebop greats, providing the buzzing nocturnal backdrop for this groundbreaking music to thrive.

This chapter will explore some of the developments bebop made to standard type tunes and some of the key characteristics of the style. The standard song forms 'AABA' and the 12-Bar blues etc remained intact but the melodies and the improvisation changed to reflect the new style. Bebop solos take the II-V-I chord progressions to their limit by imposing extra changes and chromatic decoration to the lines. This chapter will explore bebop through two of the most standard song forms – the 12-Bar blues and the chord progression and structure from **Gershwin**'s 'I Got Rhythm'.

52nd St. Blues

Whilst bebop was certainly a radical new sound it had its 'roots' in the jazz styles of the past, **Charlie Parker** and **Dizzy Gillespie** tended to use existing song forms for their tunes and re-write the head in this new bebop style. '52nd St. Blues' is a good example of this approach, it has a standard 12-Bar blues progression using only the chords I, IV, and V, as explored in chapter four. Listen to mp3 track 38 and follow through the head in the figure below.

38

Fig 10.1 **'52nd St. Blues' Head with I, IV, V Changes**

Now play the head yourself along with mp3 track 38 and try to feel the differences between this and a traditional blues head.

The three line structure of a blues tune is still used for '52nd St. Blues' – notice that the first two lines are a repeating statement of the theme with the third line acting as a conclusion. The melody is far more intricate both rhythmically and melodically than a simple blues or swing tune. The quirky three-note 'hook' in bars three, seven and eleven is a common bebop trait – the repetition of this simple phrase provides a reference point and makes the intricate tune more memorable.

Chromaticism

Using more and more chromatic notes was a feature of bebop. Musicians sought to extend the melodic options open to them by using chromatic notes which are non-diatonic notes that decorate phrases rather than using chord tones. Using these chromatic notes instantly makes bebop look more complicated as the page becomes littered with accidentals.

The first four bars of '52nd St. Blues' contains several examples of chromatic decoration: the C♯ in the pick up isn't diatonic to the tonic key of G major but adds colour to the phrase. Using the flattened fifth (shown enharmonically as C♯ in this case for ease of notation) can be seen as a reference to the blues as it is one of the 'blue' notes this is a common trick in bebop. Here is the pick-up again but this time without the C♯:

Fig 10.2a **Non-chromatic Pick-up**

Fig 10.2b **Chromatic Pick-up**

Play each of the above examples in turn a few times to hear the stronger statement of the chromatic pick-up.

The non-chromatic pick-up works perfectly well but sounds more like a standard or simple blues tune. Adding the C♯, which stands out more and sounds dissonant, gives the music a distinctive edge that the 'beboppers' were looking for.

Another popular chromatic decoration is to prepare the major third with the minor third – another possible derivative of the blues. The B♭ followed by B♮ in bar one of '52nd St. Blues' is a good example – imposing the 'dissonant' minor third quickly followed by the 'chord tone' of the major third adds another chromatic passing note and therefore makes the line more intricate. Without the flattened (minor) third the line would look like this:

Fig 10.3a **Without Flattened Third Passing Note**

Fig 10.3b **With Flattened Third Passing Note**

The flattened third passing note is also used over chord IV in this head. This is demonstrated by the F♮ at the end of bars one, five and six over the C^7 chord – the F♮ then resolves to the F♯ (the major third).

Without any chromatic decoration the first four bars of '52nd St. Blues' would look like this:

Fig 10.4 **'52nd St. Blues' Without Chromatic Decoration**

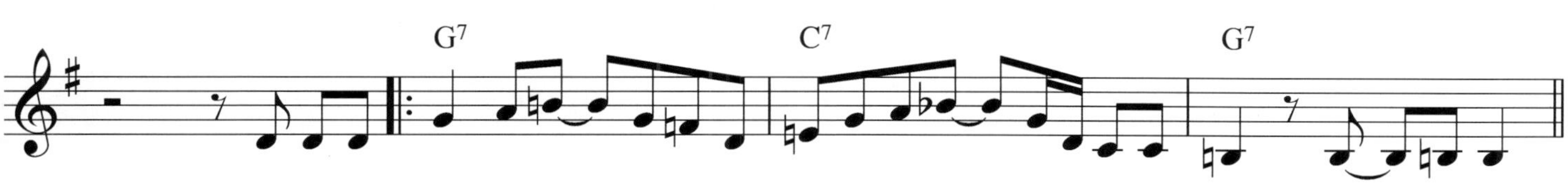

The head functions well like this but the chromatic notes, typical of the bebop style, decorate the tune and make it sound more quirky.

Articulation

The articulation and feel is all important in bebop. For the music to have the rhythmic drive and bounce, so much a part of the style, the phrasing must be correct. The crotchets should be short and accented with a definite gap before the next note. These are all marked in this head but in other compositions it may be assumed that the player is aware of this. Think of one of the scat syllables to help with the length and articulation of the crotchets – aim for a short 'da' sound rather than a legato 'laa.'

Quavers should be tongued softly to give them definition but not so short as to sound jerky. Try not to make the second quaver of each pair too short – if you start to feel as though you are using staccato tonguing, this is too short!

The Chord Progression

As well as melodic invention bebop musicians started to add extra chords and turnarounds to the long established progressions being used. The last few chapters of this book have explored the harmonic devices commonly used by jazz musicians to unify chord progressions. II-V-I, III-VI-II-V-I, and turnarounds are the building blocks of bebop tunes just in the same way they are for standards. The usual bebop blues has three main differences to its I, IV, V predecessor:

Modulation to Chord IV

At bar five the conventional blues changes chord from I to IV. This is one of the fundamental aspects of the 12-Bar blues and without it the progression would lose its identity. Chord IV could be thought of as a 'mini-modulation' and you can prepare bar five with the chords II and V of this new chord.

Fig 10.5 II-V-I to C^7

39

Because the root chord of the tune is a 7th chord adding chords II and V in bar four is a subtle addition but changes the way you can play over the progression as a cadence point has been created.

The Last Four Bars

The blues progressions we have previously looked at always used chords V and IV to bring the music back to chord I at the end. To make the chords sound more like a jazz progression a bebop blues uses the less bluesy II-V-I in the last four bars. This gives it a solid cadence at the end and makes it more in keeping with the standard-type progressions outlined in chapter nine.

To add another point of interest the progression has chords III and VI in bar eight. These create another cadence (a minor II-V-I) to A minor in bar nine. The last five bars of the progression (relative to the tonic chord) is:

III-VI^7-II-V-I

Turnarounds

A traditional blues would sometimes have a dominant seventh chord (D^7) in bar twelve to lead back to the start of the progression. A bebop blues adds a turnaround to the last two bars – the I-VI-II-V keeps the chords moving as well as preparing for the top of the next chorus with a cadence.

The Bebop Scale

Another chromatic decoration is the D♭ in bar ten, this is in addition to the usual blues scale derived notes. This passing note between the root (D) and flattened seventh of the D^7 (C) chord creates a useful 'bebop scale' – this is effectively a Mixolydian scale with an extra passing note between the flattened seventh and the root.

The bebop scale serves two main purposes – firstly the added chromatic note is in keeping with the style and gives the line a bebop 'flavour', secondly it allows the chord tones to fall on strong beats of the bar. Here is the descending line from bar ten without the D♭:

Fig 10.6 Descending Mixolydian Scale

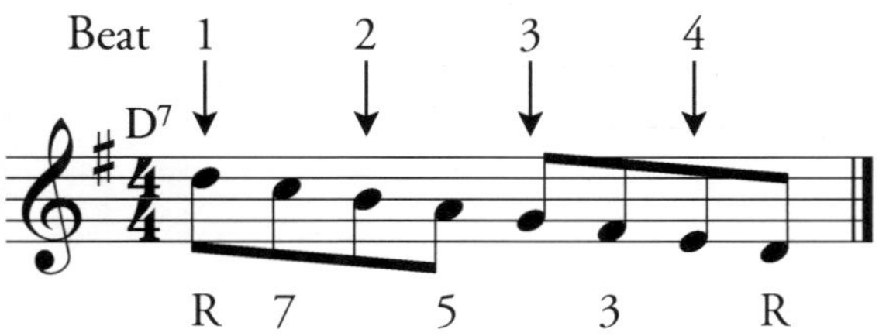

Notice that the chord tones of the D^7 chord fall on the 'off-beats' in this example. To make the harmony really clear, bebop players wanted to have the chord tones on the stronger 'on-beats' of the bar. This would make the fast-moving harmony easier to hear and the scalic lines would fit better over the chords. The major scale and its modes only contain seven different notes – to make it fit as quavers in a bar of 4/4 eight notes would be better. The logical way to do this was to add an extra note – the passing note between the root and the flat seven achieves this and moves the chord tones onto the on-beats of the descending scale.

The ascending Mixolydian scale already has root, third, fifth and seventh on the stronger on-beats and so the additional passing note needs to move the last root to the on-beat. Here is the same line but with the passing note added:

Fig 10.7 D⁷ Bebop Scale

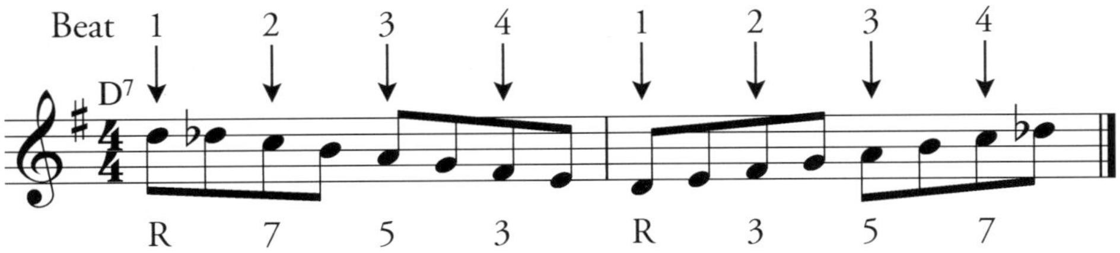

Now all the chord tones fall on the strong on-beats. This makes the scale sound neater and spells out the D^7 chord more clearly.

Assignment

Revisit the seventh chord workout in chapter four and play the bebop scale over all the seventh chords. The chromatic passing note between the flattened seventh and the root will make these into bebop scales – useful for soloing.

This chapter has examined some of the most common variations to the 12-Bar blues progression. These touches take away some of its 'bluesiness' and make it more like that of a jazz-standard chord progression. However the continued use of the 7th chord for the root chords instead of the major sevenths means that the progression still has an essential air of the blues about it. Play the head along with mp3 track 40 and listen for the effect that the extra chord changes have on it.

Fig 10.8 '52nd St. Blues' Sample Solo

40 12

Ollie Weston

1st chorus

2nd chorus

3rd chorus

4th chorus
G7 C7 G7 Dm7 G7
C7 C7 G7 Bm7 E7(♭9)
Am7 D7 G7 E7(♭9) Am7 D7
Last Head
G7 C7 G7 Dm7 G7
C7 C7 G7 Bm7 E7(♭9)
Am7 D7 G7
1.
2.

The Solo

This is a bebop style solo that exhibits some of the trademarks of the style discussed in this chapter. Listen to the solo on mp3 track 40 and try to identify the features discussed in this chapter.

Chorus One

The very opening of this solo is similar to that of the head. The chromatic minor to major third (B♭ to B♮) happens in both instances. The solo carries on the ascending chromatic line up to the D (the fifth) in bar two of the solo. The use of this chromatic line from the minor third to the fifth appears in many bebop solos where the minor third and flattened fifth are used as passing notes. There is also chromatic decoration in the third line of this chorus – the F♮ to F♯ in bars nine and ten is another use of the minor/major third shift.

The D♭ in bar ten is the 'added' chromatic passing note from the bebop scale, it makes sure that the C lands on the on-beat!

Notice the use of the B♮ and B♭ over the G^7 and C^7 chords respectively. Chapter four introduced the importance of the trade-off between the major and minor third, one that is an important part of the blues sound and maintains its relevance in bebop.

Chorus Two

The first two lines of this chorus further explores the blues aspect of bebop – the opening bar is repeated in the second bar but swapping the B♮ for B♭ which fits the C^7 chord better. This is a further use of the contrasting major and minor thirds. Notice the anticipated quaver at the end of the first bar – this really pushes into the second bar and helps the phrase to swing.

The chords III and VI chords are spelt out in bar eight. The F♯ and G♯ wouldn't be used in a traditional blues but the cadence using chords III and VI to A minor sets up the final resolution to G major. These fast moving chord progressions are typical of bebop and standards.

Chorus Three

The first two bars of this chorus introduce the dissonance of the flattened fifth (notated enharmonically as C♯ here). This jarring note can add excitement to solos when contrasted with the static fifth. Use the off-beat quavers to add rhythmic excitement to these bars too.

The G bebop scale is used in bar four – the G♭ acting as a passing note between root and seventh. The E♭ is another bluesy minor/major third example – this one over the chord of C^7. The result is a cool chromatic line making a II-V-I progression to C.

Bars seven and eight are about as far away from the blues as this solo gets. The use of the F♯ in bar seven implies a G major seventh chord rather than the G^7 written. This gives the solo a different direction at this point and a much brighter sound more akin to the jazz-standard II-V-I language rather than the seventh chords of the blues.

Chorus Four

The last chorus of this solo is more rhythm based and aims for a driving finale to the solo. The opening phrase is developed in bar five as an answering phrase much like that of the traditional blues tunes. Notice the difference in the rhythm between these two bars – the crotchet rest in bar one is adapted to a quaver rest in bar five. The shorter rest in bar five drives the music forward.

Playing the Solo

Now play the solo yourself. Technically it's more challenging than anything so far in this book. Take your time over the chromatic lines as they can be quite fiddly, get them right slowly first and then increase the tempo. Use both the demonstration track (mp3 track 40) and the track without clarinet (CD track 12) to play this solo. Playing along with the clarinet on the CD will help you to play with the correct feel and will also help with any difficult rhythms.

Remember – don't make the quavers too short, bebop should sound smooth and effortless not awkward and jerky!

Bebop Soloing

You can now use the backing track (CD track 12) for your own solos. Try to incorporate some of the new ideas covered in this chapter. Use of the chromatic notes in the bebop scale and the flattened thirds and fifths will give your solos an authentic bebop sound.

Try to add the harmonic developments too – using the III-VI-II-V-I progressions within the progression will give you many more harmonic options and enable you to incorporate the harmonic language explored in chapters eight and nine.

Don't feel that you have to play every single change in every chorus you play – the melodic and harmonic developments were incorporated as additions to the chord progression. As the sample solo demonstrates, the fundamental aspects of the blues are still in place.

Quoting from the Written Solo

To help you learn the complicated language of bebop, don't be afraid to use sections of the written solo. Take a phrase you like and try to incorporate it into your solo – be sure to play it in the right place though as a good lick over the wrong chords doesn't sound so good!

Checkpoint

Bebop's importance to modern jazz cannot be underestimated. The excitement created by the fluency and sheer virtuosity of **Charlie Parker**, **Dizzy Gillespie** and the other bebop legends inspired younger musicians and paved the way for future generations of jazz players. The melodic and harmonic innovations explored in this chapter have their role in bebop as well as the significant jazz styles that followed.

By learning the techniques we've explored in this chapter as well as immersing yourself in the style of bebop you will be developing some of the essential style of a jazz improviser.

11: Style Workout

The final chapter of this book brings together everything you've learned so far. From beginning to improvise with just the blues scale we went on to linking sets of chords together in increasingly complex ways. To achieve this we introduced the main chord types, the modes of the major scale, cadences and the most commonly used chord progressions. Hopefully you are now soloing freely and are beginning to feel the foundations of your own jazz style taking shape.

This chapter has four tunes with different styles that you may encounter in gig situations. As always each tune has a sample solo and analysis of the solo and chord progression to help get you started.

This is a bebop-style tune similar to '52nd Street Blues' from chapter ten. 'Flying With the Bird' is a tribute to **Charlie Parker** and is based on the chord progression of **Gershwin**'s 'I Got Rhythm'.

Fig 11 'Flying with the Bird'

41 13

Ollie Weston

C7
F7
Cmaj7
A
1st chorus
C
A7(b9)
Dm7
G7
C
A7(b9)
Dm7
G7
Eg. 8
C7
F7
3
Em7
A7(b9)
Dm7
G7
Eg. 9
Eg. 12
A
C
A7(b9)
Dm7
G7
C
A7(b9)
Dm7
G7
Eg. 1
C7
F7
Cmaj7
Eg. 13
B
E7
A7
3
Eg. 5
D7
G7
3
3
Eg.6
A
C
A7(b9)
Dm7
G7
C
A7(b9)
Dm7
3
G7
Eg. 10
Eg.2
C7
F7
Cmaj7

A
2nd chorus
C A7(♭9) Dm7 G7 C A7(♭9) Dm7 G7
Eg. 15
Eg. 14
C7 F7 Em7 A7(♭9) Dm7 G7
Eg. 16
Eg. 3
A
C A7(♭9) Dm7 G7 C A7(♭9) Dm7 G7
Eg. 4
C7 3 F7 Cmaj7
B
E7 A7
D7 G7
Eg. 7
A
C A7(♭9) Dm7 G7 C A7(♭9) Dm7 G7
Eg. 15
Eg. 11
C7 F7 Cmaj7

A
Final head
Cmaj7 A7(♭9) Dm7 G7 Cmaj7 A7(♭9) Dm7 G7
C7 F7
1.
Em7 A7(♭9) Dm7 G7
2.
Cmaj7
B
E7 A7
D7 G7
A
Cmaj7 A7(♭9) Dm7 G7 Cmaj7 A7(♭9) Dm7 G7
C7 F7 Cmaj7

Rhythm Changes

One of the most popular chord progressions in swing and bebop music is that based on the chord changes of 'I Got Rhythm'. The original tune was written by **George Gershwin** in 1930 for the musical 'Girl Crazy' and quickly became a hit. The jazz musicians of the day seized upon 'I Got Rhythm' and it has become a favourite standard for generations of jazz musicians.

The chord progression and 'AABA' structure of 'I Got Rhythm' have become known simply as the '**rhythm changes**' and are the basis for hundreds of jazz tunes including 'Lester Leaps In', 'Oleo' and 'Anthropology' – the theme of the cartoon 'The Flintstones' is also based on the rhythm changes.

The Head

Like many bebop heads 'Flying with the Bird' is based on a short, punchy phrase – remember that the crotchets are played shorter in bebop, think 'Da' rather than 'Laa' for the crotchets in this head. The opening two bars contain the main theme and feature some of the chromatic touches typical of the bebop style – the F♯ (the flattened fifth) adds a bright dissonance to the head, while the E♭ to E♮ is a bluesy decoration. The second four bars are similar to the first four, acting as an answering phrase.

The second-time-bar ends on the root note (C) and chord I (C major seventh), giving the phrase a strong resolution. The snappy melody at this point also works well as a really tight ending to the tune with the whole band playing it in unison.

The harmony of the 'A' section is diatonic to the key of C. The I-VI-II-V is a turnaround in the key of C – chord VI can be treated as either a diatonic minor seventh chord (entirely fitting the key) or as a seventh chord (creating a cadence to chord II).

The first-time-bar contains a turnaround in a more familiar place – leading the music back to the second 'A' section.

Bar five creates a modulation to chord IV by turning chord I into a seventh chord. Note that chord IV in the rhythm changes is usually played as a seventh rather than a major seventh – look out for the E flats in the solo!

The bridge ('B' section) uses the **cycle of fifths** as its chord progression producing a cyclic set of resolving seventh chords – E^7 resolves to A^7, to D^7, to G^7 before the C^{maj7} chord of the last 'A' section breaks the cycle. The melody mirrors the cyclic nature of the chords with a similar phrase tailored to fit the chords.

'Rhythm changes' tunes are usually played at a fast tempo – creating the lively exciting sound associated with swing and bebop. The rhythm and feel are all important, listen to the demonstration track (mp3 track 41) for a guide.

The Solo

The sample solo of 'Flying With the Bird' is a typical bebop solo. The two choruses contain many examples of the jazz improvisation techniques covered in this book – here are some things to look out for:

Bebop Language

Like all musical styles, bebop has its own characteristics. Learning the features of the style will allow you to become conversant and fluent in the language. The 'rhythm changes' make use of progressions such as II-V-I as well as III-VI-II-V, V-I, I-VI-II-V etc. This partly explains the popularity of the 'rhythm changes' as one improvisational idea can be reused on each of these similar progressions throughout.

Bars three and four of the second 'A' section of the sample solo (marked as **Example 1**) contain a good example of a bebop line. The quavers (eighth notes) spell out the I-VI^7-II-V – giving particular emphasis to the chord tones. **Examples 2**, **3** and **4** also spell out a similar progression. These three phrases could be learned as 'licks' that would work on any I-VI-II-V or III-VI-II-V progression.

The Bebop Scale

Introduced in chapter ten, the bebop scale adds a chromatic passing note to the Mixolydian mode to make an even eight-note scale that effectively spells out the seventh chord. Look at **Examples 5**, **6** and **7** for uses of the bebop scale.

Syncopation

The rhythmic interest created by off-beat quavers (eighth notes) is a big factor in the bebop sound as it gives the music a rhythmic drive that is so important to its effectiveness. Always play off-beats with an accent as they will then have more rhythmic impact. Look at **Examples 8**, **9**, **10**, and **11**, these off-beat quavers (eighth notes) are marked as accented – this won't always be the case in other tunes you may come across so try to accent off-beats instinctively.

The Blues

Using the 'blue' notes has been an important recurring theme throughout this book. Flattened thirds and fifths, when used well, always add authenticity and an element of 'cool' to your solos. Bebop often contrasts these 'blue' notes with their un–flattened versions to create chromatic passing notes. **Examples 12**, **13**, **14** and **15** highlight some uses of 'blue' notes in this solo.

Phrasing

Often at fast tempos, the temptation is to overplay – the adrenaline kicks in and all your ideas may come out at once. The opening of this solo has short conversational phrases punctuated by gaps, this allows both the musicians and the audience to follow the unfolding of the solo and let the phrases have time to register. Answering phrases are an effective way to build a solo – the second chorus begins with a phrase that is then repeated and developed at bar five shown in **Examples 15** and **16**.

Your Solo

The sample solo has introduced you to the rhythm changes progression. Now use the backing track (CD track 13) to play your own version of 'Flying with the Bird'. The form is: head, two choruses of solo and a final head.

This solo should capture the excitement of bebop in full flight. A great rhythm changes solo can be the highlight of a jazz set as a player 'burns' through the tune. Try to emulate the greats of bebop when you play both the written solo and your own solo.

Latin Music

The term 'Latin' is generally used when referring to music with a South American influence. South America has a rich and varied heritage and accordingly a huge variety of musical styles – Tango, Rhumba, Salsa and Samba all developed in this region. Much like the African music that influenced the early jazz musicians, Latin music is extremely rhythmically diverse, and it was these rhythmic features that started to interest jazz musicians. Big band composers in the 1940s started to experiment with Latin music – **Stan Kenton**'s 1946 recording of 'Machito' is an early example that combines the rhythmic excitement and fire of Latin music with the jazz sound of the big band.

Bossa Nova

One of the most successful fusions of jazz and South-American music is the '**Bossa Nova**' style. It was developed in the late 1950s and largely centred around the songs of **Antonio Carlos Jobim**. Tunes such as 'Desafinado', 'Chega de Suadade' and most famously 'The Girl From Ipanema' (featuring **Stan Getz** on tenor sax and **Astrud Gilberto** on vocals) brought a new Latin sound to jazz audiences.

Musical style

Bossa Nova fused elements of Brazilian samba music with the sophisticated harmony and song forms of jazz. The result was a relaxed style of music but with a distinct rhythmic identity. The rich string, and sometimes orchestral, arrangements of Bossa Nova have contributed to its image as 'lounge music' and while there have been some 'cheesy' interpretations of Bossa Nova over the years it remains a beautiful example of jazz and Latin music combining.

The main difference between Bossa Nova and jazz is the lack of swing – Latin music rarely has swung quavers (eighth notes). A typical Bossa Nova rhythm would have the emphasis on beats one and three as opposed to beats two and four. The rhythm of the drums in this style would feature a 'Clave' – a South-American rhythmic backbeat. Fig.11.1 shows a **two-three clave** (a group of two beats followed by a group of three) and a **three-two clave** (the mirror image – three beats followed by two).

Clap these rhythms and feel the steady backbeat they create.

Fig 11.1 **2:3 and 3:2 Clave**

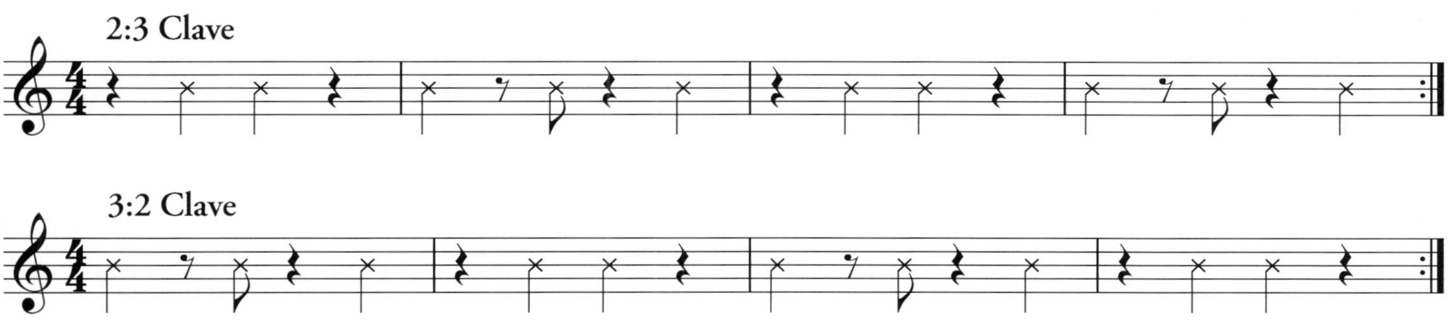

The Bass

Because a Bossa Nova isn't swung, the bass doesn't walk. Beats one and three are emphasized and are often anticipated by a quaver (eighth note) – a typical Bossa Nova bass rhythm might look like this:

Fig 11.2 **Bossa Nova Bass Line**

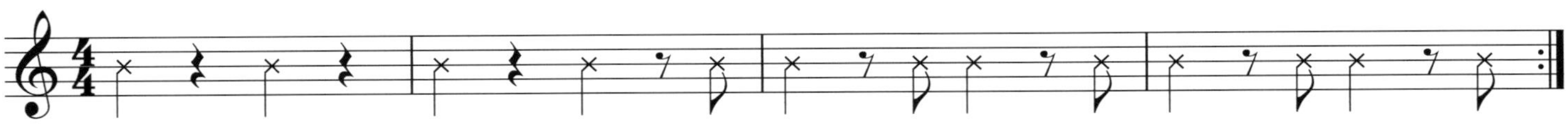

Try to clap the clave rhythm whilst at the same time tapping the bass line with your foot – not as easy as it looks!

This is a Bossa Nova tune loosely based on the often performed 'Blue Bossa' by **Kenny Dorham**. It fuses a standard jazz chord progression with the light samba-based rhythm of Brazil. Listen to the demonstration track (mp3 track 42) and notice the different mood created by the Bossa Nova as opposed to the swing feel. The eight bar introduction demonstrates both the clave rhythm on the drums and the bass pattern outlined above.

Fig 11.2a **'Super Nova'**

42 14

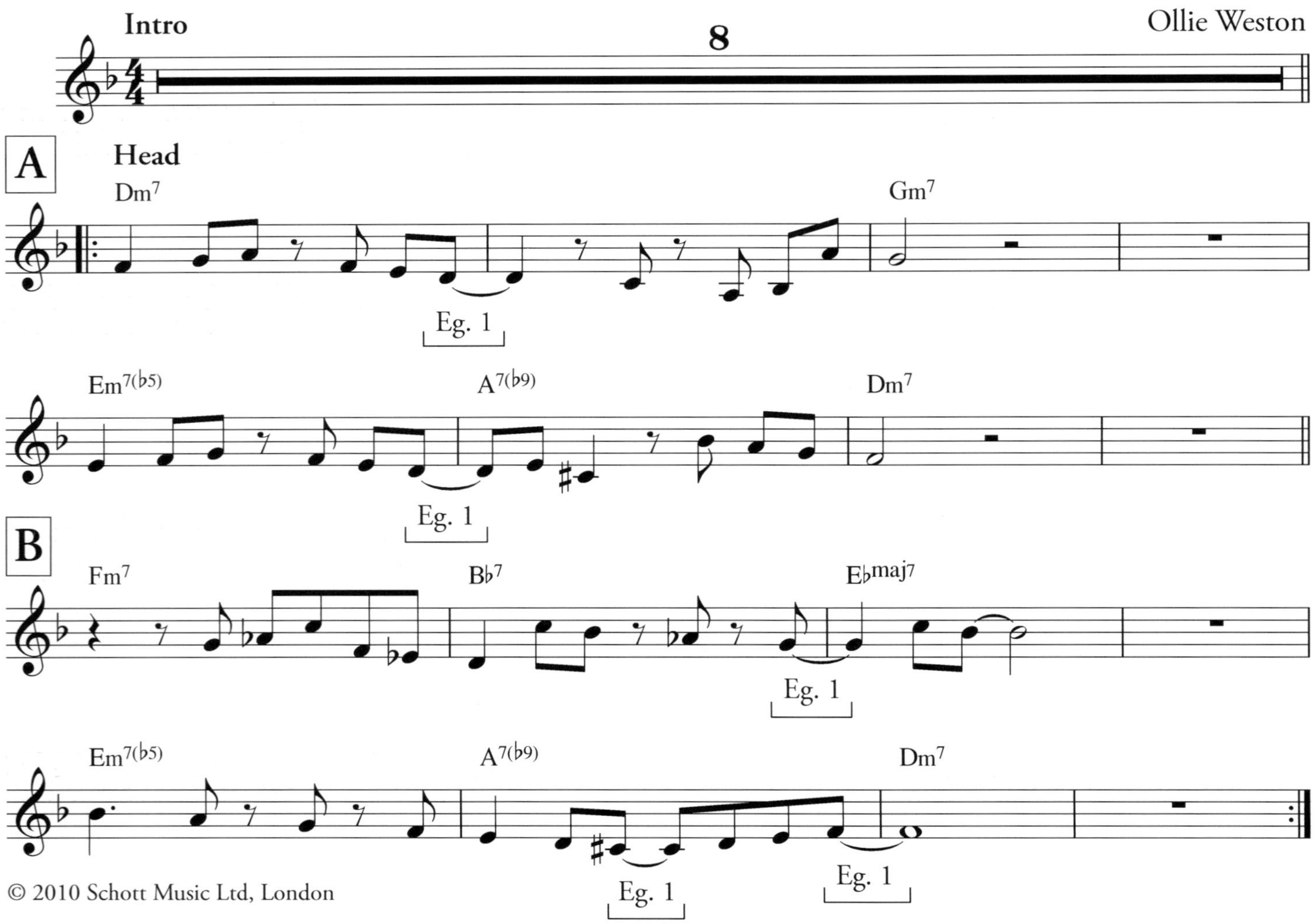

A
1st Chorus
Dm7
Gm7
Em7(b5)
A7(b9)
Dm7
Eg. 2
Eg. 4
B
Fm7
Bb7
Ebmaj7
Em7(b5)
A7(b9)
Dm7
Eg. 4
Eg. 2
A
2nd Chorus
Dm7
Gm7
Em7(b5)
A7(b9)
Dm7
3
Eg. 2
B
Fm7
Bb7
Ebmaj7
Eg. 3
Em7(b5)
A7(b9)
Dm7

A
3rd Chorus
Dm7
Gm7
Eg. 5
Eg. 5
Em7(♭5)
3
A7(♭9)
Dm7
Eg. 2
B
Fm7
B♭7
E♭maj7
Eg. 3
Em7(♭5)
A7(♭9)
Dm7
Eg. 2
A
4th Chorus
Dm7
Gm7
3
Em7(♭5)
A7(♭9)
Dm7
Eg. 2
Eg. 5
B
Fm7
B♭7
E♭maj7
Eg. 3
Em7(♭5)
A7(♭9)
Dm7
Eg. 2
Eg. 4
A
Head
Dm7
Gm7

The Head

This is a simple sixteen bar head split into two sections – 'A' and 'B'. The 'A' section is in the key of D minor, the 'B' section changes key to E♭ major – the Fm^7 and B♭^{7} chords setting up the cadence.

Straight Quavers (eighth notes)

Latin music isn't swung – the quavers (eighth notes) are played straight. Bossa Nova tunes are generally played in a more legato style than swing or bebop. Try to capture the elegant relaxed mood of the tune by playing long, even quavers (eighth notes).

Anticipated Rhythms

A feature of the Bossa Nova style is the use of anticipated or 'pushed' notes. The head of 'Super Nova' contains many anticipated quavers (eighth notes) (all marked as example 1). 'Pushing' a note usually means that it happens half a beat before the chord changes and is a common form of syncopation in Latin music. Here is the first eight bars of 'Super Nova' but this time without the pushed notes:

Fig 11.3 'A' Section Without Pushes

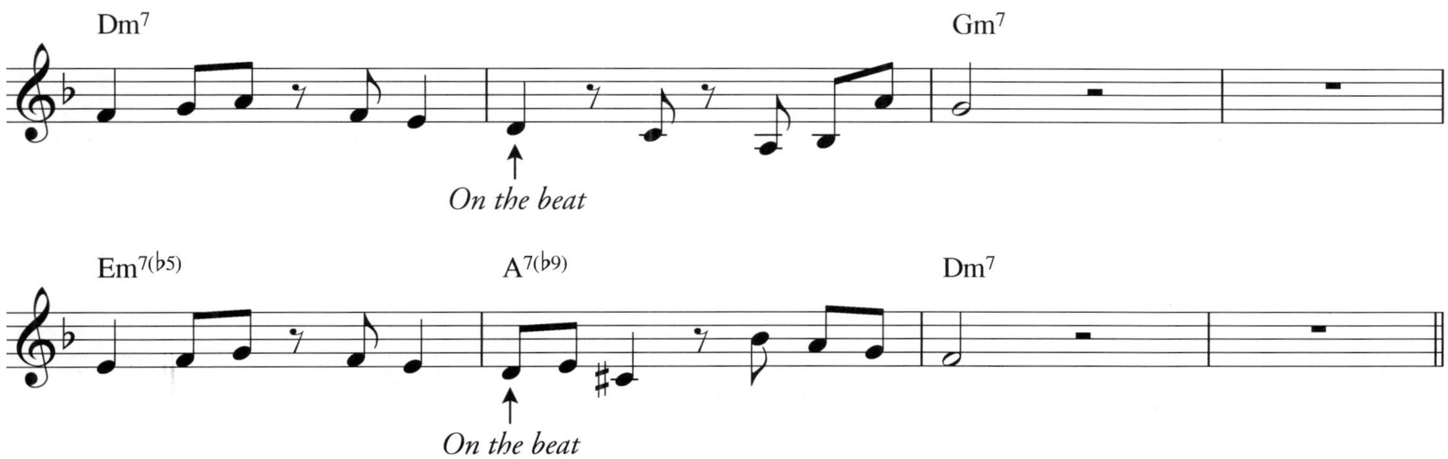

Play this version through and notice that the crotchets on the first beat of the second and fifth bar sound a little clumsy. Now anticipate those notes and listen to the difference.

Fig 11.4 'A' Section With Pushes

The Solo

The main differences between swung jazz and Latin jazz are rhythmic. The harmonic and melodic language of jazz remains the same but with the percussive influences of South America added.

The Chord Progression

It is possible to think of the whole 'A' section as being derived from F major (the relative major of D minor), with each chord relating to a mode:

Fig 11.5 Modes of F Major / D Minor

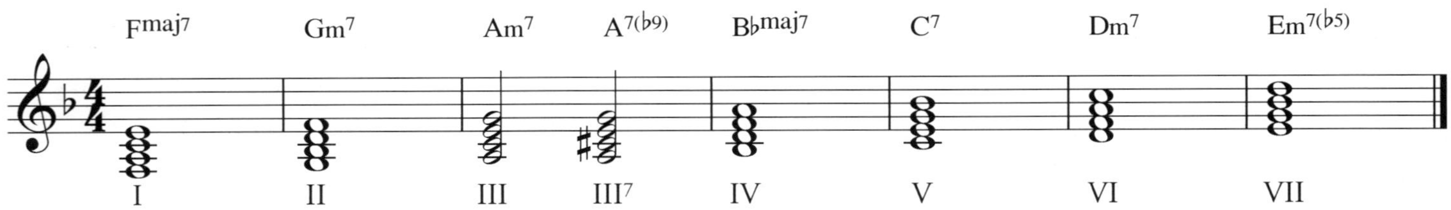

As D minor is the relative minor of F major, the two keys share a key signature and also a set of diatonic chords. The only extra note is the leading note (C♯) from D minor which turns the A minor chord to an A^7 and so creates a cadence to D minor (see the minor II-V-I – chapter eight). Here are the same chords but this time related to D minor.

Fig 11.6 Diatonic Chords of D Minor

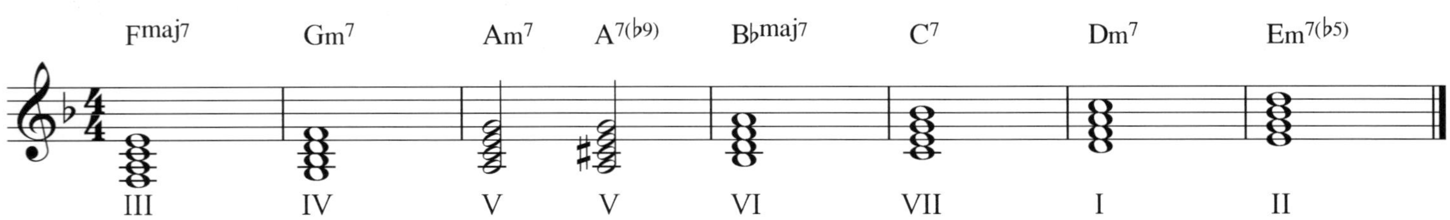

Referring chords back to the parent scale in this way frees you up to play diatonically over the progression and so with greater freedom.

Minor II-V-I

The minor II-V-I cadence is very important to this tune as it establishes the key and creates the tension and resolution of the minor cadence. The last four bars of each 'A' section contain a cadence of II-V-I in D minor. The leading note C♯ is also the third of the A^7 chord which is the chord that pulls the music back to chord I. The sections marked **Eg. 2** are strong sounding minor II-V-I ideas.

Major II-V-I

The 'B' section of 'Super Nova' changes key to E♭ major. Chords Fm^7, $B\flat^7$ and $E\flat^{maj7}$ are not diatonic to D minor and therefore suggest a change of key. The 'B' sections of the solo have a large amount of II-V-I jazz language that could be used as licks for your own solo. The sections marked **Eg. 3** are strong II-V-I lines.

Non-diatonic Notes

There are two types of notes used for decoration in this solo. The first type add colour and mood to static chords – the root chords. Once a II-V-I progression has occurred, the harmony is temporarily static and resolved – chord I can then be decorated. The A flats used on the D minor chord are the flattened fifth, a bluesy decoration of the chord as marked with **Eg. 4**.

The other decorations used in this solo are the leading notes of minor chords which give a solo more harmonic interest. Chapter eight explained how to imply a cadence to any minor chord by simply adding its leading note. In this way the Dm^7, Gm^7 and Fm^7 chords of this tune can be prepared and decorated by their leading notes. **Eg. 5** shows the use of the F♯ as the leading note of G minor and E♮ as the leading note of F minor.

Your Solo

Having learned the sample solo you should be comfortable with both the feel of Bossa Nova and the chord progression to 'Super Nova'. Use the backing track (CD track 14) to play your own version of the tune. The form this time is: head, four choruses of solo and a final head. The coda is played the last time and is a repeat of the last four bars. Try to capture the mood of Bossa Nova through a cool, relaxed solo.

Ballads

Ballads are songs that often concentrate on the emotional and sentimental aspects of life, frequently about love and loss, and these poignant songs form an important part of the jazz standard repertoire. A ballad is usually played at a slow tempo at a quiet volume, and therefore provides a contrast to other jazz styles which may make up a set. Playing a ballad well is an essential part of any jazz musician's craft, as these melancholic songs showcase the sensitive side of playing and allow you to communicate on a deeply human, as well as musical, level.

This is a minor ballad standard-type of tune inspired by 'You Don't Know What Love Is' by **Don Raye** and **Gene De Paul**. The familiar 'AABA' structure gives the tune clearly defined sections. The G minor based 'A' sections are moody and sad whilst the 'B' section offers a glimmer of happiness as it modulates first to the relative major (B♭) and then to another major key (D).

These major modulations brighten the mood temporarily before the last 'A' section returns to the minor key.

Due to the extensive amount of recorded material available throughout this book, it has been necessary to make this particularly lengthy backing track (44) as an mp3 rather than a CD track.

Fig 11.7 **'Sleepless Eyes'**

43 44

Ollie Weston

A
Gm7 E♭7 D7 Gm7 D7 E♭7
Am7(♭5) D7 Gm7 C7 Am7(♭5) D7
A
Gm7 E♭7 D7 Gm7 D7 E♭7
Eg. 1
Am7(♭5) D7 Gm7 C7 Am7(♭5) D7 Gm7
B
Cm7 F7 B♭maj7 Cm7 F7 B♭maj7
Em7 A7 Dmaj7 E♭7 D7
A
Gm7 E♭7 D7 Gm7 D7 E♭7
Eg. 1
Am7(♭5) D7 Gm7 C7 Am7(♭5) D7 Gm7

Listen to the tune and the sample solo (mp3 track 43) and then play them yourself. There is nothing technically or harmonically challenging in this tune – ballads are more of an exercise in taste and musicality than a dazzling technical display – save that for bebop!

Quavers (eighth notes) in Ballads

Because of the slow tempo of most ballads there is more room for interpretation by the performer. Quavers (eighth notes) in ballads aren't always swung – however they can be and work as swung quavers (eighth notes), so it's up to you as the musician to interpret the quavers (eighth notes) as you wish. A hint of swing over a ballad can inject rhythm into the tune, however, if all the quavers (eighth notes) are swung it can lose the slow tempo ballad feel and become another swing tune. Experiment with straight and swung quavers (eighth notes) and see the different effects of each – the recorded version of 'Sleepless Eyes' has swung quavers (eighth notes) in the bridge ('B' section) but not the 'A' section. Your interpretation might have swung quavers (eighth notes) in different places.

Use of Seventh Chords

The chords of the 'A' section of 'Sleepless Eyes' are largely diatonic to G minor. Gm^{7}, Am$^{7(\flat5)}$ and D^{7} are chords VI, VII and III (with an added F♯) of B♭ major or more relevantly for G minor they would be named chords I, II, and V.

Fig 11.7a **Diatonic Chords of B♭ Major**

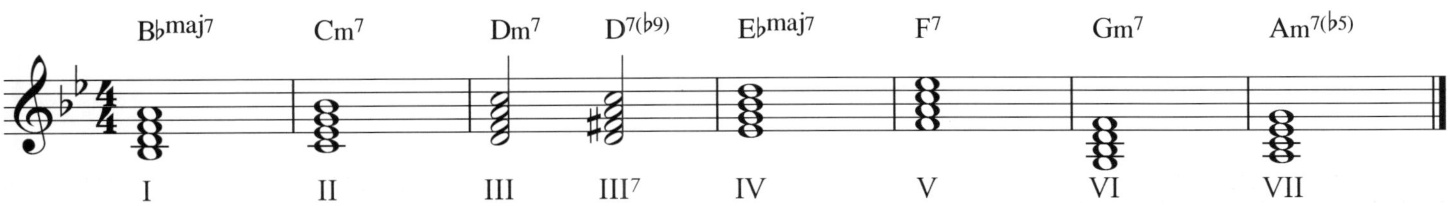

Fig 11.7b **Diatonic Chords of G Minor**

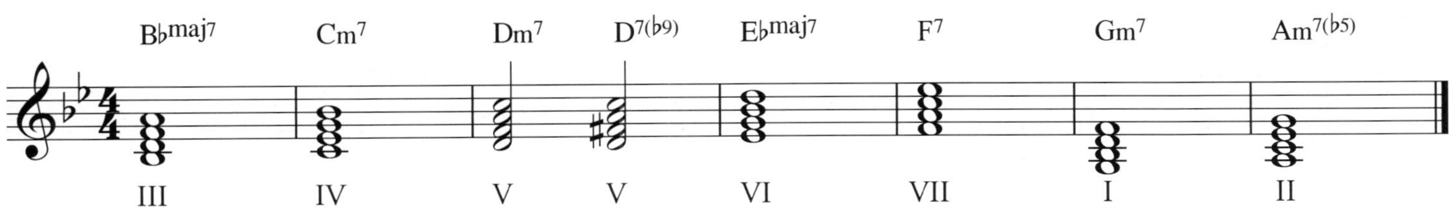

The chords based on E♭ and C are played as sevenths in this tune. If they were truly diatonic to G minor they would have been E♭^{maj7} and Cm^{7}. To achieve seventh chords from these only involves changing one note of each chord and creates colour in each. The D♭ of the E♭^{7} and the E♮ of the C^{7} chords both change the sound and the essential nature of the chords – listen out for the D flats and E naturals in the head and solo.

The use of seventh chords next to each other allows you to play lines that 'echo' one another but with the notes changed to fit the passing chords. This use of parallel phrases creates recognizable lines and a reference point for the performer and listener. The bars marked **Eg. 1** demonstrate this.

Tone and Vibrato

The great musicians are instantly recognizable by their ballad playing. Within a few bars it's possible to tell who the musician is, sometimes merely by their tone and use of vibrato. Playing ballads offers a chance for you to explore the sound you make on your instrument – hold the long notes for their full value and focus on making the sound you want. The difference between **Benny Goodman**'s sound and **Artie Shaw**'s is huge – whose tone do you like the best?

Your Solo

Because of the slow tempo there is only one chorus of solo on this tune. Try to make the solo a continuation of the head and focus on conveying as much sentiment as possible. Ballads are a great opportunity to express yourself and bring a tear to the eye of your audience!

Blues Shuffle

The last type of tune we will explore in this chapter is the Blues Shuffle. Containing as it does elements of rhythm & blues and soul music, the shuffle is a heavier version of swing. Chapter one of this book explored how to 'swing' your quavers (eighth notes) by first turning them into a triplet and then tying the first and second syllables together – the word 'clarinet' became 'cla-ri-net' and then 'cla-net' to produce the feel of swung quavers (eighth notes). A shuffle feel emphasizes this triplet based groove to produce a more intense beat – somewhere between swing and rock and roll.

Fig 11.8 **'Times Square Shuffle'**

45 15

Ollie Weston

B
1.
2.
Solo Break
Em7 A7 Dm7 G7 Cm7 F7 G7 G7
II V II V II V
D major
C major
B♭ major
Swing
Chorus 1
G7 F7 G7 F7 G7 F7 G7 F7
Eg. 2
C7 B♭7 C7 B♭7 G7 F7 G7 F7
Eg. 2
Eg. 2
Eg. 2
Em7 A7 Dm7 G7 Cm7 F7 G7
Eg. 1
Eg. 1
Eg. 1
Chorus 2
G7 F7 G7 F7 G7 F7 G7 F7
C7 B♭7 C7 B♭7 G7 F7 G7 F7
Em7 A7 Dm7 G7 Cm7 F7 G7
Eg. 1
Eg. 1
Eg. 1
Eg. 2

'Times Square Shuffle' is a funky shuffle blues to end the 'set' of tunes in this chapter. The tune is based around a simple two-chord groove played by the rhythm section – listen to mp3 track 45 and in particular to the rhythm section on the intro. The drum groove is similar to swing but with more emphasis on the triplets, while the piano and bass 'hits' form the basis of the head. This is a typical shuffle groove and should get your feet tapping.

The Head

The melody of the head is simple and catchy – the first two notes are repeated throughout the head to provide a memorable two-note 'hook'. The groove builds throughout the 'A' section and at letter B the rhythm section change from the two-chord groove to a shuffle feel – the bass locks in with the drums and the shuffle groove provides momentum. The melody takes off at this point too giving letter B a sense of release.

The whole band drops out in the first-time-bar leaving the clarinet to play the melody on its own before returning to letter A and the two chord vamp. The tension then builds again before another release at letter B for the second time. The second-time-bar has another dead stop – this time for a solo break.

The Chord Progression

This is a 12-Bar head similar to a blues in G. The 'A' section groove is based around two seventh chords – G^7 and F^7. At bar five these move up a fourth to become C^7 and $B\flat^7$ (just as a 12-Bar blues would also move to chord IV at bar five).

Letter B

This is different to a blues as there is no chord V. Instead there are a series of unresolved II-V-Is. These come in a descending sequence – each is a tone lower than the preceding one. The parent scale of each II-V has been marked at this point.

In both the melody and the solo these descending II-Vs have similar descending phrases. These parallel phrases sound great over repeated II-V lines and each one could be used on its own as the basis for a lick or pattern of your own – look out for these in the sample solo where these ideas are marked as **Eg. 1**

Triplets

Shuffle tunes rely on triplets for their feel. The drums 'suggest' triplets throughout this tune and so to make the tune rhythmically authentic it's important to pick out triplets in the solo too. Examples of this are marked **Eg. 2**

Your Solo

The backing track (CD track 15) has eight choruses of the sequence for you to play your own version of the tune. Like 'Sleepless Eyes' this tune relies on the mood you create for its effect. A shuffle blues is a fun, raucous tune and the more energy and momentum you can create the better. The progression has a natural tension and release within it – the 'A' section builds quietly over the vamp and then lets rip at letter B. You can use these inbuilt dynamics to your advantage to build your solo. Energy and excitement don't always mean volume and quantity of notes – start small over the 'A' section, where a simple funky phrase will go a long way!

Checkpoint

The term 'jazz' covers a wide variety of musical styles. This chapter has introduced you to four popular genres within jazz – bebop, Latin, ballads and shuffles – which all have a huge presence within the jazz canon, each having its own subtle quirks and idiosyncrasies. They also have a number of similarities – namely chord progressions and song forms which are alike throughout. A good jazz musician will tap into the unique elements of each genre and apply their own individual sound and style. This chapter has presented a 'set' of contrasting tunes allowing you to showcase your skills within an ever-increasing array of musical vocabulary and stylistic techniques.

Conclusion

Congratulations!

If you have reached this point by working methodically through the book you will have grown considerably both as a clarinettist and as a musician. Your technical skill, reading, theory and musicianship will all have been tested and expanded throughout the course of the last eleven chapters and you should feel proud of the results!

By using the sample solos and the play-along tracks on the CD you will have unlocked some of the secrets of jazz improvisation, and you now possess the knowledge to build your own style and to continue to develop as a jazz musician. You should have acquired the necessary skills to analyse a line and relate each note and chord to the bigger picture – you will have seen similar patterns emerging throughout the book (II-V-I, 'AABA' form, 12-Bar blues etc.) and these building blocks appear frequently in many genres of jazz.

What Now?

Whilst learning the tricks of the trade is a solitary task, jazz is rarely played alone. Playing in a group with others is one of the great pleasures of jazz. Try to find like-minded souls who share your enthusiasm for the music, and 'jam' together – it can be a funk jam on one chord or a whole bebop marathon, it really doesn't matter – just get out there and play! Look around for organised jazz groups too, a local big band or school jazz group will always welcome new faces. Jazz attracts some extremely witty and interesting people, and by reaching this stage of the book you may consider yourself one of them!

Further Study

This book aims to cover the basics and set you on your way, however there are some areas that we haven't covered – jazz has a rich heritage and a huge variety of styles that would be impossible to cover in just one book. If you are really serious about your playing, find a good jazz teacher who will inspire you further.

Transcription

The sample solos in this book are written as imitations of improvised solos. A good way to expand your musical vocabulary is to transcribe the solos you really like. This involves working out note-for-note your favourite solos and writing them down. This can seem a daunting challenge and it is indeed a painstakingly slow process at times, but the rewards are great – you are effectively training your ears to hear notes and rhythms which will turn into a theory exercise in writing them down. Once this is complete you will have a cool piece to play on your instrument and first hand inspiration from a great clarinet player. Start small – transcribe a few bars that you particularly like then build up – eventually to a whole solo.

Real Books

A 'Real book' is a collection of standard jazz tunes put together in one large book. Most real books contain a huge range of 'classic' jazz tunes from the early standards right up to useful funk and fusion tunes. I would recommend a real book as an essential purchase as once you have one of these books you will have a great resource for learning and analysing new material. You will also have repertoire in common with other musicians, allowing you all quite literally to read off the same page at a jam session!

Transposition

So far this book hasn't dealt with the issue of transposition. The clarinet is in the key of B♭ – this means that when the clarinet is playing in the key of C the concert pitch instruments (instruments that don't have to transpose such as the piano, bass or guitar etc.) are playing in the key of B♭. Transposition is common in woodwind instruments and in the case of the clarinet family it allows each member to use the same fingering and notation. If you were to pick up a bass clarinet or E♭ clarinet you will find the notes in exactly the same place as the B♭ clarinet, both on the instrument and when written down. The only difference is that the sound will be at a different pitch.

Transposition is a fact of life for clarinettists and as soon as you start playing with other musicians you will quickly learn how to converse both in your own key and in concert pitch – usually referred to simply as 'concert'. To transpose from your note or chord to 'concert' simply go down a tone – if you play a C it will sound as a concert B♭. Your B♭ will sound as a concert A♭ etc. To transpose from concert to the B♭ clarinet key, go the other way and transpose up a tone – B♭ concert will be played as C on the clarinet.

Enjoy

As I've said before, you should always try to enjoy your music making. If you are struggling with a piece or feel uninspired as an improviser, try to remember the reasons you started in the first place and appreciate how far you have already progressed. Perseverance is important – stick at it and you will achieve your goals.

History and Listening

Whilst there is much that can be written and said about jazz the best way to develop as a player is to listen to as much as possible. Like learning a language, jazz relies on hearing the subtleties of phrasing, tone and feel and can only be thoroughly absorbed by hearing the language 'spoken' by the great players. Jazz has a rich history and there are many different styles that come under the title 'Jazz'– consequently the choice of albums and artists can be overwhelming!

This chapter will give you an overview of jazz from the 1920s to the present day and outline the innovators and great recordings of each of the styles. Jazz has come a long way – each generation of musicians has absorbed the work of their predecessors and added to it. You should be aware of the great innovators and their work as they provide a constant reference and inspiration to you.

The 1920s – Early Days

The 1920s were a formative time for modern jazz. The New Orleans and dixieland styles were still popular and used clarinet as the main reed instrument – **Sidney Bechet** was a great clarinettist of the day and also later experimented with the soprano saxophone. One of the main pioneers of the 1920s was **Louis Armstrong** whose distinctive trumpet playing, singing and personality paved the way for much of the jazz that was to follow through his bands the **Hot Five** and **Hot Seven**. The bands had hits with 'Potato Head Blues' and 'West End Blues'. Pianist **Jelly Roll Morton**'s band **The Hot Peppers** were another great band of the 1920s.

Recommended Listening

Hot Fives And Sevens **Louis Armstrong** (compilation)

The 1930s – The Big Bands (Swing Era)

The 1930s were dominated by the big bands and the star soloists that they produced. As popular in the 1930s as dance music is today, band leaders such as **Count Basie**, **Duke Ellington**, **Earl Hines**, **Fletcher Henderson** and **Benny Goodman** toured America with their groups providing a musical backdrop to the thirties social scene. Many legendary soloists learned their trade with these groups including **Barney Bigard** with **Duke Ellington**'s orchestra.

Recommended Listening

The Complete Decca Recordings **Count Basie Orchestra** (Decca Recordings 1937-1939 featuring **Lester Young**.)

April In Paris (Verve Records 1955)

The Atomic Mr. Basie (Roulette Records 1958)

Mood Indigo **Duke Ellington** (1927-1931) (Columbia) (released 1992)

The Chronological Duke Ellington And His Orchestra (compilation)

The Chronological Fletcher Henderson And His Orchestra (compilation)

The 1940s and 50s – Bebop

In the 1940s, jazz moved from being popular dance music to a largely improvised music. The tight arrangements and short solos of the swing bands gave way to a music where the improvisation was the main event. Bebop scaled down the size of the band to the classic 'jazz combo' format – a rhythm section (piano, bass, drums) and one or two horns. This has been the format of the small jazz group ever since. Bebop built on the standard-type tunes of the twenties and thirties but added quirky new melodies and labyrinthine chord changes to challenge the musician and listener alike.

The legendary clubs of New York's 52nd St. played host to **Charlie Parker**, along with trumpet vituoso **Dizzy Gillespie**, pianists **Bud Powell** and **Thelonious Monk**, bassists **Ray Brown** and **Oscar Pettiford** and drummers **Max Roach** and **Roy Haynes**. The young **Miles Davis** also got his start playing with 'Bird' in New York in the 40s. Recording in the 1940s was erratic.

Recommended Listening

Bird And Diz (Verve Records Released 1952)

Sonny Side Up **Dizzy Gillespie**, **Sonny Rollins**, **Sonny Stitt** (Verve Records 1957)

Charlie Parker – Savoy Records (1944-1949) a wealth of great records usually released as compilations.

Charlie Parker With Strings (Verve Records 1949)

The Mid 1950s – Hardbop

The late 1950s marked a move away from bebop. The technical proficiency required to navigate the fast-moving chords was seen by some as a hindrance to creativity. The 1950s was the decade when **Miles Davis** came into his own – a graduate from **Charlie Parker**'s bebop groups of the 1940s, **Miles** recorded extensively in the mid 1950s with his quintet (featuring **John Coltrane** on tenor sax). They played bop inspired material that also incorporated elements of rhythm and blues and earlier swing music. This style became known as 'Hard Bop' and was characterised by **Davis**'s group as well as **Art Blakey**'s 'Jazz Messengers'.

Miles Davis struck gold in 1959 with his classic album *Kind of Blue* that abandoned the bebop approach entirely in favour of a calm, cool modal approach to music. Instead of two chord changes per bar, **Miles**'s music had long sections using only one chord, forcing the musicians to be melodically creative rather than falling back on bebop 'licks' and clichés. The musicians on the album – including saxophonists **John Coltrane** and **Cannonball Adderley** and pianist **Bill Evans** – produced a timeless masterpiece and created a move towards a more relaxed style of jazz known as 'cool jazz'. The other giant of the 1950s was **John Coltrane** who built on the bebop sound of **Charlie Parker** and **Dexter Gordon** with a burning intensity and harmonic bravado that would revolutionize jazz in the 1960s.

Recommended Listening

Moanin **Art Blakey And The Jazz Messengers** (Blue Note Records 1958)

Cookin with **The Miles Davis Quintet** (Prestige Records 1956)

Workin with **The Miles Davis Quintet** (Prestige Records 1956)

Relaxin with **The Miles Davis Quintet** (Prestige Records 1956)

Steamin with **The Miles Davis Quintet** (Prestige Records 1956)

58 Sessions **Miles Davis**

Kind of Blue – **Miles Davis** (Columbia Records 1959)

The 1960s – Modal Jazz and Beyond

The impact of *Kind Of Blue* led musicians to improvise in a looser, more textural way rather than 'burning' through chord progressions at break-neck speed. The possibilities for expression and storytelling with a few chords were explored by **Herbie Hancock** on his album *Maiden Voyage* and by **Wayne Shorter** on *Speak No Evil*. Both used modal language to take jazz to new levels of expression. **Hancock** and **Shorter** were members of **Miles Davis**'s 1960s quintet that fused elements of modal and hard bop jazz in a rhythmically advanced unit.

John Coltrane built on his work in the 1950s by introducing a level of spirituality and a meditative quality to his work culminating in his best known album *A Love Supreme* in 1964, an album that reaches an unparalled emotional intensity. **Coltrane**'s music after 1964 became increasingly experimental and with his fellow pioneers: **Archie Shepp**, **Albert Ayler** and **Pharoah Sanders**, Coltrane played music unrestricted by conventional chords – this was known as 'free jazz' or 'Avant-garde'. Coltrane also worked with saxophonist / clarinettist **Eric Dolphy** at this time, who was a virtuoso and another pioneer of 'free jazz'.

Recommended Listening

Maiden Voyage **Herbie Hancock** (Blue Note Records 1965)
Speak No Evil **Wayne Shorter** (Blue Note Records 1965)
E.S.P. **The Miles Davis Quintet** (Columbia Records 1965)
Miles Smiles **The Miles Davis Quintet** (Columbia Records 1966)
A Love Supreme **John Coltrane** (Impulse Records 1964)
Ascension **John Coltrane** (Impulse Records 1965)
Out To Lunch **Eric Dolphny** (Blue Note Records)

The Late 1960s and 1970s – Soul Jazz and Fusion

In the 1960s, pop and rock music had come to dominate the musical landscape. Jazz musicians sought to incorporate the music of the **Beatles**, **Jimi Hendrix** and **Aretha Franklin** into their compositions and so reach a larger audience. **Herbie Hancock** explored pop and soul styles through his compositions 'Cantaloupe Island' and 'Watermelon Man'. **Herbie**'s band **Headhunters**, featuring saxophonist and bass clarinettist **Bennie Maupin**, mixed rock and jazz using electric keyboards and bass with soul and funk beats – the result is a dance-friendly sound that was popular with jazz and rock audiences alike.

Miles Davis also sought to incorporate electronic sounds and rock grooves into his music. *Bitches Brew* is a moody, brooding mix of jazz and rock that concentrated on texture and atmosphere rather than the danceable grooves of other fusion bands. *Bitches Brew* featured Miles's long-time tenor saxophonist, **Wayne Shorter** and **Bennie Maupin** on bass clarinet as well as new names **Chick Corea** (keyboards), **Jack Dejohnette** (drums), also British musicians **Dave Holland** (bass) and **John McLaughlin** (guitar).

Other successful fusion groups include **Weather Report** co-founded by sax legend **Wayne Shorter** and **The Brecker Brothers** led by dynamic clarinet and trumpet playing brothers **Michael** and **Randy Brecker**.

Recommended Listening

'Watermelon Man' **Herbie Hancock** from *Takin' Off* (Blue Note Records 1962)
Bitches Brew **Miles Davis** (Columbia Records 1970)
Headhunters **Herbie Hancock** (Columbia Records 1973)

The 1980s Onwards

Since the 1970s jazz has continued to develop and has moved in varied directions. A return to acoustic, traditionally-rooted jazz was spearheaded by New Orleans trumpeter **Wynton Marsalis** (born 1961). Marsalis' **Lincoln Centre Jazz Orchrestra** recreate classic jazz from many eras with impeccable taste and respect. Following **Wynton**'s lead there are many very fine contemporary clarinet virtuosos rooted in traditional jazz and swing but with a fresh approach to the music – American **Ken Peplowski** (born 1959) has often been compared to the great **Benny Goodman** due to his fluent and hard swinging playing.

Eddie Daniels (born 1941) has had a rich and varied solo career including stints as featured soloist in both the **Thad Jones** and **Gordon Goodwin**'s **Big Phat Band**. British clarinet player **Tony Coe** (born 1934) has been a leading player on the world stage since the 1950s, equally at home in both jazz and contemporary classical music. A world class British player is **Alan Barnes** (born 1959) a prodigiously gifted player on clarinet and saxophone.

Another contemporary clarinet great is **Gilad Atzmon** (born 1963) who explores his Israeli heritage through his music and fuses jazz with Klezma and other Middle Eastern / Eastern-European styles. **David Jean-Baptiste** and **Rudi Mahall** are other contemporary jazz clarinet specialists well worth listening to.

As jazz continues to evolve it assimilates more and more diverse elements, the increasing use of technology in music finds acoustic and electronic instruments used side by side in ever more imaginative ways. Jazz has also absorbed classical and rock styles to create contemporary music with blurred boundaries between both genre and improvisation and composition.

Recommended Listening
Easy To Remember **Ken Peplowski** (2004)
This Is Now **Eddie Daniels** (1991)
In Concert **Tony Coe** (2003)
Gilad Atzmon **Gilad Atzmon and the Orient House ensemble** (2000)

Selected biographies

Sidney Bechet (1897–1959)

One of the first great jazz instrumentalists, New Orleans born and bred **Sidney Bechet** paved the way for future generations of clarinet and saxophone players with his early improvisations and obligatos in the New Orleans groups of the day. His wide vibrato and robust tone set him aside from other clarinettists of the era and his influence can be heard throughout the history of the clarinet.

Recommended Listening
The Essential Collection **Sidney Bechet** (compilation album)

Barney Bigard (1906–1980)

Barney Bigard was born in New Orleans where he learnt music as a boy before moving to Chicago in the 1920s to take up a gig with the legendary **Joe 'King' Oliver**'s band. Bigard left King Oliver to join the great **Duke Ellington**'s band and remained with Ellington for over 15 years. Bigard's woody and sultry playing were an essential addition to Ellington's compositional palette. Bigard co-wrote 'Mood Indigo' with his employer, which went on to become a great hit.

Recommended Listening
'Mood Indigo' **Duke Ellington and his Cotton Club Orchestra**

Benjamin David 'Benny' Goodman (1909–1986)

Born in Chicago, **Benny Goodman** was introduced to the clarinet when his father enrolled the 11 year old Benny and his brother at a local music school. Goodman was a quick learner and, inspired by local clarinet heroes **Johnny Dodds** and **Jimmy Noone**, was soon making his way on the professional circuit. Goodman left Chicago for New York in the late 1920s and made his name first as a sideman and later as the leader of his own group. The 1938 Carnegie hall concert cemented Goodman's place in the highest echelons of American music, as his orchestra became the first jazz group to play the hallowed Carnegie hall stage. The concert featured the orchestra's established hits including 'One O' Clock Jump' and ending with arguably their biggest hit 'Sing, Sing, Sing' a feature for the drummer **Gene Krupa**. Goodman's nickname 'The King of Swing' leaves no question as to his status as a clarinettist and band leader/composer.

Recommended Listening
The Famous 1938 Carnegie Hall Jazz Concert Vols. 1, 2, 3 (Live) (1938, Columbia)
Sing, Sing, Sing (1935)

Artie Shaw (1910–2004)

Shaw was born in New York and started his musical studies on the alto sax in his early teens. He soon switched to clarinet and at 16 left home to tour the USA and learn his craft on the road. Shaw's band was hugely popular with the 1930s swing audiences and he had great success with 'Begin the Beguine' and 'Stardust'. Shaw's clarinet playing was eventually acknowledged as equal to his great rival **Benny Goodman**, his fans dubbed him 'King of Clarinet' as opposed to Goodman's 'King of Swing'.

Recommended Listening
The Essence of Artie Shaw (compilation album)

Sir John 'Johnny' Dankworth (1927–2010)

Possibly Britain's best known jazz musician, **Johnny Dankworth** has arguably done more to put British jazz on the map than any other single musician. Born into a musical family, Dankworth learnt both the piano and violin before settling on the clarinet in his teens after hearing recordings of **Benny Goodman**. British jazz in the 1940s and 50s was often unfavourably compared with its American counterpart – the bebop emerging from New York was seen as the 'real deal' whereas British jazz was its 'poor cousin'. Dankworth could cut it with the best of the Americans and cemented his reputation at the 1949 Paris Jazz Festival when he met and played with the great **Charlie Parker**. Dankworth led both a septet **The Dankworth Seven** and a Big Band – the latter being hugely successful both in the UK and the USA where they were invited to play the 1959 Newport Jazz Festival. The band shared a stage with the great **Duke Ellington** whom Dankworth struck up a long-standing friendship with.

Johnny Dankworth continued to be prolific in Jazz, Film, TV and education; the Wavendon Jazz Summer schools were founded by him and his wife **Cleo Laine** and have inspired generations of players.

Recommended Listening
The Vintage Years (1953–1959)

Acker Bilk (1929–)

Born **Bernard Stanley Bilk** (he acquired the term 'Acker', meaning 'mate' in Somerset slang). Bilk is one of Britain's best-loved traditional jazzmen. Acker learned to play the clarinet during his army years in the 1940s and by the 1950s was playing professionally. Originally a member of **Ken Colyer**'s jazz band, Bilk formed his own **Paramount Jazz Band** in the mid 50s and has worked largely unchanged with this ensemble ever since. A central figure in the traditional jazz boom in Britain in the 1950s, Bilk also had huge commercial success with 'Stranger on the Shore' in 1962 which became his signature tune catapulted him to wider fame.

Recommended Listening
Stranger on the Shore – The Best of by Acker Bilk

Bennie Maupin (1940–)

Along with **Eric Dolphy**, **Bennie Maupin** was one of the early pioneers of the bass clarinet. Maupin's sonorous tone added an earthy and much needed acoustic quality to the dark,

electric albums of the 1970s. He was a key member of **Herbie Hancock**'s **Mwandishi** and **Headhunters** bands as well as participating on **Miles Davis**'s seminal *Bitches Brew* album.

Bennie Maupin has continued to be a unique and important voice on the bass clarinet and other woodwind instruments.

Recommended Listening
Bitches Brew **Miles Davis** (1970)
Mwandishi **Herbie Hancock** (1971)
Penumbra **Bennie Maupin Ensemble** (2006)

Eddie Daniels (1941–)

Born and raised in New York, **Eddie Daniels** career has encompassed a huge range of styles from jazz to **Mozart**. A graduate of the prestigious Juillard School of music, **Eddie Daniels** was an original member of the **Thad Jones / Mel Lewis** orchestra's Monday night residency at New York's legendary Village Vanguard Club. His performances with the band led to him winning the Downbeat Magazine's new star award for clarinet. Daniels frequently combines jazz and classical music in his concerts in an attempt to bring the music to as wide an audience as possible.

Recommended Listening
This Is Now (1991)
Swing Low Sweet Clarinet (2000)

Ken Peplowski (1959–)

Ken **Peplowski** started life in Ohio and learned his trade playing with local Polish, Polka musicians. An early starter, Peplowski was playing professional engagements whilst still in junior school. Peplowski learned many of the skills essential for jazz musicians during this time – the ability to improvise, busk and generally think on your feet. Peplowski became increasingly interested in jazz whilst at school and was offered a job with the **Tommy Dorsey Orchestra** as alto saxophonist and featured clarinet soloist. He further honed his craft with Dorsey; the band spent up to 48 weeks of the year on the road playing different venues every night. Peplowski settled in New York in the 1980s and his playing has been showcased in a variety of settings from dixieland jazz to Avant-garde. A feature on the international jazz circuit, Peplowski's shows feature elegant swinging jazz of the highest class coupled with his legendary wit and charm.

Recommended Listening
Noir Blue (2010)
The Other Portrait (1996)

Rudi Mahall (1966–)

German clarinettist **Rudi Mahall** is a contemporary clarinet player equally at home and active in jazz, classical and Avant-garde music. Mahall has specialized in the bass clarinet, playing it almost exclusively the majority of his career and has built a reputation as one of the world's premiere bass clarinet players. Mahall has recorded extensively with pianist **Aki Takase** producing a variety of contemporary music. Mahall also played on **Alexander von Schlippenbach**'s album *Monk's Casino*, a recording of the works of pianist **Thelonious Monk**. Mahall has worked with some of the top names in European Avant-garde and contemporary jazz including the **Globe Unity Orchestra**, **Sven-Åke Johansson** and **Kenny Wheeler**.

Recommended Listening
The Dessert **Mahall/Aki Takase** (2004)
Monk's Casino **Alexander Von Slippenbach** (2007)

Index

Further Clarinet Titles Available From Schott

The Jazz Method for Clarinet
ED 12440

Developing Jazz Technique for Clarinet
ED 12864

Clarinet Sight-Reading 1
ED 12834

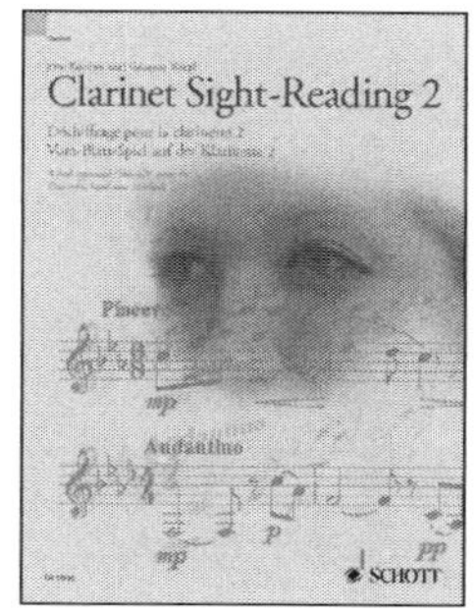

Clarinet Sight-Reading 2
ED 12835

Baroque Play-Along
ED 13152

Classical Play-Along
ED 13164

Romantic Play-Along
ED 13158

Movie Themes
ED 12981

Swinging Baroque Play-Along
ED 12959

Swinging Classical Play-Along
ED 13097

Swinging Romantic Play-Along
ED 13091

Latin Themes
ED 12994

Clarinets for Christmas
ED 12686

SCHOTT
www.schott-music.com

Track Listings

(for download code, please see p. 2)

Audio Backing Tracks

1 Major 7th Heaven (fig. 2.14)
2 So Far, So Good (fig. 3.15a)
3 Sonny's Blues (fig. 4.13)
4 Pearly White (fig. 5.1)
5 Down To It (fig. 5.3)
6 First Impression (fig. 6.9)
7 Dancing With Duke (fig. 7.11a)
8 Autumn Sun (fig. 8.20)
9 Among the Stars (fig. 9.1)
10 Undying Love (fig. 9.4)
11 Take the Express Train (fig. 9.8a)
12 52nd St. Blues (fig. 10.8)
13 Flying With the Bird (fig. 11)
14 Super Nova (fig. 11.2a)
15 Times Square Shuffle (fig. 11.8)

Demonstrations and Workouts

1 Leavin' Town (fig. 1.1)
2 Leavin' Town ('Bluesed-up' version) (fig. 1.2)
3 Write your own 12-Bar Blues (fig. 1.9a/b)
4 Sample Blues Solo – Leavin' Town (fig. 1.10)
5 Major seventh workout #1 (fig. 2.5a)
6 Major seventh workout #2 (fig. 2.5b)
7 Major seventh workout #3 (fig. 2.5c)
8 Major 7th Heaven (fig. 2.14)
9 Minor seventh workout #1 (fig. 3.4a)
10 Minor seventh workout #2 (fig. 3.4b)
11 Minor seventh workout #3 (fig. 3.4c)
12 So Far, So Good (fig. 3.15a)
13 Seventh chord (Mixolydian) workout #1 (fig.4.5a)
14 Seventh chord (Mixolydian) workout #2 (fig.4.5b)
15 Seventh chord (Mixolydian) workout #3 (fig.4.5c)
16 Sonny's Blues (fig. 4.13)
17 Pearly White (fig. 5.1)
18 Down To It (fig. 5.3)
19 Modal workout (fig. 6.3)
20 Modal progression from a static root (fig. 6.4)
21 First Impression (Head) (fig. 6.9)
22 Unresolved ending (fig. 7.3a)
23 Resolved ending (fig. 7.3b)
24 Cycle of 5ths (use for fig. 7.6, 7.7, 7.8)
25 II-V-I in twelve keys (starting from F) (fig. 7.10a)
26 II-V-I in twelve keys (starting from B) (fig. 7.10a)
27 Dancing With Duke (fig. 7.11a)
28 Minor V-I in 12 keys (from D minor) (fig. 8.13, 8.14)
29 Minor V-I in 12 keys (from A♭ minor) (fig. 8.13, 8.14)
30 Chord progression (fig. 8.16)
31 Autumn Sun (fig. 8.20)
32 Among the Stars (fig. 9.1)
33 'A' section of Undying Love (fig. 9.3a)
34 'A' section of Undying Love with II chord (fig. 9.3b)
35 Take the Express Train 'A' section (fig. 9.7a)
36 Take the Express Train expanded (fig. 9.7b)
37 III-VI-II-V-I (fig. 9.7c)
38 52nd St. Blues (head with I, IV, V) (fig. 10.1)
39 52nd St. Blues (head with II-V-I to C^7) (fig. 10.5)
40 52nd St. Blues (fig. 10.8)
41 Flying With the Bird (fig. 11)
42 Super Nova (fig. 11.2a)
43 Sleepless Eyes (fig. 11.7) Demonstration
44 Sleepless Eyes (fig. 11.7) Backing track*
45 Times Square Shuffle (fig. 11.8)

*Due to the extensive amount of recorded material available throughout this book, it has been necessary to make this particularly lengthy backing track as an mp3 rather than a CD track.

Recording Acknowledgements

Clarinet – **Paul Fawcus**
Piano – **Duncan Haynes**
Double Bass – **Dave Foster**
Drums – **Richard Barr**

Clarinet recorded, mixed and engineered by **Paul Fawcus** for Jazz Mouse Productions Ltd (www.jazzmouse.co.uk) – August 2010.
Rhythm section recorded, mixed and engineered by **Jules Jackson** at Putney Rd Studios – July 2008.